W9-CFG-933

The Civic Web

The John D. and Catherine T. MacArthur Foundation Series on Digital Media and Learning

Engineering Play: A Cultural History of Children's Software by Mizuko Ito

Hanging Out, Messing Around, and Geeking Out: Kids Living and Learning with New Media by Mizuko Ito, Sonja Baumer, Matteo Bittanti, danah boyd, Rachel Cody, Becky Herr-Stephenson, Heather A. Horst, Patricia G. Lange, Dilan Mahendran, Katynka Martínez, C. J. Pascoe, Dan Perkel, Laura Robinson, Christo Sims, and Lisa Tripp, with contributions by Judd Antin, Megan Finn, Arthur Law, Annie Manion, Sarai Mitnick, David Schlossberg, and Sarita Yardi

The Civic Web: Young People, the Internet and Civic Participation by Shakuntala Banaji and David Buckingham

Inaugural Series Volumes

These edited volumes were created through an interactive community review process and published online and in print in December 2007. They are the precursors to the peer-reviewed monographs in the series.

Civic Life Online: Learning How Digital Media Can Engage Youth, edited by W. Lance Bennett

Digital Media, Youth, and Credibility, edited by Miriam J. Metzger and Andrew J. Flanagin

Digital Youth, Innovation, and the Unexpected, edited by Tara McPherson

The Ecology of Games: Connecting Youth, Games, and Learning, edited by Katie Salen

Learning Race and Ethnicity: Youth and Digital Media, edited by Anna Everett

Youth, Identity, and Digital Media, edited by David Buckingham

The Civic Web

Young People, the Internet and Civic Participation

Shakuntala Banaji and David Buckingham

The MIT Press
Cambridge, Massachusetts
London, England

© 2013 Massachusetts Institute of Technology

For information about special quantity discounts, please email special_sales@mitpress.mit.edu.

This book was set in Stone Sans and Stone Serif by Toppan Best-set Premedia Limited, Hong Kong. Printed and bound in the United States of America.

Library of Congress Cataloging-in-Publication Data

Banaji, Shakuntala, 1971–
The civic web : young people, the Internet and civic participation / by Shakuntala Banaji and David Buckingham.
  pages cm. — (The John D. and Catherine T. MacArthur Foundation series on digital media and learning)
Includes bibliographical references and index.
ISBN 978-0-262-01964-4 (hardcover : alk. paper)
1. Youth—Political activity. 2. Internet and youth. 3. Internet—Political aspects.
I. Buckingham, David, 1954– II. Title.
HQ799.2.P6B35 2013
004.67'80835—dc23
2013007265

10 9 8 7 6 5 4 3 2 1

In memory of Vijayatara, indomitable spirit

Contents

Series Foreword

In recent years, digital media and networks have become embedded in our everyday lives and are part of broad-based changes to how we engage in knowledge production, communication, and creative expression. Unlike the early years in the development of computers and computer-based media, digital media are now *commonplace* and *pervasive*, having been taken up by a wide range of individuals and institutions in all walks of life. Digital media have escaped the boundaries of professional and formal practice, and the academic, governmental, and industry homes that initially fostered their development. Now they have been taken up by diverse populations and noninstitutionalized practices, including the peer activities of youth. Although specific forms of technology uptake are highly diverse, a generation is growing up in an era where digital media are part of the taken-for-granted social and cultural fabric of learning, play, and social communication.

This book series is founded upon the working hypothesis that those immersed in new digital tools and networks are engaged in an unprecedented exploration of language, games, social interaction, problem solving, and self-directed activity that leads to diverse forms of learning. These diverse forms of learning are reflected in expressions of identity, how individuals express independence and creativity, and in their ability to learn, exercise judgment, and think systematically.

The defining frame for this series is not a particular theoretical or disciplinary approach, nor is it a fixed set of topics. Rather, the series revolves around a constellation of topics investigated from multiple disciplinary and practical frames. The series as a whole looks at the relation between youth, learning, and digital media, but each might deal with only a subset of this constellation. Erecting strict topical boundaries can exclude some of the most important work in the field. For example, restricting the content of the series only to people of a certain age means artificially reifying an age boundary when the phenomenon demands otherwise. This becomes particularly problematic with new forms of online participation where one important outcome is the mixing of participants of different ages. The same goes for digital media, which are increasingly inseparable from analog and earlier media forms.

The series responds to certain changes in our media ecology that have important implications for learning. Specifically, these are new forms of media *literacy* and changes in the modes of media *participation*. Digital media are part of a convergence between interactive media (most notably gaming), online networks, and existing media forms. Navigating this media ecology involves a palette of literacies that are being defined through practice but require more scholarly scrutiny before they can be fully incorporated pervasively into educational initiatives. Media literacy involves not only ways of understanding, interpreting, and critiquing media, but also the means for creative and social expression, online search and navigation, and a host of new technical skills. The potential gap in literacies and participation skills creates new challenges for educators who struggle to bridge media engagement inside and outside the classroom.

The John D. and Catherine T. MacArthur Foundation Series on Digital Media and Learning, published by the MIT Press, aims to close these gaps and provide innovative ways of thinking about and using new forms of knowledge production, communication, and creative expression.

Acknowledgments

The research discussed in this book was made possible by funding from the European Commission, under the Framework 6 program for Targeted Socioeconomic Research. We owe a huge debt of thanks to the web producers in our seven countries who participated in our research, and also to the young people whose insights and input made the research so interesting. The overall findings discussed in our study are the collective work of seven teams of researchers in the UK, the Netherlands, Slovenia, Hungary, Spain, Turkey, and Sweden. We would like to thank Liesbeth de Block, Eva Bognar, Fadi Hirzalla, Maja Turnšek Hančič, Judit Szakacs, Aleksander Sašo Slaček Brlek, Liesbet van Zoonen, Tobias Olsson, Magdalena Albero-Andres, Peter Dahlgren, Asli Telli Aydemir, Francesco Fabbro, Albert Bastardas, and Fredrik Miegel for their contributions. Some of their individual work is specifically acknowledged in chapters 6 and 7, although the project involved collaboration throughout. While responsibility for the arguments here remains our own, the discussions that took place across our project team contributed in important ways to our synthesis of the data. Our colleague Liesbeth de Block also played a key role in managing the project and in keeping us relatively sane; her insights helped us pay attention to crucial areas of policy and practice in the field.

Introduction

In contemporary Western societies, there is increasing talk of a "democratic deficit." Even as we pay lip service to the principles of democracy, it seems that we are becoming less and less engaged in civic life. We are less inclined to vote, join political parties, volunteer or campaign for social causes, or place our trust in the political process. Very few of us appear to be "active citizens" in any sustained or meaningful way. These problems are often thought to manifest particularly among young people, who are widely described as alienated, apathetic, and disengaged. And if young people are no longer learning to participate in civic and political life, can there be any hope for the future of democracy?

The search for solutions to this problem has led many to look to technology, and specifically to the Internet. Politicians, activists, non-governmental organizations (NGOs), youth workers, and educators have all turned to the Internet as a means of reengaging young people in civil society. The networked, participatory potential of this new technology has been touted as creating new possibilities both for civic learning and for civic action. As well as reinvigorating the work of existing civic and political organizations, it is argued, the Internet affords new forms of interaction, participation, and engagement.

Yet this debate raises several questions. How do we explain young people's apparent disaffection from traditional forms of politics and civic life? Are young people in fact continuing to participate, but in new and different ways? Can the Internet help revive democratic participation? What counts as participation in the first place? Will technology create new forms of political and civic culture among young people, and how might we recognize these forms? What constraints and obstacles are likely to be encountered in these respects? And how do the possibilities vary across different political cultures and national contexts?

This book is based on an extensive research project that sought to address these questions. It was conducted between 2006 and 2009 and funded under the European Commission's Framework 6 program for targeted socioeconomic research. The funding of the project itself reflects the wider significance of this issue and its particular relevance to the "European project"—the desire to create a more active and effective pan-European public sphere. A good deal of the EC's work in this field has been directed toward young people, not least through the creation of websites, portals, and online networks designed to promote their understanding of European issues and their involvement as active citizens. Ours was one of several EC-funded research projects on related themes, most notably the Demos and EUYOUPART projects, although it was the only one to focus specifically on the Internet (see http://demos.iue.it and http://www.sora.at/index.php?id=44&L=1, respectively).

The project set out to analyze the potential contribution of the Internet to promoting civic engagement and participation among young people aged roughly fifteen to twenty-five years. It focused specifically on the range of youth-oriented civic sites that had begun to emerge on the World Wide Web around the turn of the twenty-first century. Such sites were being created by an increasingly wide range of organizations, from national and local governments, political parties, charities, and NGOs to grassroots campaigners and activist groups. This emerging and somewhat unstable online youth civic sphere had already been documented by Kathryn Montgomery and her colleagues (2004) in the United States, although at that point there had been very little European research.

This was an international project, if not strictly a comparative one. Our research took place in six EU member states and one applicant nation: Hungary, the Netherlands, Slovenia, Spain, Sweden, the United Kingdom, and Turkey. The partner countries were selected on the grounds that they represented very different cultural and political histories, and hence contrasting political systems and forms of civic culture (see chapter 2).

Broadly speaking, the design of our research followed the "circuit of culture" approach that is widely adopted in cultural studies (see Buckingham 2008; du Gay et al. 1997). We sought to combine and compare data about website producers, texts, and audiences, addressing a common set of research questions across a range of different types of investigation, and to set the data within a broader social and historical context. The research used both quantitative and qualitative methods and focused on three key dimensions of this phenomenon:

• the *nature and characteristics* of such websites, in terms of their content and formal features (design, mode of address, structure) and the extent to which they invited active participation among their users;
• the *production* of the sites, including the motivations, working practices, and economic models of the producers; and
• the *uses and interpretations* made of such sites by different social groups of young people, and the relationship between their online participation and their civic participation offline.

In developing our research project, we adopted a deliberately broad and open conception of "civic participation." The kinds of sites and activities we examined included the following:

- initiatives on the part of government (including the EU) or political parties (such as through their youth wings) to secure greater civic participation;
- those based on "single-issue" campaigns (such as campaigns built around globalization, discrimination, opposition to hunting, or homelessness);
- more open forums, in which young people from particular social groups (the disabled, refugees, gays and lesbians) defined and debated their own agenda of issues;
- sites promoting social activity or participation based on religious beliefs;
- sites encouraging volunteering and social or community activism;
- sites designed for specific ethnic minorities or geographically isolated groups; and
- sites addressing areas that might be seen as problematic, such as political violence or xenophobic hatred.

Such sites are, by definition, noncommercial sites created by private individuals, citizens' or public interest groups, governments, political parties, NGOs, or other nonprofit agencies. They address a range of concerns, including voting, volunteering, local community involvement, identity politics, global issues, tolerance and diversity, equity, and activism. The nature and availability of such sites vary across European countries, partly reflecting different levels of access to the Internet and partly because of differences in national (as well as regional and local) political cultures. These sites are also diverse in form. Some, such as many of those produced by governments, political parties, or activist groups wary of police surveillance, are relatively inert; they provide little interactivity beyond the mechanical means of online polls and petitions. Others make extensive use of the interactive dimensions of the medium, including message boards, chat facilities, video upload facilities, and even games. Additionally, it is worth noting that our research spanned a period during which online social networking became widespread, and our sample includes websites explicitly modeled on or including aspects of social networking sites.

In exploring this emerging phenomenon, we set out to address a range of empirical questions. How far does participation online result in greater participation offline in civic culture, or do these virtual networks constitute new forms of civic participation in themselves? How far does the model of "networked citizenship" actually correspond to the everyday practices and motivations of the majority of young people? Are some kinds of young people (for example, as defined in terms of social class, gender, ethnicity, religion, sexuality, or culture) more likely to respond to such invitations than others? Are some groups more likely to stay within traditional forms of civic participation or, alternatively, to resist them altogether? What are the social, political, and economic obstacles to such new media initiatives? And how do the answers to these questions vary across the different political cultures of our seven countries?

As well as generating insights for further research, we also sought to identify some of the issues and dilemmas faced by practitioners and policy-makers in relevant fields, and to understand some of the key characteristics of good practice in this field. We also considered how information and communication technologies—and these civic sites in particular—might be used in the context of citizenship education, not least in developing more participatory and "self-actualizing" approaches to civic learning (see Bennett 2008; Selwyn 2007).

This book is organized around the three key dimensions of our research, outlined above. We look in turn at the organizations that produce this kind of civic content (chapter 3), the young people they seek to address (chapters 4 and 5), and the actual sites or services themselves (chapters 6 and 7). To begin, we provide a more detailed discussion of the broader issues at stake in research related to new media and their potential to increase civic participation among young people.

1 Defining the Issues

By the time we began to write this book, in 2011, the issues our research was concerned with seemed to have taken on much greater urgency. Both authors were involved in the wave of protests that swept through universities in the UK in response to the government's withdrawal of funding and the consequent tripling of student tuition fees. On one occasion, we were trapped in (different) police "kettles" on the streets near London's Houses of Parliament as ranks of officers confined protesters to narrow spaces and then proceeded to ride horses into the crowd. We anxiously texted each other and our friends, who were either enclosed elsewhere in the demonstration or at home watching developments on television or online. During subsequent demonstrations, it became clear that police and protesters were playing a game of digital cat and mouse, tracking each other's movements using smartphones and surveillance cameras, Twitter and Facebook.

Meanwhile, on the world stage, a controversy erupted as the website Wikileaks published an enormous hoard of confidential memoranda and documents obtained by hacking into government computers (Beckett with Ball 2012). In an increasingly bizarre mix of political intrigue and soap opera, the embarrassment and incrimination that might have followed from the release of this material rapidly disappeared in the scandal surrounding the Wikileaks founder, Julian Assange, who was facing extradition from the UK to face charges of sexual assault in Sweden. Much more dramatically, in the spring of 2011, a series of mass demonstrations, strikes, and occupations of public spaces spread across North Africa and the Middle East. Groups of protesters came together to challenge long-running dictatorships, first in Tunisia and Egypt, and then (with much greater struggle and bloodshed) in Syria, Bahrain, and Libya. In the media coverage of what were dubbed the "Twitter revolutions" or the "Facebook revolutions," much was made of the role of technology—and especially of social networking sites—in somehow promoting or even precipitating these dramatic political shifts (see Meijas 2010).

These developments have already generated a considerable amount of academic commentary. However, they need to be set within the wider context of civic and political uses of new media, many of which are more mundane and less spectacular. Thus, while we do describe examples of civic activism, new social movements, and grassroots cultural politics, this book also considers the distinctly worthy and respectable uses of the Internet by governments, charities, and official youth organizations—as well as by established far-right groups and parties. The research on which this book is based focused primarily on what some would now identify as Web 1.0—the network of somewhat less than interactive sites that preceded the advent of social networking and user-generated content sites in the mid-2000s. However, sites of this kind continue to dominate the Web, and have not been superseded by subsequent developments; we are wary in any case of undue rhetorical distinctions between rubrics such as "1.0" and "2.0."

The kinds of dramatic events described above might be (and often have been) put into the service of telling a particular story about the relationships between political and technological change. When we look at the events more closely, however, the story is more diverse and more complex. New media technologies of various kinds were undoubtedly involved, although mobile phones, social networking sites, and computer hacking have very different possibilities and were used in very different ways in the uprisings and social challenges. Conventional media and offline contacts were also critically important in most of these instances: the events were intensively covered by traditional media such as television and newspapers, while leaflets, posters, and word-of-mouth played a key role in informing and mobilizing demonstrators. The genuine and sustained threat to authority in the UK student protests and in the Egyptian uprising—and indeed in more recent events in Greece, Spain, and Portugal—was not posed by tweets or critical postings on Facebook but by the physical presence of large numbers of angry people in the streets and squares in the heart of major cities.

Young people were also, of course, heavily involved, although we were by no means the only participants in the London demonstrations who were well past the bloom of youth. While the mainstream media and the authorities were often keen to represent such events as driven by irresponsible (and even hormonal) adolescents, the protests additionally attracted a much older age cohort, many of whom also enthusiastically tweeted, texted, and consulted the Internet on their smartphones.

These events were obviously and overtly political, not least in that they were directed toward the actions of elected (or nonelected) politicians. For many of the young people whom we met in the London demonstrations, the protests were probably their first experience of political protest, although some might well have participated in the massive (and ultimately ineffective) demonstrations against the Iraq War that took place in the very same streets eight years earlier. Again, however, it is important not to diminish the significant differences between the events of 2003 and 2011 or to pass over the very diverse causes and consequences they may have had—and may yet have in the future.

Nonetheless, the stories about technology, young people, and political change that crop up around such events have become increasingly familiar in recent years. A growing chorus of enthusiasts celebrates the power of technology to regenerate civic, cultural, and political life, to liberate oppressed populations, and to give voice to the marginalized, the exploited, and the excluded (e.g., Benkler 2006; Rheingold 2003; Shirky 2009). This story is, of course, part of the much broader wave of utopian thinking that often accompanies the advent of new media technologies. As historians such as Carolyn Marvin (1988) and Brian Winston (1998) have shown, the kinds of claims currently being made about the Internet echo those that were made in earlier generations about video recording, television, radio, the telephone, and the printing press. And while it has taken some time to emerge, the popular debate about the Internet and digital media is also now seeing a backlash: in the last couple of years, we have seen a new wave of publications that seeks to burst the bubble of technological optimism, arguing that new technologies are trivializing culture and politics, destroying our basic humanity, and undermining the very fabric of social life (e.g., Carr 2010; Keen 2007; Turkle 2011).

Both sides in these debates typically attribute an extraordinary power to technology and account for its role in highly deterministic terms: technology is seen to *produce* social change, irrespective of how and by whom it is used. Young people as emblems of the future are predictably invoked on both sides of this debate: they are at once the "digital natives," whose facility with technology is creating new forms of social and cultural participation (Palfrey and Gasser 2008; Prensky 2001), and the "dumbest generation," stupefied and terminally distracted by the flickering screen (Bauerlein 2009). Such arguments tend merely to replay the binary logic that has historically characterized responses to all new technologies (Marvin 1988): either technology will liberate us or it will enslave us; either it will expand our potential or it will reduce us; either it will revitalize our social and cultural life or it will take us all to hell.

Constructing a Problem

Fifteen years ago, one of the present authors sought to address some of these issues by means of an empirical study of young people's engagement with television, a medium that continues to occupy the bulk of young people's leisure time. The book that resulted from that research, *The Making of Citizens: Young People, News and Politics* (Buckingham 2000), began by laying out a debate whose broad terms continue to be rehearsed in both popular and academic discussions in this field (see, e.g., Bennett 2008; Dahlgren 2007; Loader 2007).

On the one hand, there is persistent concern throughout the industrialized world about a perceived crisis in modern democracy. The proportions of people voting in local and national (and indeed Europe-wide) elections have steadily decreased; formal membership of political parties has plummeted; citizens' interest in and knowledge about social and political affairs are waning; and measures of trust and confidence in politicians and in the political system are at an all-time low (Hetherington 2005; Niemi and Weisberg 2001; Putnam 2000; Whiteley 2009). There have been occasional signs of revival, for instance with the emergence of charismatic political candidates, as in the United States in 2008, or simply with the prospect of closely fought elections, as in the UK in 2010, yet the long-term trend is apparently one of continuing decline.

However, this perceived crisis is not simply about the relationship between citizens and the formal political system. For many commentators there has been a more general deterioration in what might be termed "civic culture." Civic culture is best seen as a continuum, ranging from organized public activities and associations of various kinds (which might include groupings based around music, sports, or cultural interests), through "parapolitical" activities such as campaigning, volunteering, and community activism (Dahlgren 2009), to politics in the more formal, official sense of parties and governments. Civic cultures—which are therefore broader than political cultures—depend on processes such as the public sharing of information and a commitment to reciprocity and mutual support. It is these qualities, sometimes termed "social capital," that some now see as being in serious decline (Putnam 2000).

The apparent deficit in civic culture is often thought to be most severe among young people. A good deal of research appears to show that young people are less interested in social and political issues, less knowledgeable about them, less trusting of traditional forms of public authority, and less likely to engage in civic participation than adults (e.g., Galston 2004; Gibson, Nixon, and Ward 2003; Henn and Weinstein 2006; Scheufele and Nisbet 2002; Spannring et al. 2008). There is some evidence, although it is less clear-cut, that this is a cohort effect rather than simply an effect of age differences, that the decline has been ongoing over several decades, and that it is particularly the case among working-class young people and those with low educational achievement (Bynner and Ashford 1994). It could be argued that the means by which young people come to see themselves as functioning citizens have been weakened or dislocated to the point that a sizable minority no longer has any investment in civic culture, now or in the future.

In these debates, young people themselves are often blamed for this situation: diminished civic engagement is typically constructed as the result of apathy (or even laziness or narcissism) on their part. Alternatively, the blame is placed on the forms of entertainment media or consumer culture that are particularly popular with the young (especially television: Putnam 2000), although with the supposedly mitigating factor that young people are typically seen as too vulnerable or too lacking in critical ability to resist such influences (see Katz 1997; Wayne et al. 2008).

However, some commentators argue that the problem is quite the opposite: it is not so much that young people have abandoned civil society but rather that social and political elites have abandoned—or even positively excluded—them. Politicians, according to this line of thought, have largely ignored the issues that young people are most concerned about and have failed to keep pace with social and cultural change. They fail to communicate with young people and often actively disparage them, and so have only themselves to blame (Coleman with Rowe 2005; Katz 1997). Young people, it is argued, are also systematically misrepresented by traditional, top-down media formats such as television news and newspapers (Wayne et al. 2008; Women in Journalism 2009).

From this perspective, the problem has not so much to do with apathy as with a perceived lack of relevance of mainstream politics to young people's everyday interests and concerns. Research suggests that some young people can be very passionately engaged in particular campaigns or community-based issues even if they feel alienated by conventional forms of political discourse (Gordon 2009; Sherrod et al. 2006) and that their level of civic engagement depends very much on the opportunities they are given to participate in public life—which in most cases are limited. In general, it appears that most young people are engaged not by the "macropolitics" of politicians and political parties, which are seen to be dominated by older generations and out-dated cultural modes, but by the "micropolitics" of everyday life, single-issue campaigns, and so-called DIY (do-it-yourself) politics. As such, measures such as voting figures or membership in political parties, on which most narratives of decline are based, are inadequate indicators of levels of civic engagement, particularly among the young.

Some advocates of this position go further, arguing that popular culture has now become the preeminent domain for contemporary politics. Rather than dismissing talk shows or reality TV as symptoms of the degeneration and trivialization of public life, this line of argument holds that it is in such forums that fundamental social and political issues are now being debated—if often in vicarious or symbolic forms (see Corner and Pels 2003; van Zoonen 2004). Other studies suggest that young people may learn much more about politics from satirical comedies such as *The Daily Show* than from television news (Baumgartner and Morris 2006), while yet others point to consumer-led campaigns in the field of popular culture—for example, around the cancellation of particular TV shows—as forms of active contestation that adopt the tactics of social movements and potentially empower consumers (Earl and Schussmann 2008; Jenkins 2006). Meanwhile, as Stephen Coleman (2003) and others have noted, the voting figures for programs such as *Big Brother* are often higher than those for national elections, and audiences tend to prioritize values seen to be in short supply among politicians, such as authenticity and honesty. From this perspective, popular culture is viewed as providing the possibility of new forms of "cultural citizenship" that address the dimensions of pleasure, emotion, and entertainment, dimensions largely repressed in mainstream political discourse.

Lance Bennett (2008) makes a useful distinction here between two models of contemporary citizenship. For the "dutiful citizen," involvement in political and civic life is seen as an obligation and is expressed through conventional activities such as voting and following political news: politics in this model is essentially a matter of one-way communication from the elites to the masses. By contrast, the "actualizing citizen" adopts a more individualistic approach: he or she is distrustful of traditional forms of authority and news media and is inclined to adopt more privatized responses to changing social circumstances, such as at the level of lifestyle or consumption practices. This preference for "politics by other means" is based not on the "strong ties" favored by social capital theorists (Putnam 2000) but rather on looser, more decentralized networks—and indeed, on less sober, nontraditional forms of communication. Bennett argues that young people are moving away from the dutiful citizen model and toward that of the actualizing citizen, and that this is increasingly manifested in arenas, such as reality TV or online games, that are a long way from traditional politics, although he also emphasizes the need to connect (or reconnect) such actualizing citizens to the dutiful requirements of government (see also Coleman 2008).

These developments should also be seen in the context of broader arguments about the changing social constructions of youth and the changing forms of socialization that characterize contemporary democracies (Furlong and Cartmel 1997; Wyn and White 2007). Many social theorists have argued that contemporary life courses are more differentiated and heterogeneous than in earlier times: life transitions are prolonged or delayed, and life narratives are accordingly becoming more fragmented. Young people are apparently born into a globalized consumer culture in which the resources for identity formation have proliferated, and social roles and expectations (as defined, for example, by occupational careers or religious identifications) are no longer so clearly mapped out. In this context, social theorists suggest, we have to engage more actively in a form of self-driven "identity work"—variously labeled "self-socialization" or "reflexivity"—that is characterized by diversity, fluidity, and an emphasis on "weak ties," formed through personal relationships, rather than obedience to strong authority figures (Beck, Giddens, and Lash 1994). The shift toward a more individualized or localized micropolitics might therefore be seen as characteristic of a period that is variously labeled "the risk society," "late modernity," or "postmodernity."

The broad terms of this debate are thus fairly well established. On the one hand, one line of argument tends to place the blame for the decline in traditional forms of civic and political culture among young people on young people themselves. On the other hand, critics of this view suggest that it rests on a limited and conventional understanding of what counts as civic or political practice, and that such an understanding is no longer relevant to younger generations. If we want to reengage young people in the mainstream of civic life, they argue, we will need to find new means of communication that transcend the limitations of traditional politics.

Enter the Internet

Buckingham's *The Making of Citizens* was concerned with television, and on the basis of empirical work with young people both in the US and the UK, it made some suggestions about new styles of television that might prove more effective in informing young people and engaging them in social and political debate. Recently, the focus of attention in this debate has shifted decisively toward new media. To some extent, we have seen a replaying of the earlier debate: just as critics such as Putnam (2000) saw television as to blame for the decline in social capital, some now regard the Internet as the bane of civic life (e.g., Keen 2007). The logic of this argument is partly one of displacement: the more time people spend gazing at screens of various kinds, the less they spend on the face-to-face social activities that are seen as the prerequisite for meaningful civic participation and the accruing of social capital. However, popular critics also accuse the Internet of trivializing social debate, confining people to like-minded interest groups, and promoting a superficial, "one-click" approach to politics (e.g., Carr 2010; Keen 2007).

Nevertheless, the dominant view of the Internet in this context is much more optimistic. Indeed, for some it appears to provide the solution to the perceived problem of young people's disengagement from politics and civic life. According to its advocates, the Internet offers enormous possibilities for citizens to make their voices heard, to contribute autonomously to public debates, and to play a more active part in the political process. It provides a form of "networked citizenship" that is more inclusive and more participatory than the passive, dutiful citizenship of the past. This, it is argued, may be particularly relevant for the "socially excluded" who have effectively been left behind by mainstream political discourse (Coleman with Rowe 2005; Rheingold 2008). Such arguments are frequently applied to the so-called digital generation of young people, who are apparently developing new forms of global political consciousness and activity as a result of their use of new media (Tapscott 2008). Far from dumbing down and disengaging young people, the new media are viewed as politically and personally empowering: they enable young people to become the agents or authors of civic action rather than merely the objects of adult interventions.

On the face of it, there are good reasons to believe that the use of the Internet could indeed have significant effects on civic participation and that it might at least contribute to new ways of "doing politics." If we compare the Internet as a medium with offline forms—both established media such as newspapers or television and forms of civic engagement such as voting, attending meetings, or demonstrating—several differences are apparent. Some of the Internet's most relevant characteristics or affordances in this respect would include the following:

- *anonymity* the Internet provides opportunities for trying on or trying out ideas, positions, and civic identities without the necessity of personal commitment
- *instantaneity* the Internet is significantly quicker than other media in terms of the ability to disseminate, gain feedback, and update information on a regular basis
- *accessibility* at least for the growing majority with access to the technology, the Internet is significantly cheaper and more accessible on an everyday basis than are many other forms of media
- *ongoing involvement* ease of access permits regular ongoing involvement and dialogue, compared with the episodic or sporadic nature of most other forms of civic participation
- *disintermediation* in many (though not all) contexts, access to the Internet is not controlled by gatekeepers or other intermediaries, allowing more direct access by users
- *equality* at least in principle, the Internet is an egalitarian medium in which all participants have an equal right to speak and there are fewer formal requirements for participation
- *abundance* information on the Internet is abundant, and the costs of entry for producers are much lower than in older media such as television
- *deterritorialization* the Internet allows instant access to information from all around the world, making distant events appear close, and hence offering new possibilities for transnational engagements
- *personalization* many of the above characteristics permit users to develop personalized approaches to the medium that will serve their individual motivations and purposes.

Furthermore, it is not unreasonable to expect these possibilities—what we might call the "civic promise" of the Internet—to be particularly apparent to young people. Although essentialized notions of young people as digital natives or a digital generation have been widely challenged (e.g., Banaji 2011; Buckingham 2006; Herring 2008; Selwyn 2009), it remains the case that many young people coming of age today, at least in Western democracies, have grown up with ready access to the Internet, and many of them use it more intensively (and, many would argue, more competently) than older generations.

Of course, it is important to see these technological developments in the context of broader social changes, of the kind briefly outlined above. Numerous social theorists have pointed to significant shifts in the modes of social organization and identity formation in "late modern" societies manifested in, among other things, major changes in the nature of knowledge production and dissemination (of which the

Internet is part). As a result, they suggest, the existing forms of authority invested in social, cultural, and political elites are more open to challenge—a development that some see as part of a larger move toward a more democratic, participatory culture (Jenkins 2006). These changes are often seen to be particularly apparent in young people's changing orientation toward information: they are more likely to catch information on the fly, from a variety of sources, and they are more skeptical and less trusting, more playful and less formal in their approach (Katz 1997).

These assertions are all debatable, however, and as we show in coming chapters, they do not necessarily apply in all contexts or to all users. Furthermore, their consequences for civic engagement may be negative as well as positive (Bentivegna 2006; Rice 2002). The use of the Internet may democratize public debate, but it might equally well result in superficiality, disrespect for evidence and logical argument, and an incoherent "dialogue of the ignorant" (Keen 2007). Likewise, the rise of specialist, net-savvy interest groups might prove empowering for their members, but it could ultimately undermine the legitimacy of more official forms of communication and further dissipate interest in the formal political process. The proliferation of information on the Web could be seen to promote a diversity of views, but it might equally lead to a chaotic information glut that alienates users. The lack of intermediation might allow greater freedom of expression, but concerns about the reliability of information on the Internet could equally lead to a form of superficial cynicism and mistrust. The Internet might be seen to encourage less hierarchical networks and to promote dialogue, but it has also proved to be a valuable resource for groups whose interests are distinctly antidemocratic, such as those seeking to promote xenophobic violence and religious sectarianism (Copsey 2003). Finally, while rhetorical claims about "interactivity" and "participatory culture" may appeal to libertarian political instincts, they can also be seen as a manifestation of the new business models of contemporary capitalism (van Dijck and Nieborg 2009).

So What Do We Know?

To what extent can the Internet actually deliver on the promise of reengaging young people in the civic sphere and creating new forms of civic and political culture? Research on these issues has proliferated massively in the last five to ten years, but it is possible to map the broad contours of the debate. Fadi Hirzalla (2010) makes a useful distinction in this regard between what he calls *mobilization* and *normalization*. On the one hand are studies extolling the civic potential of the Internet and suggesting that it removes barriers to access, promotes participation, and creates new forms of civic community; on the other hand are studies that see it as merely confirming existing inequalities and making very little difference to people's inclination to participate in civic and political life (see also Loader 2007). As Hirzalla and Banaji (2012) point out, these two types of research tend to rely on different kinds of evidence: studies of mobilization are inclined to employ qualitative case studies, while those that conclude in favor of normalization tend to rely on large-scale surveys. To some extent, then, we have a further binary here, although it is fair to say that most research could be located at some point along a continuum between these two positions and that there is an increasing degree of convergence between them.

Thus, on the side of mobilization, there are several studies that are primarily based on surveys or case studies of available websites. For example, the early US study by Montgomery, Gottlieb-Robles, and Larson (2004) paints a picture of a vibrant, diverse online youth civic sphere, and this generally positive account is supported by other, more detailed descriptive case studies of particular sites or initiatives (e.g., Bachen et al. 2008; Coleman 2008; Coleman with Rowe 2005; Vromen 2007, 2008). However, as Montgomery and colleagues readily acknowledge, such studies tell us nothing about how such sites are actually used or by whom, or what effects or consequences such use may have.

Also on the side of mobilization we find numerous studies exploring productive uses of the Internet by activist groups (e.g., Bennett, Breunig, and Givens 2008; Hands 2011; Kahn and Kellner 2004; McCaughey and Ayers 2003; Olsson 2007). There has been extensive documentation of the role of the Internet in social movements relating to issues such as antiglobalization, minority rights, feminism, and antiwar campaigns, as well as forms of technological "cyberactivism" such as hacking and online "adbusting"—although, as this suggests, much of the interest among academics has been in liberal or progressive politics (Cammaerts 2009; Hands 2011) rather than in the equally extensive uses of the Internet by the political Right (Banaji 2008). While some are relatively modest in their claims, such studies generally find that the Internet provides powerful means of fostering communication and building solidarity within such groups, that it facilitates transnational connections in particular, that it can provide important alternatives to mainstream media as a source of information, and that it is a valuable means of coordinating political actions that take place offline.

However, few activist groups prioritize the use of the Internet for its own sake or regard online engagement as an alternative to offline activities. Indeed, some studies suggest that the Internet may make it more difficult for people to put in the real work that is necessary for building social or political movements, and that having to engage with (potentially malicious) users (Gillan 2009) or avoid and negotiate government surveillance and censorship can prove a particular distraction. Others argue that it can militate against the formation of the strong ties that are necessary for sustained solidarity (van Laer and van Aelst 2010). Several studies suggest that the Internet may make it easier for people to confine their contacts to like-minded people and to avoid those whom they would like to ignore, although Olsson (2006) describes examples of young members of political parties deliberately using online forums on opposing websites to hone their debating skills. Meanwhile, Tatarchevskiy (2011) points to the ways in which images of "ordinary people" as activists—used in this case by the musician Bono's ONE campaign—are effectively appropriated to brand and market nonprofit organizations seeking to compete in a world of marketized philanthropy. Finally, it should not be forgotten that the Internet has particular advantages for right-wing hate and extremist groups—perhaps more than it does for political moderates or those engaged in more traditional forms of politics (Atton 2004; Caiani and Wagemann 2009; Gerstenfeld, Grant, and Chiang 2003).

By contrast, normalization studies tend to conclude that using the Internet does not make much difference to civic participation: the kinds of people who are active online are generally the same as the kinds of people who are active offline; they mostly do the same kinds of things online as they do offline; and it seems that the Internet very rarely motivates people who are not already motivated to engage in political action. Thus, when it comes to civic participation, we find numerous studies showing that the Internet is most heavily used by the "usual suspects"—that is, by affluent, highly educated young people and by those who are already interested in politics (Dahlgren and Olsson 2007; Livingstone, Couldry, and Markham 2007; Theocharis 2011; van der Meer and van Ingen 2009; Vromen 2008). Other groups, such as those from lower socioeconomic backgrounds, tend to be disengaged—at least from *institutional* politics—both offline and online (Geniets 2010). There is thus a danger that, far from overcoming inequalities in participation, the Internet may actually exacerbate them: to those who have, more shall be given.

As we discuss with regard to our own survey research (analyzed in chapter 4), young people use the Internet mostly for entertainment, academic work, and personal communication rather than for purposes that might (however generously) be defined as public or civic in nature. Studies suggest that Internet use may increase knowledge in some areas but that people generally seek out information that confirms their existing views, and Internet use therefore does not contribute to significant changes in offline political or civic behavior (Baumgartner and Morris 2010). Likewise, despite considerable optimism about the use of the Internet and other new media by political candidates (Gillmor 2006; Talbot 2008), there is little evidence that it has made much difference to people's interest in politics or their participation in elections (Baumgartner and Morris 2008; Mesch and Coleman 2007; Xenos and Foot 2007; Zhang et al. 2010). Some argue that the Internet makes it too easy for users to *feel* as though they have engaged in meaningful political or civic action, for example by filling in petitions or donating small amounts of money online, and that this kind of "keyboard activism" may be at the expense of actions that demand more sustained commitment (van Laer and van Aelst 2010).

To some extent, however, the interpretation of these findings must depend on one's initial expectations. Is the glass half full or half empty? For example, if we find that

23 percent of our sample respondents have consulted civic websites, do we interpret this as disappointingly low or reassuringly high? Likewise, when Theocharis (2011) finds that over 50 percent of his Greek sample have been involved in direct political action, such as demonstrating or occupying a building, we might well find little grounds for concluding that young people are politically apathetic. Yet at the same time, these findings point to the limitations of self-report questionnaires: consulting a civic website or volunteering or talking about politics with your friends may mean many things, and there may be a social desirability bias at work in the self-report. On the other hand, other civic activities conducted online, such as contributing to discussions about racism in football, or about bullying, or indeed about music or other leisure activities, might not be reported at all by young people as an element of their online civic participation.

Beyond the Internet Effect

As we have implied, the distinction between mobilization and normalization studies should not simply be polarized into one of cyber-optimists versus cyber-pessimists—and indeed, these two positions may not be as incompatible as they might seem. One of the fundamental problems with the debate, and with some of the research, is that it seems to be seeking evidence of an "Internet effect," yet as we know from other areas of media research, the attempt to isolate and quantify media effects in this way is (to say the least) a highly problematic endeavor, both theoretically and methodologically. In fact, as the early flush of enthusiasm has waned, much of the research in this field has adopted a more socially contextualized view. On both sides of the debate there is a general recognition of several factors that serve to qualify exaggerated claims about the likely effects of the Internet on young people's civic participation. We briefly group these points, in very broad terms, under the three themes of our research:

1. The Internet
To begin with, it is important to avoid representing "the Internet" as though it were a unitary phenomenon. To a much greater extent than measures of television use in earlier research, measures of the extent of Internet use may well be measuring very different things. The Internet includes a range of different technological affordances, genres, and cultural forms, each of which should be analyzed in its own right. Even so, it is fair to say that the Internet generally functions as a "pull" medium rather than a "push" medium: it requires individual users to actively seek out content rather than "broadcasting" it to them. As such, it may be a valuable tool for communication among those who are already active, at least for some purposes and under some circumstances, but is likely to be less effective in reaching and actively engaging those

who are disengaged when compared with older methods such as television, print media, or even public meetings or demonstrations.

2. Young People

Likewise, it is important to avoid generalized or essentialized views of young people. The continuing existence of digital divides or inequalities of various kinds is inevitably replicated in civic uses (and non-uses) of the Internet. Despite romantic characterizations of young people as digital natives, these divides are apparent in this age group as well. Even so, it is clear that most young people's uses of the Internet are for purposes related to commercial entertainment and for interpersonal communication among friendship groups. Most user-generated sites (social networking sites, sharing sites) are commercial spaces whose existence depends on selling audiences to advertisers (Andrejevic 2007; Fuchs 2010; Terranova 2000). As such, there may be few opportunities for young people to come across information on traditionally civic or political issues, and relatively few of them will actively seek it out, although there is evidence that they may engage contingently with such information in other online environments (Willis 2006).

3. Civic Participation

Similarly, there are various forms and degrees of participation. Some experiences of civic participation online may well be sustained and profound, while others are brief and episodic (signing petitions, for example) and yet others positively frustrating. In some circumstances, nonparticipation (or disengagement) might well be construed as a rational response to the available opportunities (Banaji 2008). As we have implied, a much broader view of civic engagement and participation is needed than is sometimes adopted in such debates. In our usage, "political" implies some form of agonistic or adversarial relationship (with "opponents" of some description) and an inclination to seek solidarity with like-minded members of particular social groups; whereas "civic" is somewhat broader and more elusive, implying merely some notion of involvement in the public sphere. Broadly speaking, we have followed Peter Dahlgren's (2003, 155) definition of civic as "a prerequisite for the (democratically) political, a reservoir of the pre- or non-political that becomes actualized at particular moments when politics arises." As Dahlgren suggests, participation may *become* civic—or indeed political—in particular circumstances, depending on how it is conducted and defined, and these specific circumstances need to be identified and understood. Yet self-evidently, not all forms of online participation are civic participation, either in intention or in effect, and it is important not to extend the meaning of this term too far (Serrano and Sampere 1999).

All these points emphasize that research needs to take into account the diversity of young people, the Internet, and civic participation. They also imply that we have to understand online activities in the context of people's offline engagements. And even if the broad picture is one of normalization, it is equally important to look at the exceptions to the rule. What it is that (however unusually) motivates people to get involved in civic action? Under what circumstances and for what reasons does this happen? It may be that what motivates people is not immediately perceived (even by them) as civic or political in nature. At least to begin with, it may be about other (apparently more banal, more self-interested, or more superficial) things. Equally, the reasons why people do not get involved, or why they avoid what they perceive as "politics," are not necessarily political. While we would certainly question simple assertions about an Internet effect, we do need to know when, under what circumstances, and for whom the Internet might be making a difference, and why and how such an effect may occur. To this extent, qualitative case studies of unrepresentative examples are needed alongside analyses of broader trends; and that is what we have sought to provide in this book.

Conclusion

In this introductory chapter we have attempted to map out some of the broad terms of the debate in this area and some of the key themes and findings of previous research. There are broader critical questions that might be raised about the framing of the issue itself. Is the democratic deficit simply a communication problem that can be solved by adopting different means of communication, or is it something more fundamental? What is at stake in identifying young people in particular as the focus of concern and of intervention? Are we assuming that participation is always in itself a good thing, or are we in fact seeking to promote particular kinds of participation? What do we count as civic, what are we excluding from this category, and why? These questions run through the account of our research in the following chapters, and we return to them more directly in our conclusion.

2 Researching the Civic Web

Any attempt to study even a part of the online world faces obvious difficulties. The Internet is a decentralized medium, and it is impossible to gain a comprehensive picture of everything that is available online, much less construct a representative sample of it. It is an ever-changing medium that is always "under construction": several of the sites we discuss in this book no longer exist or have changed significantly since we first accessed them. And though it is developing rapidly, Internet research still lacks the kind of shared descriptive and conceptual tools that are available, for example, in areas such as film or literary studies (see Baym and Markham 2009; see specifically in our field, Gerodimos and Ward 2007).

In our research, we faced further difficulties of the kind we hinted at in the first chapter. It was fairly straightforward to identify sites that appeared, in whole or in part, to be targeted to young people, although we had to be fairly flexible in how we defined the parameters of that category. However, it was much harder to agree on what might count as civic, especially in the context of an international project. The word *civic* does not have an obvious linguistic parallel, for instance, in Dutch or Slovenian. It also appears to have very different connotations in different contexts: in Turkey, it denotes any sphere of life not connected to the military, while in Hungary the closest synonymous term is mostly used by conservative political groups. Furthermore, the countries that were the focus of our research have quite different political histories, with the result that the terms "civic sphere" or "civil society" can mean very different things. Phenomena we might choose to categorize as "civic" are not necessarily explicitly labeled in this way, nor will they always announce their civic credentials in explicit terms. Finally, different levels of Internet access and use across different countries—and differences of scale between smaller and larger nations—result in widely different amounts and types of civic activity online.

Our Research

Our approach to the intersecting fields of civic participation, young people, and Internet use entailed several distinct but overlapping forms of investigation. We began by seeking simply to map the range of civic websites available for young people in the seven countries. This descriptive analysis explored basic aspects of both form and content, including the use of interactive features and user-generated material. The detailed findings of this survey are reported elsewhere (CivicWeb Deliverable 6), although a brief summary of the key points appears in a later section of this chapter.

Based on some of the most salient patterns we found for those dimensions, we then developed in-depth case studies of a range of civic websites (between six and eight in each country), looking further at the interconnections among pedagogy, site design, mode of address, ideological stance, and the aims of the sites. Then the case studies from the different countries were compared under the following categories: party political sites, European-wide youth sites, youth activist sites, general (adult and youth) activist sites, sites promoting civic participation more broadly, those promoting volunteering, youth council sites, sites addressing specific identities (minority, regional, national), and youth counseling sites. A selection of these case studies relating particularly to politics, activism, and identity issues is analyzed in chapters 6 and 7.

Overlapping with the survey of websites and the case studies was a series of in-depth interviews with a total of eighty-five producers of civic websites. Again, we attempted to sample producers from a range of organizations and contexts, from national and local governmental bodies and large NGOs to organizations encouraging volunteering and individual grassroots youth activists. The aim of the interviews with producers was to gain an understanding of how the producers view their sites; why they have a website, what its purpose is, and how it links to offline activities; how they make decisions about its design; how they perceive its users or participants; and how they conceptualize the civic and political sphere. Some of this material informs the case studies in chapters 6 and 7, and we also consider the cross-cutting organizational aspects, particularly with respect to NGOs, charities, and smaller activist or campaigning groups, in chapter 3.

Turning to the users (or potential users) of these sites, we again sought to obtain both broad survey data and in-depth qualitative information. For the survey portion, we posted an online questionnaire that drew more than 3,300 participants in the seven participating countries. The questionnaire elicited basic quantitative data about young people's uses of the Internet and the extent to which they engaged in episodic or sustained civic activities both online and offline. This survey questionnaire was followed by a series of in-depth focus group interviews with young people. Around ten to twelve such groups were convened in each country, for a total of seventy groups and more than four hundred participants. These focus groups covered a range of demographic sectors and enrolled young people both civically active and inactive, as well as Internet-savvy and "digitally excluded" users. The focus groups enabled us to explore young people's Internet practices in different sociocultural contexts, their motivations for political or civic engagement and ways in which the Internet helped them pursue their interests in this field, their responses to civic content online, and the role of civic or political education. Some of the quantitative and qualitative aspects of this work are adumbrated in chapters 4 and 5.

An International Perspective

As we have argued elsewhere, the role of the Internet in promoting, directing, or discouraging social, political, and civic participation depends on the offline contexts in which its use is situated. Much of the research we introduced in chapter 1 was based primarily on US user studies, and much of it appears to take for granted what we might consider to be peculiarly American values and assumptions. Yet there are notable differences between the US and Europe in many relevant respects. A concept such as "democracy," for example, means something quite different in the context of European welfare state societies such as Sweden or even the UK compared with the much more market-led system of the United States. Analyses of the decline of social capital often seem to refer implicitly to the social context of the middle-class US suburbs and are of more limited relevance to the more urbanized, socially diverse context of nations such as the UK or the Netherlands. Meanwhile, the outwardly "classless" constructions of youth that seem to inform much of the US-based research do not translate very easily to the complex and heterogeneous landscape of youth cultures that characterizes countries like Turkey or Hungary.

Evidently, differences in political systems and civic cultures, in the media landscape, and in the social position of youth have implications for the Internet's potential for promoting young people's civic engagement. As we have noted, our research took place in seven contrasting nations, and we selected the countries quite deliberately to explore some of the differences in political and civic cultures and histories and in the ways in which the Internet might be used.

To begin with, the seven countries are of very different size. Turkey, for example, has approximately thirty-five times the population of Slovenia. Some of the countries (such as Sweden) have relatively centralized political systems, while others (such as the Netherlands) are relatively decentralized. Some (such as the UK and Spain) include semi-autonomous nations or regions within their borders, while others include strong nationalist minorities (such as the Kurds in Turkey). Some are traditional immigration countries (and former imperial powers, such as the Netherlands and the UK); some (such as Spain) have only recently become a focus for immigration; others (such as Turkey) have historically been countries of emigration. As a result of population migration and the presence of strong minorities, most of these countries have become increasingly culturally and linguistically diverse, which in turn has implications for citizenship.

The seven countries also differ markedly in political history. Slovenia and Hungary, for example, made the transition from communism to a democratic, market-led system fairly recently, though in different ways. While Slovenia broke away from the former Yugoslavia at a relatively early stage in the conflict and escaped much of the turmoil, Hungary is experiencing continuing political turbulence. By contrast, Spain emerged from a right-wing dictatorship only forty-five years ago and is currently making a gradual and uneven transition from a conservative, Catholic culture to a more liberal, secular one. Sweden, the UK, and the Netherlands represent more established social democracies, although there is a notable difference here between nations such as the UK that are dominated by two main political parties and those such as the Netherlands that have a decentralized, multiparty system. Turkey, meanwhile, has a population that is almost entirely Muslim, although the state itself remains officially secular.

The media systems of the seven countries we studied are similarly diverse. Formerly communist countries tend to have relatively concentrated media systems, although here (and in countries such as the UK that have a strong public service broadcasting sector) there are growing challenges from commercial channels, several of which are foreign-owned. In other settings, such as the Netherlands, the media system is much more diversified, reflecting both political and religious differences among the country's populace. Levels of access to new media also vary considerably across the seven countries. Domestic access to the Internet is approaching universal levels in Sweden and is only a little lower in the UK and the Netherlands, while Turkey and Hungary are at the opposite end of the spectrum, with figures for home access in the mid-2000s at around 20 percent. Even so, there remain notable digital divides across the board, with poorer and immigrant communities in each of these countries less likely to have home access to the Internet.

Finally, the position of youth varies across the seven countries. Our research followed the United Nations definition of youth as encompassing those aged between fifteen and twenty-five years, although definitions of youth vary considerably, depending on national traditions and political histories, as well as features of identity such as social class, ethnicity, gender, and religious affiliation. In most of the countries in our study (with the notable exception of Turkey), the proportion of young people in the population is shrinking. Youth unemployment is a particular problem in some cases (the postcommunist nations and among immigrant communities), and young people have become increasingly dependent on their parents. In some instances (such as Slovenia, Spain, and the UK), tertiary education has rapidly expanded in recent years and is becoming increasingly marketized. The general picture of young people's lack of interest in formal political and civic activities (such as voting or volunteering for political parties) is fairly consistent in all seven countries but is particularly evident in the former communist states.

Taken together, these observations suggest that the space of civil society is differently constituted in each country. As such, the roles of political parties, NGOs, and autonomous political movements are likely to be quite variable as well. Different countries have different traditions and practices as regards political and civic activities and different levels of tolerance for the expression of dissent. Each of these differences—and undoubtedly more besides—is likely to affect the level and nature of political or civic participation among young people and the potential role of the Internet in this sphere. Furthermore, these phenomena may be accentuated or altered by immediate events. Since we undertook our research, many of the economies of Europe have been hit by the long runout of the banking crisis, and several governments (including Spain, Hungary, and the UK) have chosen to implement far-reaching austerity measures, which in some cases have met with concerted resistance and a rise in political activism, not least among young people, many of whom face a future without employment.

A systematic characterization and comparison of the history and civic culture of each of the seven countries is beyond the scope of our study. Nevertheless, an international approach helps problematize some of the routine generalizations and easy assumptions that are often taken for granted in the debate over young people's civic and political participation. The specific implications of the country differences we noted are explored in more detail as we proceed, particularly in the case studies in chapters 6 and 7.

Mapping the Civic Web

Our first aim was to generate a broad map of the online youth civic sphere. Our survey was to some extent modeled on the work undertaken by Kathryn Montgomery and her colleagues (2004) in the United States. We categorized our sample of sites a little differently, in ways that reflect salient differences between the youth civic sphere in the US and in Europe. Each of our participating countries identified eighty civic sites aimed at young people, and we applied a shared coding strategy, although each country tweaked this strategy slightly to reflect national differences. The coding covered aspects such as the nature of the organization, its mission statement, and its ideological outlook; the range of content available on the site; aspects of visual design and language; the ways in which the site addressed and represented young people; and the use of interactive or participatory features.

We subsequently categorized the sites under a series of broad (and inevitably somewhat overlapping) headings. Table 2.1 shows the number of sites in each category. As

Table 2.1

Websites analyzed

	Total
EU or EU-oriented	20
National government	55
Political organization	67
Religious organization	49
International network	54
Charity	50
NGO	187
Activist	169
Total	570

the table suggests, a number of traditional public actors are engaged in making civic websites aimed at young people in the participating countries. These actors include the EU and national governments, political parties, religious organizations, international NGOs, and charity organizations, many of which could be considered representatives of the official public sphere and civil society. At the same time, by far the most diverse and difficult to categorize websites are those concerned with grassroots, local, or temporary activism. These sites are often bottom-up efforts created by single-issue activist groups, smaller NGOs, or individuals.

While we found considerable diversity in terms of content, modes of address, design, and interactivity, it was possible to identify general tendencies and patterns among the 570 websites we analyzed. In summarizing this work, we consider two key dimensions, politics and pedagogy.

1. Politics

A spectrum of views of the civic sphere and of civic and political participation is apparent on these sites. At one end are sites produced by organizations that are generally supportive of national governments as they run at present, of the parliamentary system, and of what they consider to be the democratic institutions of each country; these websites are generally produced by national or local governments themselves, by political parties, and in some cases by NGOs or educational organizations. Such organizations may see opportunities to make things run more effectively or more equitably for some groups of people, notably young people in general or, in some cases, those from minorities or disadvantaged areas. These organizations' websites seek to provide a platform for young people, or forms of training and support, that will enhance their participation in relatively official modes of civic activity: young people are seen to be cut off from formal politics, and the aim is to encourage them to become interested in the parliamentary system, voting in elections, and debating the views of politicians. In other cases the aim is simply to canvass support for particular parliamentary parties, and this is often done in a fairly overt and propagandistic manner. Such sites self-evidently espouse highly conventional norms of good citizenship.

Somewhat more radical sites at this end of the spectrum, those of organizations generally supporting the existing political system, see young people as excluded from current debates, and aim to increase politicians' awareness of and responsiveness to young people's views. Some local government sites in this category take this stance slightly further by providing offline resources for youth and reasons for them to get involved in their local communities, where "community" is defined in terms of geographic boundaries or urban and rural zones, rather than in relation to race or religion. Despite this effort, and judging from the evidence of the sites themselves in terms of data collected and provided by producers, the number of young people in any of our participating countries who actually take up such local government invitations to offline counseling or participation is small indeed, in the hundreds.

Toward the middle of the spectrum are sites belonging to organizations that believe (or were started on the premise) that while the *ideal* of elected parliamentary democracy is good, there are huge gaps between the promises made by politicians and what actually happens. Such sites are mostly produced by global campaigning organizations, large charities, and NGOs. These sites typically point to the number of people who are not enjoying basic human rights, let alone the full array of rights promised to national citizens. For example, they invite the involvement of young people in campaigns against torture and human trafficking, or against child labor and sweatshops, and in doing so provide them with implicitly political information about how power and the social order work. The large amount of written information on the sites appears to reflect the assumption that civic and political participation requires high levels of knowledge about historical and current events, social practices, and policies. Also centrally located on this spectrum are sites that pursue advocacy at the highest levels for particular minority group rights but do not necessarily exhort young people to solidarity with other groups or seek to promote broader systemic social change.

Finally, there are a number of sites whose rhetoric and invitations to political activity are clearly driven by anti-state and anti-capitalist ideologies. It is these sites that have been joined in recent years by a vibrant if somewhat agonistic social network sphere of a similar nature. On these sites, civic participation at its most basic level is perceived as a matter of skeptical and critical decoding of mass media messages and government rhetoric, and is further manifested in forms of action such as creating alternative media, leafleting, and engaging in demonstrations, sit-ins, occupations, strikes, petitions, boycotts, and discussion meetings. A small but significant number of radical sites of both the left and the far right view these kinds of actions as old-fashioned and advocate forms of direct action that may break the law. Such actions might include repeatedly breaking "unjust" copyright legislation by file sharing, chaining wheelchairs to disabled-unfriendly roads or thoroughfares, lying down in the road in front of army bases, releasing animals destined for slaughterhouses, or preventing animal testing facilities from carrying out their work, although they might equally involve beating up ethnic minority shopkeepers or firebombing ethnic minority community centers or abortion clinics. Clearly, not all of these actions are comparable or indeed equally "democratic," although their advocates view them as legitimate forms of civic or political action. This is an approach that is becoming more widespread and intense in the wake of the anti-austerity student protests across Europe.

This spectrum of views of the civic or political domain seems to cut across national differences. As far as concerns particular national features that emerged from our survey, such as the strong presence of civic websites in Sweden or the dominance of charity websites in the UK, these seemed to be reflections of the different state of civil society in the participating countries rather than manifestations of nationally specific online civic landscapes. To the degree the latter kinds of difference existed, they seemed to be largely the result of different approaches to "e-government" (in terms of history, policy, and funding) than of other kinds of national differences. Thus, the Spanish and the Turkish websites in the sample seemed to have profited from strong government initiatives, while Slovenia and Hungary were lagging behind. Sweden, the UK, and the Netherlands have a longer Internet history and greater broadband penetration, and so have more developed sites. Yet given the overall similarities in the websites analyzed, it might simply be a matter of time before these national differences disappear.

The spectrum we have described here is primarily a political one. At one end are sites that implicitly support democratic politics as usual, while at the other are those that seek to challenge or undermine it (if from a variety of ideological positions). Yet the differences here are also manifested in the different epistemological and pedagogical approaches of the sites, and hence in the different ways in which they perceive and address their users.

2. Pedagogy

While some of the governmental and party political sites we surveyed make few concessions to their (apparently) intended youth audience, most make some attempt to address young people by adopting particular linguistic or visual characteristics that are construed by the site producers as youth-friendly. These characteristics range from the use of informal language and youth culture slang to the inclusion of images featuring young people and the use of particular graphic styles, such as fonts resembling graffiti. In several cases, sites employ games, music, and animation, as well as interactive features that are clearly included because of their youth appeal. However, these aspects are often superficial, amounting to little more than window dressing for content that is otherwise very conventional and a mode of address to youth that remains quite authoritarian, even patronizing.

Sites' *epistemologies*, their attitude to what is true knowledge about the world and what can and should be challenged, differ hugely depending on their position in the context of European and global civic movements. At one end are sites that consider the most legitimate form of knowledge to be that coming from government or official political parties, and these sites implicitly encourage young users to trust these institutions totally. At the other end of the spectrum are sites that define "the truth about the world" as de facto the opposite of what is asserted by most agencies of government, most political parties, many politicians, and most arms of the national state. These sites, by the very nature of their claims and beliefs about the political sphere, see the need for engagement and action as being far greater and wider-ranging than that envisioned by the former type. The provision of historical information that invites users to view the organization or particular campaign as part of a broader history of struggle is common to sites that view themselves as outside the mainstream. While official party and government sites do provide information to users, historical knowledge is frequently excluded as irrelevant to public debate or else is used selectively, just as debate about the "official" version is eschewed.

In terms of *pedagogy*, however, the differences are much less evident. Broadly speaking, the online civic sphere for young people in Europe seems to be dominated by institutionalized, top-down perspectives and prescriptions of what youth civic engagement means, leaving little room for bottom-up initiatives and alternatives coming from young people themselves. While there are differences in site visual design and style, these are relatively superficial. Although almost all the sites we analyzed have extensive links to other relevant sites, offer contact information, and, if relevant, offer online possibilities to join or donate money, the input of users is seldom sought. The exceptions are the websites especially designed for online participation, discussion, and the distribution of user-generated content, such as Muslim Youth or Roma.hu (two of the case studies discussed in chapter 7). Aside from these, the online civic sphere for European young people seems to be predominantly concerned with disciplining them into good citizenship rather than engaging them in a more participatory process or inspiring them to produce their own alternative understandings of civic engagement.

These pedagogical and epistemological differences are to some extent manifested in different uses of the Internet as a medium, but the picture here is complex. Internet use in the civic participation sphere also depends on the extent to which organizations prioritize online as opposed to offline participation, as well as on material issues such as funding. A further key issue is that of control. Organizations trying to maintain control over their own flow of information and communication—and hence the definition of their mission and purpose—are bound to find it hard to open up to a diversity of user statements and opinions. Particularly clear instances of this phenomenon are visible in the websites of EU, national, and local governments, but tight control can also be found among the websites of religious groups, NGOs, and activist groups.

Meanwhile, the existence of a formal offline organizational structure seems to be a key factor determining the level of online participation that is encouraged: those groups without an offline organizational presence are more likely both to promote online participation of some kind and to use bottom-up, interactive modes of communication. Nevertheless, even these websites offer fewer opportunities for participation than one might expect. By and large, civic participation is seen to take its most important forms *offline*: thus, volunteering, demonstrating, meeting, socializing, and leading a virtuous lifestyle are called for on many websites across the different categories.

This all points to complex set of potential relationships between the political or civic aims of a given site, the kinds of users that are addressed and the ways in which they are addressed, the relative significance of offline as opposed to online participation, and factors such as the potential size of the audience, the nature and extent of the funding, and the wider national civic culture and traditions in which the site is located. These all have an impact on the form, design, and structure of sites in ways that are not necessarily straightforward. A site that uses more interactive functions is thus not necessarily more "civic" than one that does not. A government site may be more self-consciously youth-oriented in its design and address than a grassroots activist site. A site that is addressed primarily to existing members rather than to a wider group may be comparatively static. A site whose primary aim is to promote offline participation may offer very little in the way of online interaction.

Of course, this kind of analysis of the content and form of the online civic sphere tells us relatively little about the ways in which people engage with it (or fail to do so). The insights gleaned from this survey—and, in later chapters, from more in-depth textual analysis—need to be complemented and extended by looking at the people and organizations that produce this content, and by the readings and accounts of young people themselves. It would be a mistake to judge the depth and breadth of an organization's civic role solely by the content—or indeed the technological or aesthetic adventurousness—of its website.

A Moving Target

In the years since our research began, we have seen a steady expansion in the use of commercial "Web 2.0" services, particularly among grassroots and activist organizations: there are now hundreds of activist YouTube channels, students' movement

Twitter feeds, and broadly civic and political Facebook groups. Mainstream organizations—governments, NGOs, charities, and others—are also making use of such services, or attempting to do so. Even so, a surprising number (around 80 percent) of the sites in our original sample are still in operation and updating their content regularly to reflect current concerns and issues, national and international. Regular contributions from young people on the forums and message boards, however, still are only apparent on those sites that initially set out to create a dialogue among their users. On the other hand, a surprising number of the sites initially established as social networking communities have now ceased to exist; this is the case with two Hungarian Roma sites that we studied, Roma.hu and Zhoriben, despite or perhaps because of the increased climate of official hostility toward Roma in many nations. It may be that such social networking possibilities are now being found on generic (if commercial) sites such as Facebook.

To take the UK as an example, eight of the eighty sites originally surveyed are no longer in existence, while five more appear to offer the same static content that they did at the time of the initial survey. In Spain, fourteen of the sites in the initial sample are no longer functional, and half of the sample sites (nearly forty sites) now sport social network buttons (for Facebook and Twitter) on their homepages. Likewise, in the UK the most notable addition to the home pages of more than thirty of the sites initially surveyed is the option to follow the organization or group via an RSS feed or to join it as part of a commercial social network. The British Youth Council site and other official sites, such as the government's site need2know, have added social networking links to their home pages. Rather than developing their own internal social networks, they are attempting to tap into the already popular commercial networks that cut across generations, although in the process they may have to deal with some kind of dilution or diffusion of their specific mission.

More generally, the civic web has also seen a burgeoning of new websites and blogs on a whole range of issues and causes, particularly in 2011–2012, following the implementation of economic retrenchment measures by governments in such countries as Italy, Greece, Ireland, and Spain. Campus groups on Facebook on virtually every imaginable civic issue now abound, and events such as the bombing of Gaza in December 2008 and the anti-Tamil violence in Sri Lanka in 2009 have prompted dozens of concerned Facebook and blog groups. The need for more static Web 1.0 sites clearly remains, partly because they represent the official online presence of an organization, but also because of their ability to host large amounts of material. However, the more sociable or participatory dimensions of civic life online now appear to be migrating to all-purpose commercial social networks.

At the same time, we are seeing a slight but distinct shift in the nature of online activism, though not necessarily in the balance between on- and offline activities. At the time our project began, it was evident that more energy and creativity on the part of activists was being directed into offline civic action than into its online counterpart. Perhaps especially in the wake of the Wikileaks case, a parallel sphere of online action has sprung up (Beckett with Ball 2012), as exemplified by the cloning of banned sites so that information remains in the public sphere, and by the attempted online boycotting of corporate sites that have succumbed to government pressure—although of course, such tactics have been countered by governments that are trying to bring down such sites. The Internet has thus become more of a focus for civic action and struggle *in its own right*. Even in these instances, however, our initial questions about the motivations for and organizational tactics, ideologies, and effectiveness of civic organizations operating online remain very relevant. It is to the production of online civic content that our analysis now turns.

3 Producing the Civic Web

Previous research on civic and political websites, whether those of governments, campaigning networks, or activist organizations, has largely tended to focus on their form and content and less frequently on their users. Very little attention has been paid to the organizations or individuals who produce such sites or to the contexts in which they are actually created. Writing about the use of the Web by antiwar activist groups, Kevin Gillan has argued that "the creation and dissemination of meaning through Internet technologies has been included among the core practical tasks of movement organizations" (2009, 26). Yet these "core practical tasks" constitute a body of labor: the work must be carried out by someone, or by a diffuse group of people, who all become de facto "producers" through their roles in building, maintaining, or contributing to a website. Case studies of civic sites (e.g., Olsson 2007; Vromen 2008) and larger-scale surveys (e.g., Coleman with Rowe 2005; Montgomery, Gottlieb-Robles, and Larson 2004) may make use of interviews with producers, but in general, the labor that is entailed in the production of such sites has remained invisible. There is a striking contrast here with the growing body of research on the nature of work in other areas of the media and creative industries (e.g., Deuze 2010; Hesmondhalgh and Baker 2011).

In an attempt to redress this imbalance, this chapter takes a detailed look at the production of civic websites for young people in the seven countries we studied. We consider the rationales for the creation of the sites, issues of funding and editorial control, working practices, organizational structures, and labor conditions. While the sites in our study were addressed to young people, production often involved multigenerational teams with their own hierarchies, which were at least partly based on age. The larger the organization, the more likely it is that the labor will be divided into different functions—for example, writing content, design, technical maintenance, and moderation—and in some instances these functions may be outsourced to independent providers. These issues clearly varied across the different categories of sites we discussed in chapter 2, although our primary focus here is on charities and NGOs, and to a lesser extent on activist and campaigning organizations. The issues we discuss here are, of course, by no means unique to the online civic sphere; and so we also attempt to set our analysis in the context of other research on working practices both in the new media industries and in voluntary and nonprofit organizations.

Defining the Field, Generating the Data

At first sight, the organizations active in the online civic sphere might seem almost as diverse as the websites themselves. Some sites we explored in our research had large offline organizations behind them, while others existed mainly online. Some were created and maintained by paid staff, while others relied on individual members or volunteers to keep going. However, closer scrutiny revealed two distinct models at opposite ends of a spectrum—one formal and sometimes highly corporate, particularly in the case of youth branches of major political parties, large charities, global campaigns, and mainstream religious organizations, and the other following an informal, sometimes ad hoc "alternative" model, as in the case of smaller NGOs and activist groups. Some of the latter were slowly moving toward a more formalized structure, with a clear division of labor, although many sites combined elements of both models or lay somewhere in between.

In his study of alternative media, Chris Atton suggests that in looking at the organizations behind such "alternative" viewpoints, we are "interrogating identities and practices that are negotiated across a third space that hybridizes practices between hegemonized and marginalized cultures" (2002, 152). This liminal "third space" is also one inhabited by many (but by no means all) of the civic and political website teams and organizations we discuss in this chapter. As such, this space is perhaps inevitably characterized by tensions—between control and openness, between hierarchy and democracy, and between management and workers (insofar as such distinctions can be sustained). These tensions are manifested in working practices and are played out in the everyday decisions and working conditions of production teams.

As we shall indicate, these tensions pose a series of stark questions for practitioners, funders, and policy-makers. The first of these questions was asked by Charles Handy (1988) more than two decades ago: "Is there lurking in the voluntary world a better theory of organizing?" How do such bodies and groups manage and organize themselves; and in what ways are their modes of organization effective, efficient, or necessarily democratic? How are decisions made, how is control exercised, and how are disagreements—for example, about ethos or ideology—managed and resolved? A second and related question has to do with work itself. Tiziana Terranova has suggested that "far from being an "unreal" empty space, the Internet is animated by cultural and technical labor through and through, a continuous production of value that is completely immanent in the flows of the network society" (2000, 33–34). Labor in this online civic space takes many forms, some of them paid and some voluntary, and some forms of labor may not even be perceived as labor at all. If this is the case, how do civic and social organizations divide and allocate the labor that is entailed? How, if at all, do they remunerate the labor they require from the young people who are being called on to participate online? How is one to separate the work of these young people from that of paid employees, part-time volunteers, and management in large organizations?

Following the broad survey described in chapter 2, we selected more than a dozen websites in each country for more detailed analysis (a total of eighty-five sites). Our sample was inevitably somewhat ad hoc, but we intended to reflect a cross section of civic or political concerns, as well as different types of organizations and sites. Although we discuss and analyze several of these sites in more detail in chapters 6 and 7, our aim here is to draw out some crosscutting issues relating to the production of such sites.

We interviewed the producers of these sites (primarily designers, moderators, content editors, or webmasters, but also sometimes organization directors or coordinators) either face-to-face or over the telephone between February 2007 and May 2008. These producers inevitably came from varying backgrounds and had some quite divergent intentions. They ranged from political aides whose aim was basically to reproduce on the Internet the information that people can find at their party headquarters or in leaflets (such as the producers of the website JERC in Spain or AKP in Turkey), to aspiring journalists (producing the website Spunk in the Netherlands) or artists (producers of Payasos sin fronteras in Spain), to professional charity workers or NGO volunteers. Others were simply individuals who had decided to share their opinions with others, as in the case of G, the founder of the website Racò Català in Spain, or people with a long history of civic work from a religious perspective, such as J, from e-christians, also in Spain.

An open-ended qualitative interview schedule was used, building on some of the issues arising from the survey. Our key questions included the following: What role does the website play in the organization's day-to-day functioning? How are key decisions made about the aims, ethos, content, and design of the site? How is the site funded? Do producers have enough funds to keep their website up-to-date and functioning in the way they wish? What roles, if any, do young people play in the creation and maintenance of the organization, its ethos, and its website? How do producers try to reach potential users of their sites, for example through promotion and marketing in both old and new media? How are contributions to the site solicited and moderated? These interviews also dealt with broader themes having to do with how the producers conceptualized their audience and their views both of the Internet and of civic and political participation; these issues are addressed in detail in the case studies presented in chapters 6 and 7.

How Are Civic Websites Born and Made?

The websites of different organizations vary considerably in their history and role, depending on a range of factors. While the longest-standing websites in our sample dated back about twelve years to 1995 or 1996, many were less than five years old at the time of the interviews. The reasons why they were launched are very diverse. Some were set up in the wake of specific historical and political events, such as the racial harassment and discrimination faced by young Muslims in the wake of the events of September 11, 2001, or out of an avowed desire to oppose particular candidates in the European elections. Others began as part of a rebranding strategy for an established organization, aiming to attract what is perceived as a more Internet-savvy generation. The editor who worked on Generation Why, the now defunct youth website of the international charity Oxfam, summed up this approach:

We had a youth strategy, basically which was to engage young people in Oxfam work, but we didn't actually have a website to support that, which was bound to be a key part of the youth strategy, to have a website which would engage them and wasn't. . . . Obviously people have a lot of different opinions about what Oxfam is, like it might be a bit old, maybe a bit untrendy and we were kind of meant to challenge those perceptions via a website that would engage young people on their level in an uncomplicated way.

In yet another rebranding exercise, this website has since been absorbed back into that of the parent organization and the production team has been redeployed or has migrated elsewhere.

By contrast, other websites have no offline component, or else have just a loosely related parent organization, and exist as virtual experiments in youth e-consultation or e-democracy. This was the case with HeadsUp, a UK government-funded site established in 2003 in the wake of the new citizenship curriculum for schools. As its editor put it, "one of the main aims of the website is to try and get parliamentarians debating directly with young people and give them a real sense of their opinions—being heard by parliamentarians." Yet other sites arise from the political motivations and skills of individual producers or teams or producers. Social Spider, another UK site, originally came together around a community-based youth media project. Here is the development director:

Initially when we were setting up we liked the idea of doing socially useful work but without the restrictions of being a charity. And at the time one of the places we were working at was offered to do this job, like a youth magazine based in Seven Sisters, and [that was] when we decided to set up Social Spider.

However, not all aspects of websites' development and evolution are planned by producers. They can be contingent on circumstances, such as who takes up the offer within the organization, the predispositions of the production team, or even historical accident, such as the coincidence of an important political event with the early days of the website. This was clearly the case with the website of Autonomous Tribune in Slovenia, where a group of young people protesting against the increasing privatization of education felt they needed a platform for the discussion and dissemination of their ideas and events. It was also the case with Rog in Slovenia, the site of a youth group occupying what used to be a large industrial space long left empty. A perception that people's suspicion of their activities—which were mainly artistic and creative— was preventing them from getting involved was a catalyst for the group to reach out to a wider public.

Economic Pressures and Working Practices

Funding is inevitably key to the survival of websites and the organizations that run them. It determines a range of aspects, from the establishment and composition of production teams to the design and technical features of the sites and the ideological and political stances producers feel they can be seen to take in the public domain. Independence is a key issue for many civic and political organizations aiming to reach young people or run by young people, but it may have to be compromised or sacrificed in the interests of survival.

A high proportion of the day-to-day work on the sites in our sample was undertaken by part-time or voluntary staff or by staff who also had many additional duties in the wider organization. The commitment and motivation of many of these staff is what sustained the sites, but the sites were often only one element competing for their time and attention. The struggle for funding creates a very insecure working environment, which can in turn lead to a disconnection between the organization's aims and the actual practices on the site. Many sites are not updated for months because initial grants funded only the building of the site and not its updating and maintenance, which are crucial to success. There is often a fairly high turnover of volunteer staff, which can lead to the closure of a site entirely. Most civic website producers have neither the time nor the money to publicize their sites adequately among those who are not already engaged; and hence the core of users remains relatively small.

Given the increased availability of social networking and Web 2.0 tools and the competitive, time-consuming nature of fundraising, it is not surprising that several civic organizations with little funding end up using free blog-style software and relying on voluntary labor. For instance, *Judapest*, a community blog on Jewish culture and identity based in Budapest, Hungary, has never achieved any funding; it is designed, run, and funded by a small group of young people, runs on a free blog engine, and is hosted on a user's server for free. At the other end of the spectrum, some organizations are skillful in raising funding from the corporate sector, with limited and easy-to-fulfill agreements on both sides. For example, also in Hungary, I-dea (Demokratikus Ifjusagert Alapitvany, Foundation for Democratic Youth) is a public benefit nonprofit organization whose mission is to create opportunities for youth to develop democratic values and skills through experiential learning; it is funded by the mobile phone company Nokia. Meanwhile, Planet, an NGO running programs to help young people going abroad as voluntary workers and professionals, received a donation from the Hungarian subsidiary of the multinational telecommunication giant T-Com. Both I-dea and Planet were satisfied with the cooperation and did not feel overly constrained in their activities by their funders. However, such partnerships with private companies are not always viewed with the same degree of comfort in other countries: organizations in the UK in particular commented on the complexity of inviting private corporate investment, and the compromises that might result.

On the other hand, commercial activities, particularly merchandising, can provide a growing form of income for some civic sites. This is especially apparent with large campaign and charity sites such as the official sites of Amnesty International and UNICEF, which market a range of "ethical" products that may in turn help promote their cause (as in the case of slogans on t-shirts or mugs). However, it can also be important for much smaller operations with different political motivations: for example, much of the funding for the nationalist tu-je.si website in Slovenia comes from "patriotic" merchandise ranging from apparel to coffee mugs and refrigerator magnets, most of it featuring the nationalistic Carinthian panther symbol. We have discussed the role of "ethical consumption" elsewhere (Banaji and Buckingham 2009), and this approach is also manifested in some of the case studies we consider in the following chapters.

More generally, many organizations find it a constant struggle to raise enough money not only to keep web-based projects running but also to improve and widen their reach. Even those youth sites that receive internal funding from their parent organization (such as Unicef Youth Voice, the UK local government site B-Involved, the Dutch site Young Socialists, or the Turkish AKP) have to justify this in terms of their aims and outcomes. Others must apply to numerous funding sources or take on paid projects and contract work (such as technology training) in order to be able to guarantee the salaries of permanent nonvolunteer staff. For instance, the environmental campaigning groups One World and One Climate have a team of fifteen part- and full-time staff, including two or three volunteers, and depend on a variety of funding sources:

In the UK it's a mixture—our partners all pay small amounts to be partners, we do have some advertisements and some donation pages but neither of those raise all that much, and then we have grants from sponsoring companies and organizations who work with us on particular projects, companies like Vodafone and BT. (Director, One World)

Social Spider's team used to depend almost entirely on being paid for the work they do for larger government-related civic organizations to subsidize their pro bono civic projects. Now they are able to apply for grants from funders such as the National Lottery and youth charities in order to continue their work. However, connections to government in terms of funding also bring certain constraints. If the designated time for a particular program runs out at the end of the funding, then the chances of continuing the work that has been started are slim. This presents particular difficulties for those organizations that hope to engage "harder to reach" young people, who might not participate in one-off or brief events and activities. Organizations like the British Youth Council described the difficulties of juggling different funding streams, which inevitably resulted in a short-term, even entrepreneurial approach.

For others, there is a precarious balance to be maintained between having adequate funding and being able to pursue independent goals and ideas, while simultaneously assembling funding from some very diverse sources, each of which may have different imperatives:

Our core funding comes from the government, from the Department for Children Schools and Families. . . . It's always negotiated every year. The core funding doesn't go very far so we've always had to look elsewhere and we've got a sponsorship deal with BT [British Telecom] and an engineering company called MWH and then we go to other pots as well, so a few things like the Youth Charity, we got some funding from there and funding from all kinds of places which we have to do just to keep it going. (Content editor, UKYP)

Yet even government funding of this kind was not open-ended or free of conditions: organizations were required to provide very detailed reporting and feedback, and the criteria in play could often be subject to change.

In other countries, government funding could be even more complex and treacherous. Some institutions are under constant pressure from restructuring, their officials come and go, and even the money won via governmental tenders remains uncertain. As one content editor from I-dea in Hungary explained,

Dozens of civic organizations go bankrupt because the State of Hungary wouldn't transfer the money. . . . They don't check submitted reports for months, therefore they cannot transfer further money. . . . The system is not exactly perfect.

As an established NGO that survives on a limited EU budget, the Civil Society Development Center in Turkey has had to deal with similar uncertainties by adopting what is euphemistically termed a more "flexible" approach to work—although this makes web management issues problematic:

In terms of software . . . one has to prepare the interface, organize the database and connect these. The beginning of it was tough, but the period following that was even tougher. We had to work flexible hours, as in the evolution panel we have just organized. My partners, C and E, are also very flexible and try to fill the gaps. However, realistically speaking, just one person working full-time would create a much better working situation in terms of web management. (Editor, Civil Society Development Center)

The theme of long hours and flexible worktime was repeated, with varying degrees of frustration and resentment, across a number of the organizations we researched. For example, J, a content editor for Save the Children in Spain, described how the increased popularity of the site had generated a need for a person dedicated to work solely on the site, but the organization could not afford to pay a salary. Currently, the same small team of people who keep the website functional have to do many other tasks, both on- and offline.

This perceived need for a more professional, specialized, and technical worker to maintain the website was a concern shared by many producers. Particularly where organizations rely on free or open-source software, there are sometimes complex issues that can only be resolved by one skilled member of a team, and this may mean that the site is out of commission for key periods, days or even weeks, until that person can be brought in. In other instances the lack of regular funding makes for an insecure working environment, with almost equal amounts of time being spent on the work of the site and in looking for funding to continue that site in the future. This situation in turn can lead to significant gaps between the organizations' initial aims and the actual practices that can be sustained on the site.

Some producers cautioned that having a website to reach young people en masse in relation to a very general issue—or even a more specific but non-time-limited one—can be a risky strategy for a low-income organization. We were told of several situations where funding had been thrown at small civic organizations to help them develop a website strategy, because it was assumed that a website would bring in new adherents, yet the way in which the practice of website presence was implemented was often poorly thought out and short-sighted, in the sense that funding involved a one-off payment. For example, LMV in Hungary had received initial funding from the National Civil Fund to set up its website but subsequently had to operate without any external financial support, and it was unable to afford paid employees or occasional expenses (for instance, to maintain the domain name) out of its own resources. For organizations lacking a budget line for technical maintenance, moderating online discussions or user input, or keeping the site up-to-date, the burden must be absorbed by a team of volunteers. Such work requires a high level of altruistic commitment on the part of volunteers or members. In other cases, the assumption that such online work could, by default, become part of the organization's other (offline) activities was very questionable. Some of our interviewees argued that, compared to the trials of running a website in such circumstances, printing several hundred leaflets and hand-delivering them to young people each month or posting them in schools and universities would be far cheaper and more effective in terms of promoting long-term participation.

Editorial Control and Moderation

Regular updating of content and the effective moderation of user contributions are obviously vital to the ongoing success of civic sites. However, the extent to which these activities are possible or practical depends on several factors, including the level of ongoing funding and the kinds of online tools that are provided, as well as the management strategy of the organization, its ethos, and how it conceptualizes democratic participation. A number of the producers whom we interviewed reported that their sites were run in an anarchic or decentralized manner, with roles and obligations being delegated ad hoc and rarely formalized. In the case of the Slovene patriotic site *tu-je.si*, for example, decision making involved giving every participant the status of "full user":

This is awarded to everybody who writes on the forum. It is not necessary that he writes much, but that he came with this intent. Some people come to these forums just to provoke.

Similarly, in the case of the Art Centre, an alternative youth arts center that had come into ongoing conflict with the Slovenian authorities, we were told that decisions were made "very democratically," and that work was divided "according to experience and abilities, about everything in between we decide collectively." Likewise, the inhabitants of the Slovenian community arts center Rog explicitly adhered to a philosophy of openness, which was also transferred to its website. However, in this case the fact that the site uses open-source software and is more complex in design means that those with specific computer skills are de facto making most of the decisions.

While these kinds of youth-led grassroots projects might at least aspire to a condition of complete democratic openness, this was more difficult for sites that were funded by government or other official sources. In the case of the UK's local government site B-Involved, for example, the tension between the site's formal connection to local government and the needs and wishes of young constituents made the use of interactive tools such as forums complicated. Several producers described moving from postmoderated to premoderated content, sometimes as a result of difficult experiences. This was the case, for example, with the government-funded citizenship education site HeadsUp, which also relied on the mediating influence of teachers who were using the site in their citizenship lessons.

However, this issue is often more than a matter of bad behavior. In the Netherlands and the UK most notably, it was a particular problem for young first- and second-generation immigrants who had established civic sites designed to challenge prejudice both within and outside their communities. Some of them had been subjected to fierce and sometimes racist critique and flaming, sometimes by organized right-wing groups. In Hungary, Roma sites had attempted to avoid this situation by having closed membership or censoring posts from racist users. Similar experiences had been encountered on sites focusing on sexuality and, in the case of Sweden, gender. Here again, after negative experiences with flaming and spam, there had been a move from postmoderated to premoderated contributions. For many producers, such moderation or even "censorship" is seen to conflict with the democratic rhetoric surrounding the Internet and can generate continuing moral and political dilemmas, yet it may come to be seen as a necessity (see Fabbro 2010). Even so, premoderation of comments could represent a significant expense, and for organizations that are concerned to maintain a consistent profile or sense of mission, encouraging open debate could create more difficulty than it is really worth.

In the case of Muslim Youth, this had to some extent been avoided through the recruitment of regular users as moderators:

We don't like to come in and moderate, so what we've done is we see that the top five users are always online and we ask them if they mind being moderators. Usually they don't mind. Some will say actually we want to be anonymous, but mostly it's just a case of going in and saying like maybe—I don't know, like bringing it back to the topic or—it's basically all self-moderation. We rarely have to go in there [to the forums]. (Volunteer content editor, Muslim Youth)

Here again, however, the site appears to rely on a form of invisible labor on the part of volunteers, which the people concerned might not always have the time or inclination to undertake.

Working Relations

While at least half the producers whom we interviewed were under thirty, almost all the teams we met consisted of people from both younger and older generations. In larger and better-funded organizations, older activists and website producers tended to be employed, either part- or full-time, while younger people were either very part-time volunteers or part of a nebulous group of youth used as "consultants" on issues of style, voice, or content priorities. People under thirty were often assigned mundane "techie" tasks, while those over thirty were given control of organizational philosophy and ideology. It was also often assumed that young volunteers did not need training in the use of the technologies or payment for running forums and editing content, while older members were guaranteed financial remuneration. Even though there were organizations where this was not the case, and the main site producer was a young person with a full-time post, these situations were less common. This clearly suggests a power differential that is roughly aligned with age and with one's position in the wider job market. Yet this was not an issue that most of the producers raised or wished to discuss publicly, either because they claimed it did not affect them or because it would have implications for their working environment.

Where an organization's entire direction and ethos, embodied for instance in statements on the website, was claimed to be open for debate and discussion with the membership, we found rather alarming differences between theory and practice. For example, the content editor of the website Young Civilians in Turkey pointed out that some twelve- to eighteen-year-olds did attend meetings alongside their families. Some of these younger people, she said, were really interested in the organization's activities; and sometimes the organization had their "memos" read aloud during street protests to capture people's attention. However, many young people in Young Civilians lived outside Istanbul, where the group is based; it was not feasible for them in terms of either time or money to participate in face-to-face offline meetings, and they could only follow the group's activities via the Internet. As a result, the most important decisions were made by a relatively small group: as the organizers admitted, "only active participants that come to most of our meetings physically have important roles in our decisions." Practices like this provide an interesting indication of the loosely concealed top-down relations in some apparently "democratic" civic groups, which are overwhelmingly defined in terms of age. Top-down relations may then be manifested on the website through an absence of dissent or debate.

In some cases, the authoritarian relationship is completely open and discussed without irony. The Turkish site AKP Youth provides a stark example of the dominance of top-down relationships in established political organizations, especially youth branches of political parties. The content editor of the youth site has a specified rank within the party: he is the research and development coordinator for the party. In his view, the party etiquette and the dominant voice of the leader should be reflected seamlessly in the website of the youth branch as well as the home page of the party. The site has to refer to the party leader's speeches and reflect his authority; and there is no scope for active participation or critique.

Nevertheless, there was a generally positive feeling about working with people from other generations, and it was only when discussing the responses of older people outside the team, either to youth in general or to the work of the organization, that intergenerational conflicts were mentioned. An example of this arose when the Youth Voice team needed to explain their work to the older board members of UNICEF, who had oversight of their funding. Another was the initial negative response of a number of older British South Asian Muslims to the issues being raised on the Muslim Youth site. However, these contentions were dealt with in a skillful manner, by keeping dialogue as open as possible without allowing the conflict to paralyze the site. Interestingly, the young people on this site often take up both controversial and authoritarian positions on religion and culture, suggesting that age is certainly not a necessary determinant of liberal values, even vis-à-vis other young people. Indeed, the Muslim

Youth site is probably the most successful example among our sample of young people being directly involved in the management of online content. Although the website was initially set up by one person and is overseen by a small funded team, it has become an online community with more than seventy regular volunteers and hundreds of contributors.

Where efforts were made to have small intergenerational teams, this was sometimes done in response to technological rather than social or ideological issues. For example, sites created by smaller NGOs or organizations in the relatively early days of the Web often seemed to give more responsibility to young people because it was assumed by older members that they were better equipped to work with technology and would require less training than those in older age groups. In some instances, if the younger people on website teams are indeed more conversant with digital technologies, their advanced skills and understanding of Web media can lead to intergenerational conflict about what strategies to adopt when trying to engage members of the public. This was the case with the website Payasos sin fronteras in Spain, as one younger member of the editorial team explained:

There are two very different generations, one old, the other one young [in our organizational team]. We're eight people in the communication department, four of us are over forty-five, and four of us are less than thirty. And, yes, we notice a generational difference, especially when it comes to the use of the Internet. The older members would never think of organizing a campaign without talking to people, either face-to-face or via the telephone. For us, though, this is not a problem. On the contrary it's very practical, easy. . . . [However], not too long ago, we proposed to have a blog on our site, the older group don't want to hear about it. They don't understand that the site we have now does not offer any option for people to communicate directly. But it is difficult to make them understand the need for a blog. (Editorial team member, Payasos sin fronteras)

In other organizations, while the paid team itself is often composed of those under thirty-five, an ad hoc group of sixteen- to twenty-five-year-old "consultants" may be called on to contribute content or make design suggestions. In these situations, there is an unsurprising lack of wider involvement of young people in the day-to-day running of the sites. Even for small teams, democratic decision making can be complex and difficult, time is scarce, and agreement about the direction a site should take is often essential to its daily functioning. Consultation and full participatory democracy may be luxuries that less well-funded producers can ill afford.

Who Are the Workers?

These age differences were in some cases compounded by other differences having to do with social class and ethnicity. In some respects, the situation here mirrors that in the media industries more broadly, where financial and political pressures have led to a widespread "casualization" of the labor force. In this context, employment is often unpredictable and insecure, and mostly takes the form of short-term contracts; there are few opportunities for training, working hours may be long and conditions poor, and extensive hours of unpaid overtime may be expected (Deuze 2010; Hesmondhalgh and Baker 2011). Access to jobs in these industries is becoming increasingly difficult, and many of them are dominated by middle-class university graduates (see Bateman 2011; McLeod et al. 2009; Paterson 2010).

Similar points apply to the growing world of internships, which are very common in the NGO and charity sectors. In the UK and the US, it has increasingly become a necessity, not least for university graduates, to undertake unpaid work in their chosen field in the hope of obtaining more permanent employment, although this option is one that largely depends on the possibility of parental support and is therefore more readily available to those from more wealthy families (Perlin 2011). In this context, employment appears to be becoming a buyer's market, and there are numerous instances of unscrupulous companies taking advantage of the situation to ensure a continuing supply of free labor. Yet these practices are, ironically, sustained by the possibility that such exploitative (and self-exploitative) conditions might eventually lead to "cool jobs"—or to more socially worthwhile jobs—in a more egalitarian, noncorporate working environment (Ross 2003).

Some of the young volunteers and interns whom we met described the vicious circle of never having enough experience to get employed for advertised posts but never having enough money to volunteer long enough to get the experience. This situation may be seen as a serious and practical barrier to sustained active participation:

A: I was an intern for [organization] for three months after I graduated, I wanted to work for them obviously long-term and it said "experience necessary." . . . But every post is different, yeah, and I never had the right kind of experience for any posts advertised. My mother got fed up supporting me and I ended up working for [a big retail chain] to pay my rent on that crappy room. . . .

N: It's a vicious circle. I always knew I wanted to work in graphics [design] . . . but then I'd volunteer because I was interested in something and to get some experience—and they'd only pay my bus fare. I would have volunteered much more because I believed in the cause [a British children's charity] and they never have enough hands on deck, but I had no money and B couldn't go on supporting me. So, that's how I ended up working here [at a small business] and just sort of coasting, without really believing in what I'm doing. (UK, Facebook users group)

The class dimensions of this kind of exclusion may also be reinforced by forms of racism, if often of a polite, middle-class variety. L, who was involved in a Dutch environmentalist group, expressed her discomfort with this as follows:

It is simply too bad that our organization is working with just three people from ethnic minorities within the whole of Environmental Defence. Apart from that, no one. I was at a member's day. Once a year we have a members' day and often this is in Schothort estate in Amersfoort, very beautiful. [That time], two Surinamese women entered. Then immediately one of our members went up to them and said like "umm, sorry, this is a closed meeting. It is for Environmental Defence only." Then that [Surinamese] woman said like, "Really? I know." They didn't challenge anyone else like that, only them, because they thought those two women were in the wrong place. Yes, it is quite unfortunate actually when you look at our organization, we are quite an elite, highly educated, white group.

This reflects what we see as a much broader failure on the part of mainstream civic and political organizations to promote the participation of the groups of people facing the most discrimination, and on whose behalf the action is often carried out. As a member of the Dutch Young Socialists expressed it:

I often think that the people who it [the struggle] is really about, that we don't reach them and so there's a very small group we really focus on. . . . We try to find the link to that large group . . . for example immigrants from Amsterdam Oost, or Slotervaart, we try, but as an organization we don't have the feeling yet that we are getting there.

Design

While few of the producers whom we interviewed undertook solid market research before designing their websites, some have done so to see how their website could be improved and made as attractive as possible for the young people they hope to work with. If web producers do such research, they mostly do it at the beginning of the design process. Furthermore, the research that is done tends to have an ad hoc character and is mainly based on short interviews. R of the Dutch National Youth Council explained:

We are now developing a corporate communication plan, and that also includes a website proposal. For example, our logo at the top of the website now includes a picture of a bunch of young adolescents, but we feel that this image no longer fits with how we work and what we do. It looks old. That's why we have thought about a new logo, one with a woman, or a girl, who shakes her head, and then her hair will just fly around. That new image exudes a sense of strength, we think, the ability to achieve things. And, yes, we asked young people on the streets about what they think of this new image. Most teenagers really loved it.

However, our research suggests that most web producers in this sector have had their website designed either by a professional design company with little or no interest in the causes and ideologies of the organization or by volunteers with limited software and funding. As a result, most of the people who maintain the content on civic and political websites do not design their sites themselves; and therefore the design is not necessarily based on their own experiences with or inquiries among young people. As N of Young Amnesty in the Netherlands expressed it,

Our website is designed by a communications agency. They advised us to make a separate website for young people, and they also made it for us with this look and feel. . . . They did not show us four or five options, they just offered us one website, and we accepted it.

In other instances—as with the site Deadline in the Netherlands—the producers had been invited to choose between different options. Nevertheless, their website was not so much the result of discussions with young people at a local or national level but more the result of a quasi-professional partnership with the advertising agency, which also sponsors the organization. By contrast, the UK B-Involved website, which at first had little interactive content, was built by older adult designers sitting alongside the young people working for the young mayor of Lewisham team. The new approach to the site uses a wiki, along with a few information pages, and is almost entirely based on the young people's input and wishes.

However, the design of a site does not necessarily reflect what website producers themselves think is an appealing website for young people, let alone what real groups of young people want. This can be accentuated because of the fact that staff turnover is high, and different web editors with different outlooks and goals may maintain the same site over the course of time. Some of the current web editors whom we interviewed did not even know who had originally designed their site, and even members of the same team did not necessarily express coherent and homogenous views about design. Some did not seem to know why their site had a particular design—although others were more vocal on this topic than on questions of ideology, pedagogy, or ethos. In some cases this seemed to come down to personal preference rather than any more elaborate ideas or knowledge, let alone systematic research. This diversity of approaches in the design of sites, and the different working relationships that may be entailed, needs to be borne in mind when we make claims about the intentions or the textual meanings of site designs (see chapters 6 and 7).

Promotion and Marketing

Broadly speaking, the Web is a "pull" medium rather than a "push" medium: people are much less likely to visit a website if they do not somehow already know it is there. There was broad agreement among about half of the producers whom we interviewed that getting the website and the organization's brand or name into the traditional media—the press and television, or even posters and leaflets—is both important and necessary. In some cases this publicity also plays a role in fundraising since it acts as a way of advertising the site and its aims to potential funders or stakeholders:

We have a strong "old media" strategy as well, in terms of reaching out, advertising that way, and getting a fair bit of coverage actually. . . . Obviously we're set up to help engage young people, reach young people themselves, but we had to set up the brand first—the big people with money basically, and the people with the sort of reputation to be affiliated with us, so that would attract people to invest in us so then we could reach the young people. (Director, Catch 21 Productions)

For others, getting on the TV news or into the newspapers is a way of raising the profile not only of the organization but also of the causes it is championing. Particularly in the case of charities and organizations in the area of social justice, there is a sense in which on- and offline media are not entirely separable: work on climate change, poverty, and AIDS, for instance, has to be promoted in as many arenas as possible. However, it is generally very difficult to get into any form of mass media, including online newspapers, simply by announcing the existence of a website; offline events are perceived as much more likely to attract attention. Again, the larger organizations have strategies and resources to ensure their presence in other media, although they sometimes choose not to pursue traditional media because they do not think the young people they are targeting will be taking note of mainstream newspapers and television. I from Jove.Cat in Spain explained this approach:

We need to place our ads not in a newspaper such as *La Vanguardia*, but in places where young people will read it—blogspot, fotolog, Google . . . and besides, this is less expensive. (Content editor, Jove.Cat)

United Smile in the Netherlands provides another good example of a belief that strategic promotion depends on "following the audience." To widen their support and participant base, the organization has begun to use Hyves, the most popular Dutch social networking site:

We first wanted to use our own website as a platform, but we soon noticed that you could reach youth much easier and quicker with Hyves than with our website. So, we decided to make an account on Hyves, and we have now 6,700 members on that account. That is quite a lot. If you have such a big audience, it is also easier to make calls or recruit volunteers. (Content editor, United Smile)

Additionally, there are a number of civic websites that enjoy "free publicity." In the Netherlands, the websites Spunk, Vote Match, Maroc, and Islam Index generate public discussions by engaging in activities that are considered controversial among some sections of the population. While the publicity is sometimes a by-product of the organizations' aims and activities, seeking out controversy can also become a promotional strategy, as it is in more mainstream media such as television and some sectors of the press.

Other website producers do not pay overt attention to marketing or the use of old media for promotion. These include producers for organizations whose aim is to target a highly differentiated or limited section of young people within a specific community (for example, sexual, ethnic, or local). In other cases, producers have simply been too busy campaigning or setting up a site to pay attention to promotion. Further, some find the notion of marketing itself ideologically suspect. In Turkey, most of the activist producers whom we interviewed were openly uninterested in marketing their websites in any formal sense; although they did engage in more targeted forms of promotion through the use of links from other sites that were ideologically and politically similar to their own. An exchange of links benefits both parties and is perceived as a cheap and easy way to reach potential users, although the benefit obviously depends on the numbers of users on each of the cross-linked sites. In the UK, sites with large or well-funded parent organizations were also helped by cross-promotion between regular offline publications, such as a newsletter or newspaper, and their online presence and campaigns.

As this brief discussion suggests, promoting a website and its goals across a range of media is not always possible or desirable. However, where such marketing could be effective, there is sometimes neither the time nor the funding to make it happen, and in these instances organizations revert to long-standing tactics such as printing leaflets or word-of-mouth—or merely waiting and hoping. However, several producers argued that the "build it and they will come" model is hopelessly flawed. Regardless of how anti-capitalist a group's goals may be, and regardless of whether one uses the ideologically loaded terms "marketing" and "promotion," getting one's message across and engaging young people necessarily entails a strategy that goes beyond the production of the website itself.

Even so, there were several cases of production teams who at first believed only in traditional offline activism and created the website just to circulate or spread information. It took time for them to discover that the Web could attract people who were not previously interested in getting involved. For example, some producers mentioned that the Internet enabled them to do things that the very basic infrastructures of their organizations and their limited budgets and funding expectations would otherwise have made very difficult. However, we also found many producers who argued that the website was not in fact an essential tool for their organization to carry out its day-to-day activities; this was particularly the case in well-established offline organizations such as the AKP Youth branch in Turkey and Youth Action Northern Ireland.

Tricks of the Trade, Hazards of the Game?

To what extent are the working practices and dilemmas described here unique to organizations that operate online? Are they not also apparent in other civic or political organizations or groups, such as radical activist networks or NGOs, that operate primarily offline? Alternatively, to what extent are these issues specific to the new media sector? Might we find similar pressures and experiences in other areas of web production that do not have any explicitly civic or political dimensions? In this closing section of the chapter, we suggest how insights from research in these related areas might shed light on the practices we have outlined.

More than twenty-five years ago, the UK consultancy organization Comedia produced a controversial polemic titled *What a Way to Run a Railroad: An Analysis of Radical Failure* (Landry, Morley, and Southwood 1985). Based on their experience of a range of politically and culturally radical or "alternative" organizations, the authors pointed to some endemic problems that tend to undermine such work. They recognized that it is "difficult. . . to sustain a critical and oppositional project in a society which is structured at all levels against it," and that "many of these publications and organizations were ludicrously under-resourced in relation to the scale of the issues with which they were trying to grapple" (2). However, they also argued that such organizations could be their own worst enemies. Among the potentially self-destructive practices, the Comedia authors pointed to the lack of financial planning and management, the lack of attention to target audiences, forms of "cultural snobbery" that inhibited the use of any means of generating revenue that could be considered "capitalistic," and the ideological censorship of conflicting or contrasting viewpoints, which limits both the appeal and the audience of the organizations. Perhaps most relevant to our interests here, they drew attention to working practices that rest, at best, on forms of "self-exploitation" and at worst on the unspoken exploitation of volunteers, who often did not know when they volunteered what would be required of them. They argued that the lack of time, even on the part of those who have volunteered to do specific jobs, could lead to "tension between those who know they will be doing the work and those who are there only for the generalized discussions of overall policy" (38).

The Comedia authors warned that the resulting disillusionment may lead the radical voluntary sector to lose its most talented and imaginative participants fairly swiftly to private firms, where innovation and long working hours are apparently rewarded. In place of the ideologically exclusive critiques of capitalist practices adopted by these radical collectives, Comedia proposes a more professionalized and accountable style of management, and a more flexible approach toward ideological debate and critique. They recommend that radical organizations move away from the margins toward the center ground of politics in order to engage a broader range of potential supporters; and that organizations take greater account of the role of target audiences in making "choices" about the media they consume. Although Comedia's argument has both factual and polemical aspects with which one might take issue, and one might challenge some of the recommendations, many of the civic organizations discussed in this chapter appear to have moved in precisely the more mainstream, professionalized direction proposed in *What a Way to Run a Railroad*. At the same time, there are continuing echoes in our research of several of the problems that the authors identified, particularly in respect to working practices, management hierarchies, and funding constraints.

This finding is particularly ironic in light of the egalitarian rhetoric that characterizes so much discussion of the Internet. While the Internet was hailed by many of those whom we interviewed as an inexpensive means of disseminating ideas and information, as a decentralized, democratic network, and as a source of "collective intelligence," online civic practices have also stubbornly retained some of the characteristics attached to running organizations and campaigns—whether alternative, radical, or mainstream—in the offline world. This is particularly apparent in relation to funding and promotion, where the lack of steady income and poor budgeting strategies (including assumptions of "no-cost" maintenance) have proved massively problematic for some civic and political youth websites.

Such issues are equally apparent in the world of start-up IT companies analyzed by authors such as Andrew Ross (2003). Here, too, young entrants into the industry are encouraged to give their time for free (for example, as interns) or to work punitively long hours in a situation where security of employment is scarce indeed. In this case, the appearance of flattened hierarchies and informal working relationships can mask the continuing inequalities that characterize such apparently "cool" and creative working environments. Even in the context of profit-making enterprises there may be similar tensions between small organizations and their much larger and less accessible corporate funders, and this can make it frighteningly difficult, as Charles Handy puts it, "not to become the servants of [your] paymasters" rather than of your cause and your principles (1988, 7).

Whether in commercial or nonprofit organizations, apparently informal organizational structures and the appearance of participatory and democratic decision making can mask the continuing existence of hierarchies and elites, as well as much hidden and unacknowledged labor. In the case of website production, this labor may belong to interested young people who enroll as volunteers or interns and who do not know how to say no, spending far more than the time they initially envisaged. However, it also belongs to those who actively contribute online via their postings to lists, discussions, or forums or by sharing "user-generated content": these practices can also be seen as forms of labor (Terranova 2000). As we have indicated, there are significant differentials in these organizations between those who get paid a living wage and those who do not (or who get paid nothing at all), and such payment inequities usually fall along lines of age. Particularly now, in a time of austerity across Europe, when volunteering is being hailed as a duty while offline spaces for voluntary work disappear, the importance of equality and solidarity in youth civic teams will be key to keeping alive the goals and principles of many of the organizations discussed in this study.

4 Young People Online and Offline

How do young people in Europe use the Internet, and to what extent do they use it for civic purposes in particular? How does their use—and non-use—of the Internet fit into the context of their everyday life? How does it connect—or fail to connect—with their offline social and political concerns? Are there specific types of online civic activity that are most relevant for particular groups of young people? To what extent do the differences among young people in these respects reflect broader social inequalities? And what about those who are not regular Internet users—are they thereby also excluded from civic participation?

We have seen a range of assumptions about these issues in the overall debate about young people, the Internet, and civic participation. Such assumptions are also apparent in the practices of producers of online content, as we saw in chapter 3 and explore further in chapters 6 and 7. On the one hand, we find the argument that young people are politically apathetic, even irresponsible; on the other, the claim that they are more likely to be civically engaged than adults and more passionately committed to particular causes. Some argue that the Internet will immediately motivate young people, that it is *their* medium, and that they already have the skills to use it. Others assert that, like other media, the Internet has merely distracted youth with trivial entertainment and become a substitute for real politics. Such assumptions are apparent not just in how we talk about young people but also in how we talk *to* them—in particular configurations of entertainment and education, or in the use of official or alternatively "cool" or "youth culture" modes of address, and in the ways in which we enable them to speak for themselves, for instance in forums or through user-generated content.

So, are young people civic slackers or civic activists? Are they digital natives or digital dunces? Is the Internet "dumbing them down" or is it empowering them to create new forms of civic culture? In this chapter and the next, we use two contrasting types of data to shed light on these issues: data from a large-scale survey undertaken across all seven partner countries and some evidence from in-depth focus group discussions. These quantitative and qualitative data give us access to different aspects of the topic, but they are also complementary.

The Big Picture

To obtain a broad view of these issues, we undertook a large-scale online survey of young people aged fifteen to twenty-five years in the seven participating countries. The survey was distributed in the autumn of 2007, in most cases through a link from the website of MTV Europe. Participation was incentivized with a prize drawing. In three countries it was additionally linked to nonentertainment Internet platforms with a broad appeal to students or brought to the attention of teachers in schools, although we made no attempt to carry out the survey offline. The responses we received were not evenly distributed among countries, with the UK, the Netherlands, Turkey, and Slovenia among the larger response groups and Sweden, Spain, and Hungary less well represented.

The respondents obviously formed a self-selecting sample. They were recruited in an opportunistic way rather than through rigorous random sampling. The use of online methods—and of a mainstream entertainment site as the primary means of distribution—inevitably excluded some potential participants. The uneven distribution of respondents from the selected countries also makes it impossible to compare findings between countries reliably. However, the limited resources available to us meant that a systematic, representative sample was simply out of the question. On the positive side, our sample was comparatively large: we received valid responses from 3,307 young people. It was also more diverse than in many other studies in this field, which have mostly been carried out with highly circumscribed cohorts, especially university students (e.g., Calenda and Meijer 2009; Gerodimos 2009). As such, the survey does enable us to make some reasonably valid claims across the whole cohort.

The average age of our respondents was 19.2 years. Fifty-five percent of them were female, and about 10 percent were not born in their country of residence. Fifty-six percent said they had a full-time or part-time job. Fifty-seven percent reported they belonged to a religion; of these, the majority cited either Christianity or Islam (respectively 32.3 percent and 20.1 percent of all respondents who chose to say they belonged to a religion). Overall, most respondents had completed some ten years of education, and the majority (70 percent) reported they lived with their parents and depended on them financially.

Patterns of Internet Use

We need to understand the potential civic uses of the Internet, first, in relation to Internet use more broadly. This is partly a question of access—where and when young people are able to get online—but also of the extent to which their use is controlled by adults. To what extent do we encounter "digital divides" or inequalities in these respects between different social groups of young people?

Ninety percent of our respondents said they used the Internet most frequently at home. On average, they reported using it on 6.2 days per week and for 3.3 hours a day, although some used it considerably more and some far less. About 74 percent asserted that they were allowed to use the Internet as they liked. On average, our respondents said they had already been using the Internet for some seven years prior to 2009, and with few exceptions, most maintained they felt confident in doing so.

Of all the possible sociodemographic variables that we correlated with Internet use, gender most often produced a significant correlation, predominantly in the direction one would expect on the basis of the digital divide literature (Haddon 2011; Lee 2008; Warschauer 2004). Thus, girls and young women said they felt less confident than boys and young men in using the Internet, had fewer years of experience, and used the Internet somewhat less intensively. In the Netherlands and Turkey in particular, female respondents were also more likely to report that their Internet use was controlled by adults. The respondents from the UK constituted the most striking exception to this general observation: in the UK, gender came out as unrelated to almost all the questions, and in fact, UK girls and young women were somewhat *less* likely to report that there was control over their Internet use than were boys and young men.

Social class was a further predictable dimension in relation to Internet use. Those from lower socioeconomic backgrounds reported less intensive Internet use and lower levels of access. Working-class youth were also more likely than middle-class youth to use the Internet outside the home. However, they also reported a stronger interest in civic issues, both online and offline. By contrast, upper-middle-class youth were far more likely to report an interest in institutional and electoral politics, although they were also the least likely to express an interest in or to participate in social justice and generic youth campaigns either offline or online.

Ethnicity was another demographic variable of interest, given the extensive literature on digital divides in this regard (e.g., Hoffmann, Novak, and Schlosser 2001; Tsatsou 2011). We found a significant correlation between years of Internet experience and belonging to an ethnic minority: in Slovenia in particular, but also in some other countries, ethnic minority youth reported fewer years of Internet experience. However, with respect to other questions on Internet use, there were no perceivable general tendencies related to ethnicity, nor were there specific national differences in the data except in relation to social class.

By contrast, belonging to a religious group appeared to affect patterns of Internet use among young people in our sample to a far greater extent than did belonging to an ethnic minority. Especially in the Netherlands and Turkey, young people with a religious affiliation said that adults were more likely to control their Internet use. This might account for the fact that such young people also reported using the Internet outside their homes more often than young people from nonreligious households. On the other hand, young people who belonged to religious communities also reported more years' experience in using the Internet than peers with no religious affiliation. However, in Sweden we found no correlations at all between Internet use patterns and reported religious affiliation, and in the Netherlands only in relation to the question of adult control. This might suggest that the relationship between religion and Internet use partly follows a north-south divide in Europe; although such a hypothesis would need to be followed up with further research.

Next to social class and gender, the living situations of our respondents appeared to exert most influence on their Internet use. Most of the young people using the Internet at home did so at their parents' house. Even controlling for age, young people who were living with their parents had the longest experience of using the Internet, but they also reported a lower chance of being able to access and use the Internet intensively. These three findings together suggest that a majority of fifteen- to twenty-five-year-olds in Europe gain access to the Internet through computers that are monitored by older family members. While this probably facilitates early acquaintance, it might also result in less intensive and potentially less exploratory use (as compared with those who have a means of access outside the home). Furthermore, in Turkey and the Netherlands, this also appeared to result in less freedom to use the Internet in ways that they liked and enjoyed, as measured by responses to questions about the frequency, types, and intensity of social and leisure activities undertaken online.

The factor of age revealed some strong and predictable tendencies in these respects, all of which were also clearly referenced by young people during interviews and focus groups. Older respondents used the Internet less frequently at home; they reported more freedom in how they used the Internet than younger counterparts, both at home and outside the home; and they claimed a greater degree of Internet experience and greater confidence in using the Internet. Intensity of Internet use was also positively, if less clearly, related to the age of our respondents, with older respondents tending to remain online for longer each week and in each session.

Unsurprisingly, with the exception of our Turkish cohort, the length of respondents' education correlated positively with years of Internet experience. However, in the Netherlands, Slovenia, and Spain, those with more years of education also reported experiencing more control over their Internet use. This reveals a pattern of adult control that has serious implications for online civic participation, particularly that aimed at younger age groups. This issue was explored in more detail in the focus groups, discussed in the following chapter.

To sum up, young people who reported using the Internet most confidently and intensively and with least interference from older adults were in general more likely to be older, better educated, male, and from higher socioeconomic groups. Where they were living at home, parents may potentially have controlled or restricted their Internet use; this was especially the case for younger users, as well for some older female users and those who reported a religious affiliation.

What Young People Do Online

Unsurprisingly, our young respondents were mainly interested in websites dealing with entertainment, communication, lifestyle issues, and shopping. While this might be attributed to the fact that the survey was distributed primarily through the MTV sites, it is unlikely to be a consequence of this alone.

Figure 4.1 shows that sites dealing with music, movies, and news were reported to be the most popular among our young respondents. Quite strikingly, and oddly given the anonymity granted by the survey process, young people in our sample reported least interest in websites about romance and dating or pornography. The strong interest shown in news websites was confirmed by our focus group research and supported by accounts of even greater interest in and time spent watching television news. More predictable was the low rating given to political party sites.

When we categorize the sites young people identified as those they would regularly visit, six categories emerge:

- entertainment, including movies, music and sports;
- lifestyle, including fashion, consumption, romance, and chat;

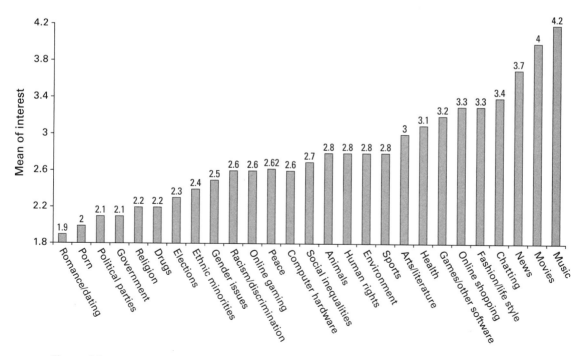

Figure 4.1
Interest in types of websites

- digital culture, including on- and offline games, hardware and software;
- social justice, relating to issues such as racism, sexism, discrimination, human rights, and social inequalities;
- new social movement and spiritual issues, for example the environment, animal rights, religion, and health;
- electoral politics, including elections, political parties, government, and news.

In this categorization, the civic and political potential of the web pertains primarily to the latter three categories—social justice, new social movements and spirituality, and electoral politics. Around 40 percent of our respondents expressed some *active* interest in at least one of these kinds of sites on at least one occasion in the preceding months, for instance through forwarding emails, signing online petitions, or taking part in an Internet poll. While interest in institutional politics was lower than in the other areas, around 20 percent of our respondents expressed *strong* interest, particularly in environmental, new social movement or spirituality-related issues, and 15 percent expressed strong interest in all three kinds of sites. This might be seen to contradict studies that perceive young people to be manifesting a generalized apathy about politics and the civic sphere.

In table 4.1 we summarize whether and how different groups in our sample expressed interest in these types of civic sites. This shows that the interest in civic and political websites appears to be stronger among older respondents in our sample, those not living with their parents, youth who report coming from religious backgrounds, and girls and young women. Class is statistically significant as a variable only in that respondents from higher sociodemographic backgrounds appear to have a significantly higher interest in websites about electoral or institutional politics. Again, our

Table 4.1
Association between interest in civic websites and sociodemographic variables

	Gender female	High socioeconomic background	Ethnic minority	Religious background	More years of education	Not living with parents	Older
Social justice	+		+	+		+	+
New social movements and spirituality	+			+		+	+
Institutional politics		+		−		+	+

Note: + in a cell indicates a significant positive correlation between interest in the type of site and the variable at stake, while − indicates a significant negative correlation.

more in-depth qualitative focus groups, discussed in the following chapter, shed more light on some of these correlations, particularly the positive correlation between several of the sociodemographic variables and an interest in social justice issues, new social movements, and spirituality, and the corresponding lack of interest in institutional politics.

Using the Civic Potential of the Internet

While the majority of our respondents expressed a strong interest in lifestyle and entertainment websites, just over 20 percent asserted an equally strong interest in civic websites or blogs, and this figure rises to 40 percent if we include those showing "some" interest. Yet do we see the same patterns if we look at the civic and political websites that the respondents tell us they have actually visited? And how do they report that they use the Internet for political and civic participation?

Figure 4.2 shows that between 6 percent and 20 percent of our respondents reported visiting websites in each of a range of areas of political and civic interest. Since each

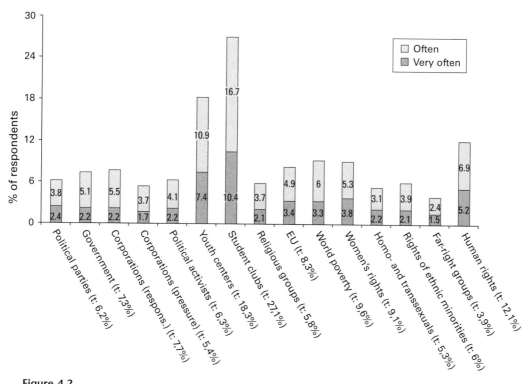

Figure 4.2
Visits to civic or political websites

respondent reported using or visiting more than one type of civic website, as well as participating in activities like the forwarding of civic emails (10.2 percent), editing civic content (6.7 percent), or signing e-petitions (10.4 percent), it is not possible to place a precise upper figure on young people's participation here. However, it is clear that there is a range of civic websites that attract between 10 percent and 20 percent of our sample. This broadly mirrors what young people reported about their interests (see figure 4.1), with occasional participation from about 20 percent and more sustained and energetic participation online from a further 15–20 percent.

However, apart from youth centers and student websites (generic sites that could broadly be said to serve different socioeconomic groups of young people), few other types of civic or political sites drew a proportion larger than 10 percent. Whether the glass is half full or half empty is open to debate; but given that each of these issues might draw the interest of a *different* 10 percent of young people, the use of civic sites appears surprisingly widespread—although it should also be noted that almost everything to do with party politics and government attracted the least interest and activity.

For ease of discussion, we have distributed the civic sites that young people actually reported visiting into three categories: social justice issues, youth sites (a slightly broader category than new social movements and lifestyles in table 4.1), and institutional politics. Older respondents within the fifteen- to twenty-five-year age range and those not living with parents reported visiting all these sites more often than younger respondents and those still living with their parents. Again, in line with our discussion earlier in this chapter, young people with more years of education were somewhat more likely to visit sites about institutional politics, and youth websites (which includes student websites), although they were *less* likely to visit sites on social justice issues. Girls and young women reported visiting websites about institutional politics less frequently than boys and young men, while respondents from ethnic minority backgrounds reported visiting social justice websites more often than respondents who did not categorize themselves as being from an ethnic minority. While these differences might be seen to reflect digital divides, they clearly also reflect differences in both personal and social interests. These patterns are summarized in table 4.2.

In addition to visiting websites, forwarding emails and signing online petitions were reported to be the most popular forms of online participation. By the time we conducted our focus groups across Europe in 2009, social networking applications were also becoming an increasingly easy means for young people to show interest in or to pursue particular political and civic activities. Those not living with their parents and those reporting religious backgrounds apparently engaged in such activities more often than others, as did the older and more educated groups among our respondents.

Table 4.2

Reported use of civic websites and sociodemographic variables

	Gender female	Higher socioeconomic background	Ethnic minority	Religious background	More years of education	Not living with parents	Older
Social justice		−	+	+		+	+
Institutional politics	−	+	+		+	+	+
Youth		−		+	+	+	+

Note: + in a cell indicates a significant positive correlation between interest in the type of site and the variable at stake, while − indicates a significant negative correlation.

Relations between Online and Offline Participation

To what extent does young people's online participation (visiting websites, signing petitions, contributing to civic content online, e-mailing politicians, and so on) replace or complement forms of offline civic participation? We asked the respondents to report any involvement in the following forms of offline participation in the twelve months preceding our survey: calling or sending a letter to a politician or a government official, organizing or participating in a demonstration, strike, or protest, working for a voluntary or charitable organization, attending a public meeting or event in their local area, boycotting a product, donating money or contributing to a political party or a charitable organization, displaying a campaign badge, working for a political party, speaking at a student council, and giving out leaflets. Clearly, this is a fairly conventional list and does not include many civic and political activities that might be engaged in by either the far right or the far left, or indeed by other political groups (such as environmentalists) and minorities. Figure 4.3 shows the distribution of offline participation across these different activities.

These figures show that around 13 percent of respondents reported participating in one or more form of offline activity either often or very often. The least popular forms—contacting a politician and going on strike—attracted only 2 percent and 4 percent of our sample, respectively, while the most popular—volunteering, donating and boycotting—attracted between 10 percent and 13 percent each. Those not living with their parents and those from religious backgrounds reported doing these things more often than others, as did those in the older age group, although the level of education of the respondents did not appear to make a difference in this respect. Methodologically, it is quite possible that the online means of distributing the survey militated against the gathering of responses from young people who are highly active offline but not at all or rarely online.

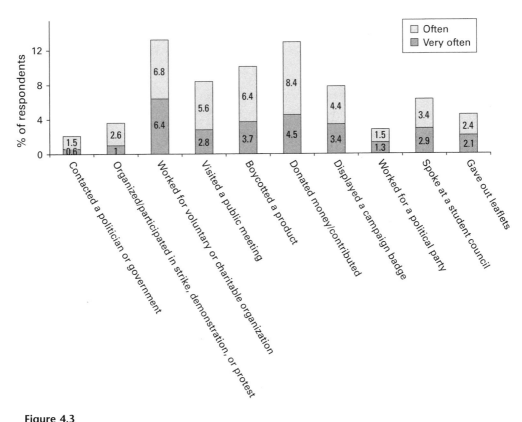

Figure 4.3
Participation in types of offline activity

To ensure that our definitions of participation were not excluding young people and misrepresenting their levels of engagement, we used *political discussion on- or offline* (or what we will refer to later as "civic sharing") as a further indicator of participation. We asked the respondents how often they talked with friends, family, and colleagues about social problems or political issues, such as unemployment, the environment, politicians, human rights, and so on. Thirty-six percent said they did this sometimes and just over 40 percent did so often or very often; only 6 percent said they never did so.

Finally, we also asked our respondents several questions about their views on what a "good citizen" is, with a view to estimating their motivations and priorities in relation to civic and political participation. The results are summarized in table 4.3 below. Supporting people who are worse off, forming an independent opinion, and being well informed were overwhelmingly identified as important traits of good citizenship. Voting received a very respectable 65 percent—notable given that the fifteen- to sev-

Table 4.3

Attitudes toward citizenship

To be a good citizen, how important would you say it is for a person to:	Not important	Hardly	Neutral	Quite	Very important
Support people who are worse off than themselves?	2.8%	4.1%	16.3%	34.6%	42.1%
Vote in elections?	6.2%	8.9%	20.4%	24.9%	39.6%
Form their own opinion, independently of others?	2.8%	4.3%	13.8%	27.4%	51.7%
Be active in voluntary organizations?	8.3%	16.5%	36.1%	24.6%	14.5%
Be active in politics?	19.5%	25.3%	34%	13.4%	7.8%
Be informed about what is going on in the world?	3%	4,1%	15.3%	30.4%	47.1%

Table 4.4

Correlation between online and offline participation (using Pearson: 1 indicates full correlation and 0 indicates no correlation)

	Offline participation	E-petitions, forwarding emails, donating, etc.	Visiting civic and political websites
Offline participation	1	.639	.569
E-petitions, forwarding emails, donating, etc.	.639	1	.608
Visiting civic and political websites	.569	.608	1

enteen-year-olds were not yet able to vote—although being active in politics was valued less than other items.

The data discussed thus far suggest that there is a strong correlation between offline and online participation, as we summarize in table 4.4. These statistically significant correlations clearly show that even within a survey aimed mainly at young people who are already online, online and offline civic action complement rather than replace each other. This also confirms our earlier point that an a priori distinction between online and offline civic and political activities is far from helpful in understanding civic participation among young people (a theme discussed further by Hirzalla and van Zoonen 2011).

When analyzing these activities as combined means of civic participation, four different types of engagement defined by clusters of activities emerge from the data. Although there are clear overlaps and nuances that are not as easy to capture here, our colleagues Hirzalla and van Zoonen (2011) have described these heuristically in terms of four categories: social activism, civic sharing, socially conscious consumption, and lobbying. *Social activism* refers to more structured and collaborative forms of civic or political activity, such as protesting, striking, or organizing events. *Civic sharing* consists mostly of talking or writing about political and social issues to or with family, friends, and colleagues, either in real life or online via websites, messenger chat, or social networking sites. *Socially conscious consumption,* or what we have defined elsewhere as "ethical consumption" (Banaji and Buckingham 2009), involves addressing social and political issues in making decisions about what to purchase or not to purchase. *Lobbying* involves contacting politicians, government, or other officials with a view to arguing for changes in policy or practice.

These types of engagement typically operate both online and offline. Thus, for example, in our sample, the most likely form of activity for those with an interest in electoral politics or for those who actually visited sites of or about governments was lobbying (that is, contacting politicians and government officials). Yet while there are clear connections between what people do online and offline, there are also some aspects that do not correlate so straightforwardly (see table 4.5). For example, socially conscious shopping is connected especially to an interest in what could be labeled "new age" websites, but much less to an interest in electoral politics or visits to websites about political parties and institutional politics. By contrast, civic sharing—the discussion of civic or political issues and events with family and friends—extends more or less equally to all civic and political interests and visits to websites. Finally, offline activism pertains in particular to social justice and social movement interests and actual visits to websites about social justice and institutional politics.

Of these four categories, our respondents reported engaging most often in civic sharing and socially conscious consumption. While this finding is unlikely to be strikingly different among other age groups, such a conclusion would need further research

Table 4.5

Form and content of online and offline civic and political activities (using Pearson)

		(7) Offline activism	(8) Civic sharing	(9) Socially conscious shopping	(10) Lobbying
Site interest	(1) Social movements	**.256**	.437	.269	.167
	(2) New age	.196	*.330*	**.335**	.131
	(3) Electoral politics	.216	.411	*.111*	**.183**
Site visits	(4) Social justice	**.386**	.528	.227	.326
	(5) Institutional politics	**.384**	.515	*.153*	**.425**
	(6) Youth	.292	.390	.179	**.167**

Note: Boldface indicates a strong and notable relation; italic indicates a less common relation.

to establish. The majority of respondents reported little interest in traditional politics and government and basically did not seek contact with politicians or government officials, either offline or online. Offline activism, including leafleting, protesting, striking, or organizing civic events, ranked only a little higher. There were clear differences on this measure between males and females, with girls and young women reporting more engagement in civic consumption and civic sharing and less in lobbying activities than boys and young men. In addition, young people describing themselves as religious also reported more engagement in all types of civic participation, while living alone and being older appeared to have a positive relationship to all forms of civic participation, with the exception of socially conscious consumption. Interestingly, the latter type of participation, although requiring an input in terms of capital, was negatively correlated with high socioeconomic status. All these patterns are summarized in table 4.6.

Explaining Participation

How can we use these data to explain the ways in which young people make use of the Internet's civic and political potential? First, it is worth emphasizing that participation in offline activities and participation in online activities were statistically significantly correlated in a strongly positive manner in our sample. Online and offline

Table 4.6
Civic and political activities and sociodemographic variables

	Gender female	Higher social class	Ethnic minority	Religious affiliation	More years of education	Living at home	Age (older)
Offline activism				+		+	+
Civic sharing (discussion, debate, on- and offline)	+			+	+	+	+
Socially conscious shopping (on- and offline)	+	−		+			
Lobbying (on and offline)	−			+		+	+

Note: + indicates a significant positive relation; − indicates a significant negative relation. An empty cell indicates no significant difference.

civic engagements and activities are complementary to each other, and rather than seeing them as mutually exclusive (or indeed replacements for each other), it makes more sense to trace the connections between them.

Contrary to pronouncements that cast all young people as a digital generation, equally comfortable with email, web chatting, RSS feeds, and uploading user-generated content, the analyses here have shown enduring digital divides among the respondents in all countries along the lines of gender, social class, and education. Unsurprisingly, our respondents also reported that they primarily used the Internet for leisure and entertainment. Among the older respondents, however, and especially among the older young women and religious youth, there was a clear interest in civic and political sites, especially those covering social justice, spiritual, or new social movement issues.

Of the four forms of engagement that emerged from the data, civic sharing implies both knowledge and engagement and has implications for democracy that go far beyond the traditional divide between formal politics and social activism that seems to be suggested by some of our findings. Interestingly, civic sharing also turned out to be a participatory form that was more or less evenly connected to substantial declarations of interest in and reports of visits to actual civic and political websites. It is especially striking that so many young people claim to participate in discussion and passing along of information with regard to noninstitutional politics and the civic sphere, regardless of the type and frequency of civic and political activities in which they actually participate.

This finding might in turn allow us to think beyond the binary of the actualizing citizen and the dutiful citizen, as conceptualized by Lance Bennett (2008) and discussed in chapter 1. Rather, we might see citizenship more in the manner conceived by Engin Isin, as something that is constantly reaffirmed or denied via numerous acts of citizenship (Isin and Nielsen 2008). In this formulation, discussions of public and political events or processes, whether arising from viewing news, exceptional circumstances, or personal experience, are neither straightforwardly dutiful nor necessarily active. They represent *choices* about whether to take up a position in relation to a specific aspect of civic or political life. These choices or decisions might contribute to formal politics—for instance, when it comes to voting for particular leaders or their policies—or they might lead young people to take up particular forms of social action.

We could conclude from our data that most young people, like older adults, seem to be neither permanently active nor monolithically passive as citizens. Rather, they engage in fewer or greater numbers of *acts of citizenship*, partly according to circumstances and opportunities. These acts can, in their turn, be seen to build a sense of external and internal *efficacy*—a sense of being able to affect the outcomes of political and civic processes or the sense that one has participated in something meaningful and made a contribution regardless of the outcome.

Respondents to our survey were asked three questions designed to elicit responses about this. The first question was, How often does politics seem so complicated that you can't really understand what is going on? The second question was, Do you think that you could take an active role in a group involved with political issues? The responses to these two questions were roughly balanced: aside from those who were "not sure," around half indicated some sense of political efficacy and around half did not. However, the situation was rather different in relation to our third question: Do you think that politicians care about what people like you think once the elections are over? Here, fully 86 percent of respondents responded that only some, few, or hardly any politicians care about them when elections are over, suggesting a low sense of external political efficacy. On the other hand, of the many statistically significant relationships between variables in our sample, the one between (self-reported) civic sharing and (self-reported) internal political efficacy is one of the strongest.

This finding has been extended and explained further by Fadi Hirzalla, Floris Müller, and Liesbet van Zoonen (2009) in a close analysis of interviews with young people regarding civic and political efficacy. These authors argue that what surveys about civic participation do not show clearly enough is the *type and extent* of efficacy felt by young people who opt to take particular kinds of civic and political action, or indeed to participate at all. They show that external efficacy—reaching desired goals or a feeling of having affected an outcome—is not usually a motivation for initial participation among young people in any of the four modes outlined in this chapter. Meanwhile, feelings of internal efficacy—having shared or taken part in something, experienced feelings of solidarity, righteousness, or having tried one's best or participated regardless of the outcome—seem to be far more evident in young people's situated talk about their motivations for civic participation.

As this implies, quantitative surveys of the kind we have described here are bound to have limitations, especially when it comes to capturing people's motivations and their lived experience. The descriptors and variables we have used, both in the survey itself and in our subsequent analysis, inevitably oversimplify the complex processes at stake. As we have acknowledged, our survey also had particular limitations in respect of its representativeness. One key constraint here is that we did not consider young people who were *not* online, even though this is the group at whom most of the concern about "disaffected youth" appears to be directed. Indeed, there has been relatively little research on this group, especially when compared with the large number of studies of youthful activists—a phenomenon that may say much about academics' wishful thinking (exceptions here include Geniets 2010; Longley and Singleton 2009; Warren 2007). We would argue that it is just as important to understand the reasons for non-use as well as for use, and both need to be understood in the context of people's broader social circumstances and motivations. This is a key focus in the following chapter, where we discuss qualitative data from our focus group discussions.

5 The Young Civilians

In this chapter, we provide a broad overview of the data gathered from our focus groups. We explore these young people's motivations for both on- and offline civic participation and the social circumstances in which this participation occurs, as well as their responses to particular forms of civic content. As far as possible, we attempt to set this information in the context of their everyday uses of the Internet and in the wider context of national and international civic traditions and movements.

The interviews discussed here were conducted in the seven participating countries between April 2008 and February 2009, with diverse groups of young people between the ages of fifteen and twenty-five years. We convened a total of seventy focus groups of different sizes, attempting to cover young people in both urban and rural areas and those who claimed long acquaintance with the Internet as well as those who were rarely online. The composition of the groups also reflected issues specific to the different national contexts, such as the rise of Islamophobic politics in the Netherlands, Catalan nationalism in Spain, anti-Roma and anti-immigrant sentiments in Hungary, conflicts between Catholics and Protestants in Northern Ireland, and the growth of neoliberal economies alongside democratic politics in Slovenia and Hungary. We also convened groups to address specific issues relating to the Internet itself, such as Internet censorship in Turkey and music downloading in Sweden. The composition of the groups also reflected the logistics of the researchers' working lives and locations and the exigencies of specific research situations: far-right youth in some countries refused to be interviewed, for example, while young mothers and young carers often did not turn up at focus groups despite multiple rearrangements.

Our focus groups therefore included:

• young people who were active in traditional politics (for instance, in youth parliaments, political parties, fringe political groups, or local government);
• those involved in traditional civic organizations (global and local charities and voluntary organizations, counseling centers, student unions);

- those who were active in new social or civic movements (independent musicians, environmentalists, peace campaigners, housing campaigners, citizen journalists or bloggers, anti-immigration campaigners);
- young people who were self-avowedly not involved in civic or political activities either offline or via the Internet (young people just out of prison or living in hostels, school students using youth centers, "average" university students).

Our lines of questioning in these groups were probably as diverse as the groups themselves. However, the research team agreed on a range of broad areas for discussion, covering basic information about the young people's everyday lives and interests, their uses of the Internet, and their views about civic and political issues (broadly defined). We set out to explore—although not always explicitly or directly—the range of concerns discussed in previous chapters, for example in relation to young people's motivations and reasons for participation or nonparticipation, their perceived apathy toward or distaste for politics, their preference for entertainment rather than political websites, and their apparent lack of political self-efficacy. In most instances participants were also able to explore various civic and political sites on computers made available at the location. This practice allowed us to glean information about the kinds of design and interactive features they might find attractive or off-putting and how they responded to being addressed, for example as fun-loving young people, as formal political subjects, or as challenging activists.

In light of the focus of our discussions, it might have been expected that some young people would choose to present a worthy or even self-righteous image of themselves as political actors or good citizens. In addition to constructing themselves as "young civilians"—as civically minded, responsible, and active—some of our participants rehearsed general complaints about *other* young people's tendency to apathy and ignorance, although they often extended these criticisms to adults as well. Yet while this kind of response was sometimes heard at the beginning of a session, participants generally relaxed as the discussion proceeded, particularly in the case of the nineteen- to twenty-five-year-olds, who were perhaps less inclined to defer to the adult authority of the interviewer. Instances of responses in this chapter have, therefore, more frequently been drawn from later in the discussion, when the focus group participants were no longer attempting to establish their positions quite so self-consciously.

The Banality of the Internet

Much of the early literature on Internet use and affordances was extremely excited about the miraculous possibilities of the Internet for young people, and for some commentators this still appears to be the case. Popular "Internet evangelists" such as

Don Tapscott (1998, 2008) continue to enthuse about young people's natural skills with and affinity for the Internet and their ability to use it in democratic, creative, and active ways. In addition to its apparent propensity to encourage playful learning, the Internet is also seen to be engendering new, nonhierarchical forms of politics and civic participation that particularly appeal to the "Net Generation." In the same vein, Marc Prensky (2001, 2012) has spent much of the past decade popularizing the notion of a universal generational divide in relation to digital technology in his widely cited distinction between "digital natives" and "digital immigrants."

Whatever the evidence to the contrary, in political and educational circles there appears to have been a widespread acceptance of the idea that human brains are "plastic" and that they "mutate" in response to technology, a capability that leads those who use this technology most heavily (still mainly considered to be young people) to process, access, and use information in fundamentally different ways from other generations (see Selwyn 2009). Ideas of this kind often take time to diffuse across disciplinary and professional borders, but once they do, their effects can sometimes be felt long after their originators have moved on or their critics have proved the flaws in the logic. As we have seen, a number of commentators have argued that the comfort and confidence (some) young people display around new media can be employed to improve their relationship with traditional political processes and their participation in civil society. But what evidence is there that the Internet is regarded in this quasi-magical way, or that it plays this role, in the lives of a majority of young users?

In line with a great deal of other recent research (e.g., Ito et al. 2010; Livingstone 2009, 2011), results from both our survey and our focus groups suggest that the Internet has become a naturalized, almost mundane part of most young people's everyday lives across Europe. These fifteen-year-olds from a technical high school in a small town in Slovenia are fairly typical of their age group:

A: I have had the Internet just for three years. I use it for downloading movies and then, I don't know, Messenger, something for school, if I need it, and for playing online games.
P: I've been using the Internet for about seven or eight years. . . mostly for MySpace, YouTube, Messenger, for downloading movies, listening to music.
J: I have had the Internet for about five or six years and I use it for downloading movies, games, music. I'm on a website called Izklop [an entertainment portal] a lot. I use it for everything.

Meanwhile, another group of underprivileged school dropouts at a youth club in another part of Slovenia described searching for ways to grow soft drugs ("herbs, in the closet"), looking at pornography ("those beautiful pictures"), and trying to "meet girls" as among their everyday online activities. Across other focus groups, especially in urban areas, young people frequently asserted that going online was no longer novel, generally exciting, or even interesting, and in fact could be quite boring. The

Internet was generally something taken for granted and yet difficult to imagine living without.

In Hungary, as in most of the other countries we studied, young people from higher socioeconomic backgrounds were the ones in whose lives the Internet was most embedded:

M: What do you do online?

P: What *don't* I do! . . . Shop. . . .

A: News, studying, activism. . . .

P: Exhibitions, tickets, e-mail, poker, IWIW [a social networking site].

A2:   Critical Mass [a civic group of cyclist activists].

All: Yeah, that's default.

A: Reading the news, opinions on blogs, cycling-related news on Critical Mass.

P: Chat.

A2:   IWIW. (Hungary, urban cyclists)

This sense of the ubiquitous and yet mundane character of the Internet was especially well expressed by one of our Turkish respondents:

A: It is almost the same with going out for me. When you go out you share something, you see different things and enjoy yourself. This is the place where you can do things all together. Like a world. I am joining the world by joining the Internet. I like it like this. Where there is regret as much as joy. And there is also news and information. There is boredom also. It is same as the world. (Istanbul, AKP youth branch)

For this participant, as for our sample in general, any binary distinction between online and offline, or between the Internet and the "real world," was effectively meaningless. The Internet exists in the real offline world: it is a part of that world, rather than a separate space or something that competes with it.

These expressions of the normalization of the Internet in everyday life stand in stark contrast to the eulogies of youth and technology mentioned above. The Internet's interactive features are perceived as generally useful and entertaining, but also as banal: they are not seen to provoke extraordinary creativity and sociopolitical engagement or change *in and of themselves*. As in our survey, the Internet practices of the young people in our focus groups (even of our young activists) were dominated by entertainment and by socializing or communicating with friends and family. Nevertheless, they also included educational and pedagogical purposes; the solving of everyday problems in relation to travel or health; consumption, both socially conscious and mundane; discovering news online and occasionally reporting news items or uploading newsworthy photographs; and participating in organizations for civic as well as leisure purposes.

Restricted Access

Nevertheless, some young people in the focus groups experienced common problems in going online. Lack of stable housing, leading to lack of access, lack of formal literacy training and education, and parental restrictions were the barriers most frequently cited. While these factors related to various crosscutting issues, such as age, ethnicity, and religion (see Dolnicar 2011), the most crucial limiting factor across most of the countries was lower social class.

Some of the most socially deprived groups we interviewed had very limited access. For example, in the case of one group of impoverished young offenders from Northern Ireland, limited literacy and a dearth of opportunities for free access led them to dismiss the Internet as largely "boring" and irrelevant. These young people expressed a thoroughgoing sense of alienation from the political process and a powerful resentment of most forms of authority, yet the Internet did not seem to offer a possible way out of their situation, or even an especially attractive leisure-time pursuit. By contrast, another group of working-class youth from Manchester in the UK used the Internet at their local library, both for school and leisure purposes, although much of their information about politics was derived from television rather than from the Internet. Young people in both groups spoke passionately about social and political issues, and there was little sense in either group that such issues would have to be dressed up as fun or entertaining or promoted alongside entertainment in order to grab their attention.

In other instances, aspects of educational aspiration (informed by social class) conspired to reduce young people's possibilities for accessing the Internet at home. For example, these high school students from a less well-to-do neighborhood in Istanbul tended to access the Internet outside their homes for a range of reasons variously connected to the economic and cultural anxieties of their parents:

G: My mother cut off the Internet because my brother had been spending too much time on it. It has been three and a half years since I first started using Internet.

Moderator: How old is your brother?

G: Eight years old.

F: We haven't got Internet at home, but still I have been using Internet for two years.

Moderator: So how do you connect?

F: From houses of close relatives.

A: I have been using it for eight years. We used to have Internet at home, but they cut it off because of me. I wasn't studying my lessons well.

B: I have been using the Internet for four years. But these days I am in trouble with my parents because I am not doing well in my lessons. They disconnected it. But I am still using the Internet [in Internet cafes].

C: I do not have a connection at home, but I have also been using the Internet for four years.

A clear pattern of parental restriction and youth circumvention is evident among these working-class and lower-middle-class families, where the parents were variously small tradespeople or manual workers. The parents appeared to lack the confidence and time to restrict Internet access differentially or to provide an aspirational educational environment that included digital technologies. Rather, they handled what they saw as the negative influence of the Internet on their children's educational prospects by removing it entirely from their homes. Nevertheless, it was a matter of pride for their teenage children that they could escape parental surveillance by accessing it elsewhere.

However, this was not so easy in areas where the poor quality of broadband and working patterns combined to undermine young people's motivation for going online:

E [Young Farmers, UK]: I have the Internet at home, but it's difficult to be patient to wait for it to connect every two minutes . . . you can see what it's like. We mostly don't get a signal, and sometimes [when] we do, it gets cut off again.

G [Rural youth, Spain]: The connection speed is very slow. And it can be frustrating. You decide to make contact in some other way.

Q [Uniactivity, Turkey]: In Eastern Turkey [outside the metropolitan areas] we are struggling because Internet usage is low . . . and the reason Internet usage is still at considerably low levels is because of economic reasons.

In addition to class, age, location, and parental restrictions, other accessibility issues were raised in particular groups, as in the case of this young participant from the blind citizens focus group in Spain:

F: Yes [the Internet is an everyday part of my life]. The only problem of surfing the net with Jauss, Hal, Orca or MVD is the little image codes that many sites ask for in order to register. . . . Technically this is known as a CAPSA or ANTIBOT mechanism. Essentially it restricts automatic registrations. Supposedly it's to make sure a real person is registering, so robots can't automatically open accounts. . . . But neither can blind people!

As these examples imply, however, access is not an either/or matter: there are degrees and levels of exclusion that reflect a range of social, individual, and technical factors, as well as young people's personal interests and everyday routines.

Young People, Politics, and Democracy

Most of the young people in our focus groups had a very negative view of traditional governmental or party politics. Most saw politicians as corrupt, argumentative, unresponsive, and deliberately misleading, or simply boring and hard to understand. They were perceived to be working only for their own interests and to be far removed from the everyday needs and realities of common citizens and of youth in particular. Such distrust and criticism were most sweeping in Slovenia and Hungary, where the focus groups repeatedly characterized political parties, politicians, and government using terms such as "chaos," "scandal," "losers," "stealing," "corruption," "conflict," "lies," and so on. Yet lest this distrust of politicians be perceived as an Eastern European or Central European malaise, it must be noted that it was widespread across all the countries. Here, some young people from the Netherlands comment on their government:

C: [The Dutch Prime Minister] is able to avoid saying the important things.

M: Yes, he talks a lot, but he doesn't say a lot, you think . . . why don't you just say how it is! He talks a lot, all [politicians] are able to talk a lot, that is why they are in politics, because they are so good at gabbling. But it's not like . . . okay folks, this is it, and the book is open.

J: . . . and a lot of what they [politicians] say, they just begin with talking, they'll tell a story for ten minutes, and after that we still don't know anything. That's politics in my view. That's why politics is not interesting to me.

M: And they simply don't tell the whole truth if bad things are happening. If something happens, well, perhaps they will open the book a little bit, but not totally. (Youth Club, Netherlands)

While not all the young people in our groups mentioned the issue, many brought up the word "democracy" spontaneously, and discussed it with some passion—and in some cases, strongly opposing views. Many of our young people participated in volunteering activities within their communities. Yet although they shared certain basic premises—for instance, they explained that they were attempting to construct a world with better social relationships—they often seemed to have divergent views about the meaning of democracy:

I: I think "democracy" is when . . . when an individual has a right to choose their destiny. . . . But the versions of democracy out there aren't to me what my version of democracy is in my mind. . . . I don't think an ideal society exists. I think with the democracy we have it's a case of the majority just get to elect the minority who then get to decide instead of letting us decide. That's just my viewpoint on it.

Moderator: Is democracy your favoured form of government?

H: I don't really have a clear definition of what kind of democracy, but I guess there was like maybe about *fairness* really, but I don't know if that's actually the case [here]. There is no ideal [country] out there, that has democracy, that is fair.

I: I think on a local level you have much greater chances. . . . I saw people around me who weren't achieving to the best of their potential and it's a case of showing these people, just because of what is happening around the world it doesn't mean that you can't still achieve. So it's about giving you the chance actually to make the most of the opportunities that are available to you. Because as much as people might moan, if you live in a country like Britain you do have access to a free education system and the opportunities you have are immense.

P: But they're not mutually exclusive, so you don't have to do one or the other, you can do both. (Young Muslim volunteers, UK)

For some, then, democracy entailed a belief in fairness, people living their lives as they wish, self-determination, and egalitarian policies. For others it was defined almost as a form of communism, though as an ideal rather than as a lived reality. Some emphasized the need to challenge the current status quo, to engage directly with those in power; while others stressed internationalism and anticolonialism. Some were unsure, but seemed to take for granted that the traditional system worked better than some systems in other parts of the world, while others appeared resigned to just voting and leaving everything else to the politicians, whatever one might think of their policies. In general, however, the act of voting was regarded with ambivalence: as we have seen, most politicians were viewed as corrupt, self-centered, and untrustworthy. One might vote, but it was difficult if not impossible to control or influence what would happen after that; on the other hand, voting was the only means of removing a disliked government. The need for continued influence (between elections) over the democratic process was seen as being key to its success and to sustained involvement; but there was a general belief that after gaining citizens' votes, politicians ceased to listen to them in a meaningful way:

N: To me right now the first thing about politics, the first series of pictures that occurred to me was the prime minister's face turning to crying when he made his speech about yesterday's train accident.

B: Yeah, I'm sure they wrote it to him in parentheses "crying" [general laughter].

N: Yeah, I can imagine that he got stuck [in his speech] and then he pretended really well that in addition to his lots of problems, this [accident] really touched him. And to me this is what occurred about the word politics.

B: That it's a sham.

N: He really sold it.

M: I see it as very entertaining, as a cabaret, what's going on here. . . . I see it as a high-quality Hungarian cabaret. . . . Like when István Nyakó [spokesperson for the ruling Socialist party] calls someone something one day and then the opposite the next day, and then he explains why he was right the first time and the second time, too. (University students group, Budapest, Hungary)

M: I don't feel the least represented by the political class, because I don't find any political party that works for . . . well, that represents my interests, you know? And young people's interests, even less. Politicians talk a lot about . . . many general things that, perhaps, are very important for the adults, but for us, for young people, no. . . . I mean, they say "We're going to do this, we're going to do that," but then you see that they don't do what they say they were going to do . . . and also, on the other hand, I also see, I don't know, everything is quite fake, you know that . . . well, it's a little bit like theatre. (Young Farmers group, Spain)

While there can be a somewhat ritualistic dimension to these denunciations and expressions of distrust, in most cases they were not simply knee-jerk rhetoric but were supported by detailed examples, both historical and from the immediate context. The satirical humor and irony here have their own dynamic, but they also reflect a deep-seated sense of desperation and a lack of efficacy. This was aptly summarized in the following exchange between two Hungarian school students:

N: We can't do anything really. Politicians decide and then that's the way it is.

K: It's sad that we have had this experience at the age of seventeen.

Even so, the relationship between this apparent lack of trust in the political process and civic engagement is complicated. At least half of the civic and political activity described by the young people in our groups was deeply intertwined with—or even arose from—their avowed distrust of politicians and the mainstream broadcast media and from their concerns with the inadequate functioning of democracy in their locality, nationally or globally. It was precisely this that made participation so necessary; and in several cases it was in order to confirm or allay this distrust and to find like minds that young people reported turning to the Internet, perhaps skeptically and reflexively, but in increasing numbers.

The European Dimension

This general dislike of formal or institutional politics because of its association with hypocrisy and "spin" surfaced most starkly when it came to the European level. Most participants displayed either a lack of knowledge about European politics or a sense of distrust about it. While there was sometimes a sense of motivation in relation to and affiliation with politics and the civic sphere at the national level, and more frequently at a local or regional level, this was rarely apparent when discussing the notion of "Europe." Indeed, throughout our focus groups European politics were rarely discussed spontaneously except when young people were specifically asked to do so by the interviewers. Nevertheless, in some cases the issue of European politics arose in relation to legislation or potential legislation that was threatening the livelihoods of certain young people. For example, a group of young *diables* (fire-throwers) in Spain were concerned about this aspect:

N: There's this European proposal that will regulate certain uses of pyrotechnic material. And supposedly Spain must follow it. . . . In a way, they're severely limiting what being a *diable* means. Being a *diable* without being able to be among the people is just not being a *diable* at all.

X: And the law also talks about minors.

N: Yes, it says that those who are under 18 cannot use pyrotechnic material, which means that all the youth *diable* groups would have to cease to exist. It would erode many national traditions.

Moderator: And this is at a national or European level?

N: European.

X: But it's in the Catalan countries where fire is a strong component of traditional festivities. . . . It's not really an issue in Belgium, or wherever.

N: And that's why we organized a protest in Berga against this proposal. We have to make sure that our precious cultural heritage isn't destroyed by some European directive. (*Diables* community group, Spain)

In this instance, the potential threat had motivated members of the group to become involved in the political process—and to use Facebook to connect and organize their campaign.

On the other hand, a small minority of the respondents felt more positively that European identity or identification was a way of avoiding aspects of national cultures and traditions they wished to get away from or were critical about. Several members of the student activists and the musicians' collective focus groups in the UK mentioned that if pressed to choose to call themselves British or European, they would choose the latter. In the words of one young interviewee, "it means that we are less connected to the history of British colonialism, to British wars overseas fought for American oil interests." In this sense, choosing to be European rather than British citizens was seen as a pragmatic step closer to being world citizens, especially on the part of young people with left-wing affiliations.

Some of the more activist young people in our sample also placed a high value on grassroots connections with other young people across Europe. The Internet, and civic organizations more generally, were seen as providing access to different views and perspectives from young people in other countries and thereby informing common struggles and debates. For example, a young Slovenian blogger described how her civic organization had enabled a cross-European discussion on the issue of the privatization of universities:

K: Basically we wanted to show that the process of privatization is not happening in Slovenia alone, that this is some wider trend of neoliberal politics in Europe and beyond. There are fights against privatization going on also in other areas. . . . [Therefore we need to] connect with others. So that they could support us and we could support them, so we can share our experience. . . . So you don't stay isolated within national borders. Connecting is good. . . . It was [also] good when an Erasmus exchange student from Spain told us her opinion on what happened in Spain. She said that they promised them delayed [university] fees, but once fees were introduced, she said, additions to the law were introduced and quietly, by stealth, privatization is happening step by step. She said that now there is some sort of segregation going on between people who can afford it and those who can't.

As this comment also reminds us, the digital divides discussed earlier in this chapter reflect broader inequalities, not least in access to education—inequalities that are undoubtedly growing as a result of neoliberal economic policies such as privatization.

Motivating Civic Engagement

These examples clearly confirm that the key motivation for civic engagement—for seeking to connect with and learn about civic issues—is generally a matter of concrete personal experiences rather than an abstract sense of duty or responsibility.

Previous research suggests that the role of the family is crucial here (Greenstein 1965). Young people with educated or professional parents, or those who watch and read the news and discuss it with their parents, are obviously more likely to be politically informed and engaged. However, other family experiences—of eviction, police raids, injustice, or extreme poverty—can also be of paramount importance. School and university education may either confirm or counteract disillusionment with government and authorities or channel it in particular directions. In some cases, key teachers or youth workers seemed to have had an exceptionally strong impact on the civic and political horizons and aspirations of economically and socially disadvantaged young people, although in general, parents seemed to play a greater role for middle-class youth.

Across our focus groups, civic engagement and the motivation to participate were frequently related to having family members, peers, or a close community interested in the same issues and concerns. Fathers and mothers were referenced repeatedly, as were teachers. There was no sense from any of our participants that older adults—parents, carers, teachers, lecturers, youth workers, older siblings—had ceased to play an important role in their lives or in the formation of their concerns and values. While many mistrusted or criticized one or another of these groups for being too controlling or not available enough or not sufficiently well informed, there were always some other adults who were identified as having assisted in getting them to the positions and beliefs they now held. By contrast, on the Internet, virtually none of the young people in these focus groups had much contact with people outside their peer group or age range. Several of the younger ones were shy or uncomfortable at the thought of online cross-generational contact, particularly because of the scares around online predation and the fear of being patronized for not knowing much about traditional political issues.

In our discussions, political debates were frequently informed by economic anxieties and concerns about personal security—issues that were often directly related to each other. Many groups expressed a fear of being attacked when outside the home, either by other groups of young people or by random strangers, while girls talked about the possibility of sexual attacks on them or their younger siblings. In the UK in particular, they discussed "hanging around" outside in groups because of the lack of indoor facilities for youth activities, but also being afraid to pass other groups of young people on the street when alone. They wanted places to socialize together in safety, but such opportunities were almost always beyond their means: most of them were worried about finances, jobs were scarce, and their parents seemed to be financially stretched and insecure. This issue of class and financial anxiety arose repeatedly even when an initial question had steered them in a different direction, as in the following extract from a group of school students in a small UK town:

Moderator: So do you ever go on any news websites on the Internet?

P: The BBC sometimes, when I go onto my Internet sometimes it will pop up like a latest story so I'll go onto there and then I'll just look through and see some stories and I'm just reading and sometimes I get quite annoyed about it and sometimes I agree with things, and then other times I just go off of the website and go onto something else to check if it was true and maybe to see if I can do something about it.

Moderator: What kind of thing might get you quite annoyed if you were to read it on a website?

P: Probably if it was saying about wages being cut or something like that because obviously all of my family work and if the wages were to be cut and the taxes were to go up and the prescriptions and the university fees are imposed I think I would definitely e-mail the government and say something about it because I don't think there's any need for it. . . . And we catch the bus in the morning like when it's cold weather but it's getting more and more expensive because every time the petrol goes up a couple of pence so does the bus fare and the train fares, but they go up even more.

D: What I find quite annoying . . . it's like the bus fares and like the cinema, we have to pay adult prices and I always thought technically we weren't adults until we were eighteen, I mean we can't vote either and there are other things we can't do.

T: We're not adults until we're 18, I don't think—until we're allowed to vote legally, they don't perceive us as adults, we're just "teens."

P: Obviously we may go on to university but . . . we also need to earn and work and live. Not all of us have parents who can pay for everything. (UK, small-town school students)

This group was by no means the only one to raise these kinds of economic issues. What is especially notable here is how the participants articulated these concerns specifically as young people, pointing to adults' selective use of the categories "adult" and "child" and the issue of adults' economic and social responsibility in relation to future generations. Paying increased university fees, for example, seemed to be a prohibitively difficult thing for them to take on in terms of debt and future prospects.

Echoing these sentiments, a youth focus group in Slovenia complained about migrant Bosnian labor being employed rather than Slovene labor. Debating this among themselves as an economic choice, the participants went on to discuss the effects of low wages on their daily lives and those of their families:

P: Just look at my mum. . . . If you get 500 euro monthly, and you have to pay 300 for your place to sleep and 200 for the bus for both [parents], and other costs. And half of the apartment is 180 euro monthly and more. Then children's allowance and what my father pays for two—37,000 tolars [around 170 euros]. That is *nothing*! That is *everything* that we get. If my mum wasn't so good at saving money, I know that I wouldn't make it through the month with so little money. I would be hungry the last week. It is hard to talk about this. (Youth club group, Slovenia)

As these discussions imply, young people's everyday concerns with economic issues can take on an explicitly political dimension in particular social and historical contexts—and it should be noted that most of these discussions took place before the current recession. The crucial question in terms of our concerns here, however, has to do with how and why these kinds of everyday concerns might translate into more overt forms of civic or political action, that is, how *engagement* might lead to *participation*. In order to explore this, we need to turn more directly to the "young civilians"—to the relatively untypical minority who are civically active.

Forms of Participation

F: At home, well, we've always talked about political issues, or even town issues. And we talk about how people criticize lots of things, and then you see that it does also have some positive aspects. There's a little bit of everything. And not everything is negative. (Spain, seventeen-year-old)

P: They talk about politics a lot at my place. Even more so since my older sister has gone to study at law school. I was at least that much interested to get her to explain about it and then I decided [who to vote for] by myself. . . . We all have the same convictions, so . . . I was raised in that direction. (Slovenia, twenty-year-old)

A: I knew as soon as I volunteered there that it was using more of my skills and satisfying me more than the jobs just in media relations, which my degree suited me to. I was being socially useful to people with mental health problems in the area, and creative, and also [doing something] unexpected at the same time. (UK, twenty-three-year-old)

Our focus groups included a number of young people who were participating in their local communities, through volunteer activities, groups, and causes in their local areas, schools, and religious bodies, as well as in civic and social debates among friends, within families, and sometimes internationally. While the position of the "young civilian" might be seen as a socially desirable one, our data here are drawn from the heart of focus group discussions, when participants were relaxed and there was less need to present themselves in such ways for the benefit of the moderator or the others present.

These young people's civic and political participation predominantly concerned issues of immediate local or personal proximity. This proximity effect was itself debated by some participants, as among this group of volunteers for a global human rights organization in the Netherlands:

P: I think that these congresses, well, they are focused on national or international things. I think that young people find local issues more appealing, for instance, road thresholds, or. . . .

J: I remember well that we were very active with that Tibet campaign, I think it was in Groningen. Well, that's so nice, but Tibet, well, I don't want to be a prick, but that's very far away and we can't do anything about it. That's just like a reflection, you know. We cannot change anything in Tibet, you know, it has been the same way since 1948 or whatever.

D: But a lot of people joined us because of what we did in Groningen.

Some confusion is evident here: there is a consensus that local action offers the most scope for motivating young people in general, but less acknowledgment of the fact that this local action may well, as in the case in point, be about a global or international issue. Indeed, this interest in taking local action to show solidarity with a global situation—such as a campaign over democracy in Tibet—suggests that while local activism is crucial to creating a sense of efficacy, global concerns are not necessarily less interesting to young people than they are to any other generation.

Nevertheless, much of the civic interest evinced by young people in our interviews related to individual and group identities, for instance those built around race, religion, sexuality, music, political beliefs, or language, and involvement around such areas was often linked to a sense of injustice. Whether the issues at stake were primarily local, national, or international, what particularly appeared to motivate engagement was a sense of inequality, discrimination, or hypocrisy. This applied to the wars in Iraq and Afghanistan—"one million in the streets and the government did not listen"—and to the creeping privatization of higher education—"the politicians made promises which they never intended to keep." It applied to hearing politicians and representatives of big companies—"the bankers and the politicians who don't pay tax"—blatantly lie on television and seeing their statements pass unquestioned. And it also applied to the death of two local cyclists at a dangerous road intersection, and to being shouted at on the street for holding hands with a person of the same sex. Perhaps predictably, young people were especially motivated by the experience of being discriminated against *as young people*, while also being disenfranchised: "the blatant hypocrisy of charging young people as adults for films and transport but not allowing us to vote." Aside from the rejection of politicians, there was considerable resentment of police harassment and brutality, especially among young activists and youths from ethnic or religious minorities. Even more traditionally politically active students, of both center-left and right-wing dispositions, criticized what they saw as the hypocrisy of the state.

In fact, our discussions with civic website producers (see chapter 3) and with the focus group participants about their families suggest that these characteristics may not be unique to young people; they may also obtain for most older adults' civic and political engagement. Certainly, the notion that young people are somehow more averse to political discussion and mobilization than older generations was overtly challenged in a number of focus groups. In the Casal Lambda gay activist group in Spain, for instance, K asserted that

our generation is much more vocal. . . . Older generations are more afraid of publicly saying what they think, mainly because of what they have lived through.

His view was supported by fellow participant G:

When I first started studying political science, my eighty-year-old aunt warned me not to get involved with any of it because she feared the return of an authoritarian regime.

As this implies, generational differences may also reflect particular historical circumstances. Parents' and even grandparents' fears of surveillance and blacklisting were recounted particularly by young Spaniards and Hungarians, although they are now equally a fear for young British activists, who find the police tracking their activities on Facebook, Twitter, and email. Yet in case this may seem like a kind of generational posturing, easy enough in front of a moderator in a closed discussion, both these young activists went on to describe their daily challenges in the small town from which they hailed:

G: Since we're talking about homosexuality, in Vic, for example, which is like a small town, it's like homosexuality is invisible. I think it is probably still forbidden by some law, because you never see any gay people around. When I walked through the streets with my boyfriend, sometimes I have been insulted. So yeah, that definitely needs to change in that town. And also racism, which is rampant over there, and I think it might end up very badly, especially now that the economy is weak.

K: Yes, there are many biased opinions. Immigrants are the scapegoat for all the troubles. (Casal Lambda group, Spain)

Of course, such issues may cut both ways; and we again caution against the assumption that civic participation is necessarily always pro-democratic or benign. In the following extract from a focus group in Slovenia, the issue is a border dispute between Slovenia and Croatia over a one-kilometer strip of sea—an issue whose racial dimensions are highlighted by the intervention of a Croatian-born girl in the group, who, apparently for the first time, drew attention to her discomfort at having to listen to racist remarks:

A: We are not disturbed by the fact that there are all these "Čefurji" [a pejorative word for immigrants from the former Yugoslavia]. It bothers us that there are so many "*smart-ass* Čefurji."
B [a Croatian-born teenage girl]: Yes, but I was never a smart-ass. . . . I am a full-blooded Croatian. And I hear a lot of times "Oh these Croats! These shit, these insects," you know. And I remain silent.
C: But no one called you that.
B: But it starts then, you know, "Croatians and the sea." Croatians and I don't know what, shit, manure, and I don't know what else.

In this case, it is hard to disentangle nationalism from racist xenophobia, but it is clear that there is a problem not only with immigrants per se but with "smart-ass" immigrants who are perhaps too inclined to assert themselves. Politically, this extract contrasts markedly with the comments of the Casal Lambda group, although it also confirms that, whatever its motivation, political participation needs to be motivated by more than a generalized or worthy sense of serving the public good (however that is defined), or indeed of duty or responsibility. On the contrary, it often seems to require an element of conflict: it is perhaps by definition contested and agonistic.

Participation and Efficacy

Whatever initially happens to motivate it, a sense of efficacy (both internal and external) is likely to be a key factor in sustaining civic and political participation, whether it occurs offline or online. If young people perceive little purpose to participating or think that what they do is unlikely to make much difference, they will not be inclined to pursue it. A large proportion of participants in our focus groups argued—in some cases forcefully and cogently—that things in society needed to change, but many insisted that they themselves were unable to effect such changes. This applied to a range of issues, including social inequalities, corruption, lack of housing and job opportunities, high prices, religious, ethnic, or regional discrimination, police harassment of civil protest, government censorship of the Internet, and so on.

This perceived lack of external political efficacy was often related to their feelings about the unresponsiveness, untrustworthiness, and distance of politicians (and, on occasion, of other authority figures, such as school principals or university vice chancellors). As one UK participant suggested, politicians of different parties were often equally to blame:

C: A lot of the time it's like no matter what the politician in power has done, the other candidates, even though they would have made the same decision, would still go "oh why did you do that," even if they were going to do it themselves, like "why did you go to war?" When clearly the [opposition party] would have done it as well!

In several instances, actual experiences of having participated (for example, on school councils, through online petitions, in picket lines or demonstrations) had also proved disappointing: several participants spoke of having been consulted or encouraged to "have their say," but of not being listened to or managing to change anything. Some also voiced fears about how active participation or political critique might affect them as individuals, making them targets of the state, school authorities, the police, or other aggressive citizens with opposing views. As another UK participant suggested:

D: . . . things that dissuade you from trying to make a lot of social changes and that, I'd have to say police brutality. It is used, it does happen. I was sixteen and it happened and that did stop me from going to any marches after that. . . . Yeah, I thought it's my health or . . .

W: That was really horrible that, he got trampled by a horse and then hit.

D: No. After *that*. There was a van of police guys, you know the wrestlers in police uniforms, they decided to set up a barricade across where a load of us kids—this is when the kids walk out from school thing happened—they decided they were going to set up a barricade across a group of kids moving down the street so they virtually just flung whoever was in the way and then set up this barricade but during that there was a bit of a scuffle, I was trying to stand up and got kicked down a couple of times. So then when I actually got back to my feet I was face to face with the guy who was hitting me and I was, like, "do you know how old I am?" I was like 16 or something and he was, "I don't care mate, I don't care." And I was, like, "look what you've done!" and I showed him bruises and stuff, and he'd ripped my shirt and I was, like, "are you going to sleep tonight?" and he was, like, "shut up, mate, I don't care how old you are."

Nevertheless, several young people described how their involvement in civic activities—particularly related to their immediate or local contexts—seemed to have increased their sense of efficacy and confidence in their own ability to change things. Much of this seemed to relate to the experience of solidarity, of making common cause with others. For instance, this Slovenian student spoke about an experience of trying to make changes in the systems operating in her faculty and university:

J: I was first active in my faculty. And I did that because I noticed that a lot of things could be done better, and it was great because I met a bunch of people. And then I saw . . . you've created a network, you've reached, and you saw that actually the things that you thought you can change in a faculty, you can't. Then I tried out the university and now here, and then you see that you in fact can't do a lot by yourself and that is it is great if there is a network of people, so we can do a bit more, although we are very weak in certain things, because you can't change the system.

As this implies, the experience of having organized an event or campaign, whether online or offline, and of receiving some positive feedback from peers or older adults seems to generate a sense of internal efficacy that encourages and motivates further participation, even if the overall campaign did not achieve its broader goals. As participation develops, online and offline initiatives can feed into each other, and the sense of efficacy can transfer from one domain to another. For example, the same young person may work in several different organizational realms or roles, bringing concerns or insights from one realm to the other, as in the case of this young socialist activist from the Netherlands:

M: I am also vice chairman of a platform of empowerment of Avantis Hogescholen, fighting for the rights and information for students with disabilities or study restrictions, and I have voluntarily worked for Amnesty, providing training in secondary schools and telling young children something about human rights, so to speak, because I find human rights very universal and very important. Also because this topic is often missing in secondary schools. And I really inherited from [my family] . . . that you are not born to make yourself free, but you are born to put your talents and qualities . . . to the cause of bettering society or the world, and that is what I want to do. I do not want a job . . . to be rich, I want a job that can help the world as much as possible.

The Potential of the Internet

In line with many of the studies discussed in chapter 1, our research confirms that the Internet can be an important tool for young people who are already civically engaged. In focus groups with our "young civilians," the Internet was constantly presented as an important hub or node for civic or political activities. Indeed, these kinds of uses were also mentioned occasionally by "average" or less active young people, especially in relation to using social networking sites to mobilize action around local issues such as the provision of public facilities for youth, or in relation to volunteering or finding out about activities that were available in the area. For those in political and civic groups, such as political parties' youth organizations and established activist networks, the Internet appeared to have become an indispensable tool. For instance, the young file sharers in Sweden who ultimately formed their own political party concerned with issues of Internet freedom (see Miegel and Olsson 2010a) could not have made contact or conducted many of their activities offline (see chapter 6). Likewise, the young environmental activists whom we met in Turkey and in the Netherlands relied heavily on the Internet for keeping in touch with global campaigners and national branches of their own organizations, as well as for posting information about their latest concerns and offline meetings or actions.

As we have noted, the Internet can be a particularly important resource for minorities (political, ethnic, regional, or religious) in terms of promoting civic and political action. The young people who volunteered for or posted in the forums of the help site MuslimYouth.net in the UK or contributed to the blog *Judapest* or the social network Roma.hu in Hungary relied heavily on the Internet as a place for socializing, communication, information, and debate, particularly with those situated geographically at a distance. Again, such uses are by no means confined to the political left. For instance, young members of the Spanish right-wing Partido Popular were emphatic about the benefits to their movement of interactive applications online, pointing to their use of live video feeds and "cutting-edge design." While some such groups, such as Opus Dei in Spain, may utilize the Internet to consolidate well-established offline identities and to rehearse authoritarian political or religious positions, others use these online spaces to open up debate within offline communities. Several of these cases are discussed in more detail in the following chapters.

The Internet may also be an important way in which young people seeking information on one topic become aware of the existence or activities of other like-minded individuals, whom they may or may not then contact either online or offline. This may not always involve expensive interactive applications, as this Turkish activist explained:

C: It is sometimes too hard to moderate a forum. Instead of spending that time, going onto the streets is sometimes much more effective. Mail groups are much better than forums. They are always active. You can convince people on the net . . . announce your plans. Two years ago, there was a peace festival right before actions against the war. I received their e-mails. I went to both of the events even though that was not what was on my mind in the beginning.

The decentralized structure of the Internet might well be seen to facilitate such haphazard discoveries. We were told of several instances of young people looking online for one type of information (to do with leisure activities, for instance, or language learning) and stumbling on the website of a related civic or political group, organization, or movement, which they then went on to join. For example, in Hungary it was reported that, having searched for information about how to repair a particular kind of bicycle, several young people discovered the website of a large and significant cyclists' movement, which they became interested in and are now enthusiastic members of. This was also reported to be the experience of a number of young lesbian, gay, and bisexual people in the UK, Turkey, and Spain. In some instances they had clicked on a link for a party or a music event they had particularly enjoyed and been led to check out the organizers, and from the organizers' website to become involved in an LGBT group or network.

The Culture of Politics and the Politics of Culture

Many activities in which young people are likely to participate may have civic or political dimensions or motivations, even if these are not made explicit or readily apparent to outsiders. We met several groups of young people who were actively engaged in cultural activities in fields such as journalism or music that had strong but implicit civic dimensions, and that often functioned both offline and online. For instance, in the case of a young musicians' collective in Manchester, UK, their work in making and promoting music was explicitly connected to civic sharing, the development of alternative lifestyles, and anti-capitalist politics. They used websites and social networks (both commercial and alternative) both for socializing and promoting their music and also for mobilizing support for civic and political action. Initially through MySpace and subsequently through their own site, they have sought to develop an alternative economy that bypasses the control of big companies. Especially for younger performers, the use of the Internet—social networking, email, instant messaging, downloading—clearly makes a DIY (do-it-yourself) music culture much more of a possibility. However, while the offline and online actions of their group are intimately related, offline events—live music in affordable venues—do appear to take priority:

Moderator: Keeping the collective together, what does that require of you now in terms of work and resources?

D: Just making sure we've always got another event to work towards and make sure there's always another thing that's going to keep [the collective] in people's heads, which people don't forget.

R: And lose direction.

J: I think the website will really help, because we put on such diverse types of music and we never really had any sort of proper branding or logo, all that artwork has been totally different for every single event that we've done. Which has always been part of the point—

D: —getting people's artwork out as well as the music.

J: But it meant that we were always starting from scratch with each event, whereas now with the website at least with each event we've got somewhere to direct people so they can find out about the next thing we're doing.

R: It's all changed now, isn't it, like there is an idea of a brand, there is an idea . . . the website is the branding.

In this case, the use of the Internet seems to be encouraging a process of "branding," if not commercialization—although the collective remains a nonprofit activity. It might be argued that, despite their criticisms of the exploitation practiced by the mainstream music industry, these young people are simply building up their own small business, though couched in an ethical and egalitarian rhetoric. Yet this was an explicit concern for the collective itself:

J: The idea is to draw people to the site with all the free downloads but then start putting out some commercial releases as well. . . . [Pricing] will be more based on how much it's cost us to produce it and then how much we'll need to do another one.

Moderator: So a kind of fair trade music?

All: Exactly.

Having built their own, this group had learned that it was important for sites to be "fit to purpose," that even a small site, which is constructed with less money, can suit a particular organization or campaign because it does what the group needs it to do. By contrast, they argued that some sites attempt to target the youth audience too obviously and end up emphasizing style over content: there can be a sense of straining to communicate ideas, of "trying too hard," which young people in particular are likely to find artificial and alienating.

The Ambivalence of the Internet

As these examples imply, the Internet can indeed serve as a form of public sphere, opening up spaces for civic activity and discussion between young people, even if such spaces are not obviously labeled as civic or political. Of course, it is important not to overrate the significance of such a public space, or to regard it as politically homogeneous. As we have seen, relatively few young people participate in these kinds of ways, and even the ones who do participate most often tend to do so sporadically. Furthermore, not all online civic activity is necessarily democratic either in intention or in practice.

Furthermore, it would be mistaken to suggest that high levels of Internet literacy and political or civic awareness always go hand-in-hand. In fact, many of our respondents displayed a high degree of critical reflexivity about the Internet as a medium, both in general and specifically in relation to civic and political participation. Some of their concerns here were to do with its limitations as a medium for socializing, and hence for campaigning: for example, it was argued that "the Internet is not that good for discussions as they quite often become very heated," "you can lose casual acquaintances and offend friends by putting your real political opinions as a Facebook status," and "it's better to meet face-to-face than to discuss things on the Internet." Other concerns were more explicitly political: "you cannot really trust your sources on the Internet," "on the Internet your actions are easily monitored," and "just clicking a petition doesn't mean that anything will change." In the following sections of this chapter we explore some of these concerns in more detail.

Despite the rhetoric of a "digital generation," young people often voice criticisms of the Internet that echo those of older generations. In fact, some of our focus group participants described the Internet as undermining authentic social interaction. As one group of young Dutch people said:

G: I am not a big fan of the Internet . . . because it says something about society, it is individualizing, you know, and that has only become worse with the Internet, and I really don't like that people don't see each other any longer and only see each other on MSN to chat. I just don't like that. People don't value personal contact any longer.

R: I would never read stories from somebody I don't know about his holiday. But if I would meet him in a bar or wherever, then I would be really interested in his stories.

Meanwhile, several bloggers in the Netherlands and Sweden were quite candid about the self-centered and even escapist nature of their engagement with blogging, both in their own writing and in keeping up with the blogosphere:

G: I think it is really great to have [a blog], just log in . . . and have 300 unread [updates] and have a cup of coffee and just sit and read blogs, it is relaxation for me.

M: Yes, it can really be relaxing . . . but it is a good way, in a way, a kind of escapism, that you kind of—

G: [interrupting] It is like reading a magazine. (Young bloggers, Sweden)

The view of social media use and volunteering as a way of building a CV or of pursuing one's own ambitions (which we saw in relation to NGOs in chapter 3) was supported by other young people, such as this Slovenian university student:

F: And in the end you discover that besides what we have already talked about, building your social network, you work on yourself, your competences, that actually by working for others you work mostly for yourself. . . . I mean [laughter] indirectly, because you form yourself and acquire knowledge, a broader view, a social network.

Although they were expressed with considerable ambivalence, these views reflected much broader critiques of the role of technology in contemporary formations of identity, such as that the Internet is helping to promote a new level of individualization, even of narcissism, and that it encourages an intensified form of self-promotion or "work on the self" (see Buckingham 2008).

The Politics of Online Interaction

The nature of online interactions was also seen to have more explicitly political implications. As we have seen, the Internet's open architecture—the fact that it allows voices to be heard that might be suppressed offline—can provide new opportunities for expressions of identity, in ways that the traditional media often have not. Yet not all of these expressions are necessarily pro-democratic or altruistic. For instance, some of the young people posting in the forums on the website Muslim Youth expressed quite conservative views in relation to sexuality and women's rights, views that elicited debate from their peers. Equally, some of the posters in the forums of Gay Youth UK have at times vociferously expressed and debated racist opinions in relation to Muslim immigrants in the UK.

Meanwhile, being attacked online was a fairly common experience for young people belonging to minorities, be these sexual, religious, ethnic, or political. The young gay people in Casal Lambda in Spain, young feminist bloggers in the UK and Sweden, young Jewish bloggers in Hungary, young Moroccans in Maroc in the Netherlands, and our Roma interviewees in Hungary all gave examples of homophobia, sexism, and racism they had experienced online. In some instances, particularly where their work online was an explicit intervention in the politics of identity, this had extended to their offline lives. Others pointed to the ways in which Facebook could be used cynically and simplistically to discourage offline civic action, to bully or "out" politically opposing factions. Perhaps for this reason, many members of such groups said they preferred anonymous interaction or highly moderated communication to named posting and unmoderated communities.

Interactivity has been much touted as a key factor in online engagement, yet most of the young people we interviewed still appeared to spend most of their time online reading, viewing, or downloading content rather than making, altering, and uploading it. Only a small minority of our respondents made and uploaded video or audio content, and an even smaller minority did this for civic rather than entertainment or CV-building purposes. Although by 2013 Facebook and social networking have caught up in popularity among some web producers, forums are still the most common places for the contribution of user content. As we have argued, not all interactivity is benign, and there can be an element of aggression about such interactions: "destroying one's enemies rhetorically" and "pointing out stupidity and tearing it to pieces" were given as reasons by some young people for interactive postings in forums and to blogs. Yet for others, it was precisely this possibility they found intimidating and that tended to discourage them from participating. User control—the ability to navigate around easily, to understand where you were at a glance, and to switch off unwanted functions—was rated very highly by everyone. However, there was no evidence that young people in general were more attracted to websites that had the latest technological tools than to those whose content and interactivity were tailored to fit the needs of specific groups.

This was also an issue for young people involved with political parties, who were often wary of the ways in which those with opposing views used the Internet to engage them in what might become humiliating and time-consuming polemic (see Olsson 2006). For example, a group of young people belonging to the Socialist party in Catalunya used the Internet extensively for messaging, commenting, and disseminating information, but emphasized the difficulties of such online engagement:

A: For example, when you're checking out the forums or the comment section under a news story, sometimes it feels like there's a bunch of people who just go there and say whatever crosses their mind.

D: That's precisely one of the things that people find most attractive in the online world. . . . I mean I've read so much crap. . . . Since people know they are protected, they sometimes go crazy and end up overcrowding forums or comment sites with petty, provocative messages.

This was a point strongly endorsed by young people in the Socialist Party in the UK, who did not see the lack of interactivity on their own party website as a problem since the party newspaper contained information and discussion, and selling the newspaper enabled face-to-face contact.

Some of these concerns were elaborated among one of our Hungarian focus groups:

N: I don't usually do that [commenting] because it is a bit . . . it scares me away when I see there are two hundred comments and I know it really is pointless because nobody is going to read it.

M: The problem with comments is that if the blog is big and has no full-time moderator then anything, I mean anything, goes, really. For example at the *Antagon* blog we see this now that we would want to have posts about the printed media. So when we say that Paul Lendvay is not qualified to be the ombudsman of *Népszabadság* [the Hungarian daily with the biggest circulation], then everyone gets there and starts going on about what a big "commie" this Paul Lendvay is . . . and they don't get that that's not the point. . . I think all those spam comments really scare people away.

B1: There was this post about cartoons. And then these people came, about thirty of them and started calling each other names back and forth. . . . And I can imagine them sitting at a table and beating each other up, and I didn't dare to write anything. I had an opinion, but I knew both sides would say I am stupid. And I didn't want to get into this.

B1: In every single discussion, no matter what the post is about, right around the thirtieth comment someone would start going on about the Jews or the commies. (Győr, young bloggers, Hungary)

On the other hand, there was a danger that political arguments could be won or lost simply on the basis of one's use of the medium rather than on the basis of the quality of one's arguments. In one instance in the UK, a group of pro-democracy student activists who worked for greater political participation by all students in their students' union found themselves outmaneuvered by their more Internet-savvy political opponents. In preparation for a referendum on students' rights to attend meetings and to vote on issues relating to their interests, the "No" campaign, which wanted closed meetings for a twelve-person committee, held parties, took photographs at these parties, and put them up on Facebook, tagging dozens of students and then posting the photographs on the "No" campaign Facebook page. While the "Yes" campaigners were busy leafleting and going door-to-door explaining why it was important for all students to have a voice and a vote on each issue rather than giving up their votes to a committee, the "No" campaign almost effortlessly reached several hundred students on Facebook with its message of "students just wanting to have fun" and leaving the "hard work of politics" to the committee. The "No" campaign narrowly won the referendum, and students at that university quietly gave up their right to participate in decision making, prompting the pro-democracy campaigners to ponder the power of the Internet:

A: This is an example of where Facebook was a bit of a bizarre phenomenon. . . . I was like "look, just ignore it, it's just Facebook" but actually I really regret saying that because the [right-wing faction] absolutely used it against the pro-democracy voters.

K: [They made a] shit video.

A: They tagged people . . . you know you can tag photos, they tagged all of their mates in these photos, they came up on everyone's profile and all these things.

K: Anything that is a cynical argument is so much easier to get over on the Internet because you don't have to explain the nuances or subtleties of why something doesn't work, you can just say a really reactionary statement and that's it. . . . So Facebook is dangerous almost.

M: This referendum has been a really good eye-opener for me about how the Internet works. Because yeah, their "No" campaign was based on the Internet, they mobilized from the Internet—and have a look, there were people making comments at four in the morning to debate. As a person who's busy out campaigning, doing . . . a job, I've got things to do. . . . You can't keep [doing that]. . . . We're going to have to discuss . . . how we're going to deal with [the Internet]. (Students union activists, UK)

It may indeed be the case, as this group suggests, that young people with anti-authoritarian politics have more elaborated and extended arguments to make about democratic processes and hence do not come off well in the quick sound-bite world of social network sites and forums. Yet their conclusion was that this was inescapable: ultimately, they would have to engage with social networking in their campaigning. They would need to campaign online, despite their preference for face-to-face contact, leafleting, meetings, and debates—and despite their feeling that the older, more traditional methods could reach people, particularly working-class people, that the Internet could not.

A further disincentive to online participation was the potential for surveillance. If we project from these accounts, it appears that a number of young people do not participate, despite a wish to do so, because they are fearful of the consequences of active participation and dissent. This anxiety over the potential difficulties of being perceived as having strong political views can be seen in online forums run by youth organizations, as well as in postings to civic websites. The website Muslim Youth was one of several sites that felt the need to remind users that posts discussing violent civic action might be taken down, while even mild forms of youth dissent such as swearing are not allowed on other forums. As Starr and colleagues (2008) suggest in relation to the US, this may reflect a broader "rationalisation of repression," whereby dissent itself is becoming criminalized and young people are blamed for "provoking" police intervention, for example through their actions at demonstrations.

The Internet in Context

As the previous quotations indicate, there was an interesting preference among several of these civically active groups for using traditional media, and for more traditional methods of campaigning. Some participants pointed to newspapers as a more reliable source of information than the Internet, although they acknowledged that the quality of news varied among different newspapers. Contradicting the common perception that older media no longer attract younger audiences, they frequently referred to television as their preferred entertainment and news medium: many said it would still be their first port of call, even if it meant watching a television station streaming its broadcast on the web, rather than seeking an online-only news source. Meanwhile, focus groups of young students and activists, for example in Turkey and the UK, repeatedly contrasted what they saw as the "passivity" involved in surfing the net, even for political or civic news or in order to comment online, with the positive or "real" activism of offline participation.

This preference for older media of communication was also apparent when it came to organizing political campaigns, as one activist involved in resistance to the "Bologna process" in universities explained:

A: Yeah, well, there's two goals [of the occupation of university buildings]. One . . . is to attract media attention to our cause, and the other is that the occupation allows us to have a space where we can coordinate our efforts at a national level. It's like our headquarters, in a way. And sure, sometimes people complain we're not too efficient, since we only make decisions in an assembly manner. But we want to reflect the voice of all the students, so it might take us a little while longer than if we took decisions unilaterally.

In fact, there were no notable instances across our research where attractive website designs appeared to have inspired civic engagement and participation in their own right. There were some cases of Internet practices themselves motivating participation: for instance, civic and political movements that had grown up online around issues relating to file sharing, the threat of surveillance of the Internet, and political censorship of particular websites. These are clearly political and civic engagements that would not be possible but for the Internet. Yet we did not find examples of a specific website per se (for instance through its interactive facilities or its attractive design) having led young people to become civically engaged where they were not already so engaged in the first place.

What appeared to be more effective was creating a dynamic relationship between online and offline activities, including those involving old media and face-to-face communication. This was true not only of activist groups but also of formal politics, especially at the local level. Both in Sweden and in the UK, schemes like the local young mayor or youth branches of local government did provide opportunities for some young people to air their concerns, and provided a moderately independent use of small budgets to spend on youth issues and youth involvement in training and community-based projects. In Lund, Sweden, this led to a "green" environmental stance in relation to buying supplies that subsequently spread to the adult council; while in Lewisham in London it involved the funding of several local sporting and "regeneration" projects for youth. In each of these instances the projects would have existed without the Internet or the website in question, but they would probably not have been as public, as widely acknowledged, or as successful.

Asked whether the Internet might actually diminish young people's involvement in political and civic issues, M and E from the website Young in Lund responded that "it's important to base democracy on something offline too, you have to meet, to discuss and learn and practice a lot." Nevertheless, the website could also play a role:

[we hope to] have a great webpage for young people in Lund, which will influence issues, where you can participate and have an impact and understand that you can have an impact, to find direct channels, find support for your ideas, support on how to solve a problem or do a project you want to start. . . . School, public transportation, housing issues. . . .

These examples support our broader finding, echoed by many of the web producers cited elsewhere in this book: most of the civic and political participation, especially sustained participation, that we identified appeared to *begin and end offline*. Such participation is based in local communities or communities of interest that exist in real physical spaces and thrive on face-to-face contact, even if the Internet has provided an additional space, a tool, or a focal point for aspects of this participation. The problems and issues debated and engaged online usually exist in circumstances offline, and the kinds of changes to society and the civic or political sphere that much of the engagement is aimed toward are changes that would affect the everyday, offline "life worlds" of young people.

Here again, we need to avoid the binary opposition between online and offline. The Internet's potential for supporting civic engagement and participation should not be viewed separately but alongside the offline activities, interests, and multiple civic and political exclusions of young people. Offline experiences are of far greater weight in forming young people's civic and political trajectories than is their level of comfort or expertise with digital technologies. The detailed fine-tuning of online platforms, or the implementation of ever more elaborated forms of technological interactivity, is no substitute for g addressing young people's concerns and the distinctly undemocratic structures that hold many of them in place regardless of their levels of civic engagement.

Conclusion

The interview data discussed in this chapter point up some of the exciting potential of the Internet for promoting civic engagement and participation but also underscore the medium's difficulties and limitations. Our aim in this chapter has partly been to offer a balanced assessment in the light of what we know from the survey of online civic content and of young people, discussed in previous chapters: the glass is both half full and half empty.

Many youth civic organizations that have an online presence tend to aim at a generalized and universal "young person" rather than at specific young people. In fact, the type of young person conceptualized by many online civic producers is implicitly middle class, cosmopolitan, and highly literate, in addition to having a high level of unrestricted access and technological competence. These notional young people are predominantly seen as being already interested in social justice, as well as in urban popular culture: they are fun-loving, but also caring and committed. Yet data from both our survey and our focus groups suggest that appeals constructed with such an audience in mind are effective only with a minority of young people. They may form a significant minority, but it is nevertheless a small one, and they tend to be privileged in other areas of their lives as well.

Our focus groups show that Internet use or non-use needs to be understood in the wider context of young people's everyday experiences. The same is true of civic engagement: life circumstances and life chances play a critical role in determining how far young people might be motivated to engage in civic action, whether online or offline. Young people may have a range of civic and political concerns, and indeed some passionate commitments, but these are for the most part based in local communities and experiences. In some instances, they might connect with broader formulations of the issues and with wider political movements, but often they do not.

This is not a matter of laziness or stupidity but of lack of opportunity. Some of our focus groups were intensely aware of broader political issues but beset by a sense of disempowerment that was profoundly debilitating. What appeared as cynicism and apathy—and quite frequently as anger—reflected the constraints of their social circumstances, and the genuine limitations of their political agency. In this context, the Internet might serve as a marginal resource for entertainment or socializing; but in civic or political terms it is an irrelevance. Just like traditional news media, it simply fails to connect.

With regard to mainstream media, many of the young people whose views we canvassed expressed serious concerns about media reporting of themselves, their localities, their political interests and everyday concerns. They showed low levels of trust in mainstream news media and politicians with whom they were familiar. They supported their affective judgments with both anecdotal and academic evidence of bias and collusion between media and perceived national or international elites. Contrary to many civic engagement studies, which take trust in institutions as a significant measure of civic engagement, however, we have shown that these expressions of mistrust and disaffection are actually examples of critical civic engagement and, in some cases, monitorial citizenship (Schudson 1998). Nevertheless, paradoxically, where their distrust was overwhelming, it appeared to decrease their sense of civic and political efficacy, and thus to fuel the feeling of disempowerment.

There are, of course, exceptions. The affluent economic and social backgrounds of some focus group participants provided them both with the necessary access and with a belief in their own ability to make a difference. Young people in these favorable circumstances use the Internet to support their civic participation, though not in spectacularly innovative or extensive ways. In a sense, they are already well served, both by traditional media and by the other opportunities for participation that are available to them. The Internet just provides them with even more, should they choose to use it.

Although our survey only provides correlations between variables, in combination with the focus groups it seems fair to conclude that it is generally civic commitments that are formed offline that drive online civic engagement, rather than the other way around. The sense of political efficacy—the feeling that one's individual action can make a difference—also emerges both from the survey and from the focus groups as a key determinant of civic engagement (whether online or offline); although clearly there will be both vicious and virtuous circles here, as positive experiences reinforce the sense of efficacy and vice versa. In fact, our survey provides evidence that young people experience efficacy as a result of sharing civic information or participating in civic debate; and this can take place online or face-to-face.

Broadly speaking, then, our research confirms that the Internet can play an important role as a tool for those who are *already* participating in civic or political activities, although even these "young civilians" are very well aware of its disadvantages and limitations. For those who are not already civically engaged, however, and particularly for those who live in socioeconomically disadvantaged circumstances, the Internet is currently all but irrelevant as a civic and political tool.

Although the Internet could easily become useful for such people, for instance for educational or leisure purposes, the obstacles that prevent civic participation offline also apply online. Despite the hype about interactivity and ubiquitous access, there are few effective efforts to include disadvantaged young people in the online public sphere. As things stand, much more would be gained for these groups by funding traditional, locally based civic initiatives such as youth centers, as well as providing free and unrestricted Internet access at libraries and other public buildings, than would result from setting up expensive civic websites to "give them a voice." A high level of experience and literacy and a sense of personal efficacy and confidence are needed for young people to create and post their own civic or political content online. The ones most likely to do this, and most likely to become involved and remain involved in both online and offline organizations, are those who already have substantial amounts of social and educational capital—factors that again are related largely to economic issues. As such, there is a distinct risk that the Internet may merely reinforce existing inequalities in participation.

However, our broader point here is that we also need to challenge the common formulation of the issue—the view of the Internet as the potential "solution" to the "problem" of young people's disengagement. The implicit assumption here is that we have a communications problem that can be solved by a communications fix: the problem is not primarily or fundamentally to do with the political system as such but with the way in which people are able to engage it. From this perspective, one can imagine that the problem could be solved simply by changing the mode of communication: politics (or democracy) as usual plus the Internet should do the trick. Yet this solution neatly relieves us of the more difficult necessity of addressing what might be wrong with democracy as it actually exists, and as young people in particular experience it.

6 Politics Online

In this chapter and the next, our focus of attention shifts more directly to the Web itself. Picking up on the brief overview in chapter 2, we present a series of case studies of civic websites targeting young people in our seven partner countries. Chapter 7 examines religious, ethnic, and regional identities online. This chapter focuses on organizations, networks, and groups whose online activities deal more or less explicitly with politics. It covers a spectrum of websites, from those of mainstream political parties to independent activist groups, from the far left to the far right, and from well-funded projects to those that are run entirely on voluntary labor.

Method

The analyses presented in this chapter and the next were initially undertaken by our international team of researchers over a one-year period between May 2007 and May 2008. Since that time, approximately 10 percent of the sites we studied have ceased to exist, or else they have disappeared and returned several times in different forms. While this is an inevitable hazard of Internet research, we have selected these examples to illuminate broader themes that were apparent in our overall survey and in our larger sample of more than fifty detailed case studies (see CivicWeb Deliverable 8 2008 and CivicWeb Deliverable 14 2009). All the existing sites were reanalyzed and contextualized in 2012 in light of ongoing historical and political events and recent scholarship, and the arguments and interpretations presented here are our own.

Our initial analyses took the form of "thick descriptions" of individual websites, based on a shared framework of questions. In many instances, these were supplemented by interviews with the site producers (including editors, designers, and others). The topics covered included a range of aspects of form and content, including the following:

- *aims and functions* as obtained from explicit statements on the site, as well as interviews

- *operation* the history, financial background, and management of the site
- *content* the issues and topics addressed, the "voices" present
- *discourse* how the issues were framed and defined, and the overt and implied discourses in play
- *civic participation* the modes of civic participation that were represented and invited
- *address* the implied or target audience, style and mode of address, and the representation of "youth"
- *design* the use of verbal, visual, and sound modes, structure, and navigation
- *interactivity* the use of interactive applications, and the degree and nature of control of communication.

In organizing this account, we have selected and grouped our chosen case studies in order to address a range of broader themes and questions. Our analysis is comparative, on two levels. Each chapter presents groups of case studies of particular types of sites—for instance, in this chapter we begin with political party sites and then move on to activist sites. This allows us to identify issues that are specific to these types of sites, while the comparison between the different types of sites across the chapter as a whole provides the basis for addressing broader questions—in this instance, in relation to different forms and styles of politics.

The Civic and the Political

In identifying our focus here as *political*, we inevitably beg the question of how this is defined—and in this context, how the "political" relates to the "civic." As we saw in chapter 1, the term "civic" is often seen to be broader than the term "political." "Civic cultures," for example as Dahlgren (2003) defines them, include a range of activities—such as volunteering, debating social issues, or participating in community organizations—that might be seen as "parapolitical" or even "prepolitical." That is, they may have potentially political dimensions, even though these are not necessarily made explicit. Both the civic and the political involve forms of collective (rather than merely individual) action. However, what seems to distinguish political action is its articulation as part of an explicit program or ideology and, in many instances, its overt attempt to influence public policy and government. We might say that actions *become* political both when they are defined as such and when they are seen in relation to broader patterns of power and authority.

To this extent, the civic is not always political. Yet is politics then merely a subset of the civic? Discussions of the term "civic" often seem to have recourse to some idea of the common good (Montgomery, Gottlieb-Robles, and Larson 2004), although it would be almost impossible to agree on a definition of the common good beyond the most basic level of human survival. By contrast, politics typically involves an explicit intention to bring about social change in some form—or alternatively, to prevent things from changing in ways that are deemed undesirable. Yet in pursuing such goals, politics may not necessarily function in support of the common good, and it may use methods that, however well intentioned, directly undermine the common good. It would thus be incorrect to assume that politics is necessarily or inevitably civic, either in intention or in practice. The two categories may overlap, but the one is not a subset or a precondition of the other.

With this in mind, we have cast our net fairly widely here. The first part of the chapter looks at sites of the youth wings of established political parties. While we have deliberately chosen parties from the left and right, all of these sites represent a relatively formal conception of politics, if one that is inflected (sometimes in fairly minimal ways) through its address to a youth audience. The second part of the chapter looks at activist sites, run by groups whose activities mostly take place well beyond the formal political process, even if they are partly seeking to influence it. These sites represent examples of the "new" forms of politics—variously labeled as "new social movements," "do-it-yourself" (DIY) politics, or the politics of the "actualizing citizen"— that some have seen as characteristic of a networked society. In the final part, we offer two case studies of sites that are less overtly political, in the sense of offering a program that explicitly addresses government and public policy. However, these sites offer an interesting contrast to both the more formal and the activist conceptions of politics that we present in the first two parts of the chapter.

The comparisons among our case studies, both in each part and across the chapter as a whole, are therefore designed to address the characteristics, and indeed the limitations, of the various forms of politics we consider. Of necessity, this involves us in discussions of the sites' political aims, both overt and underlying, and so we will discuss their conceptions of democracy, rights, and citizenship, for example as expressed in the rhetoric of mission statements or "about us" pages.

However, politics is not simply a matter of overt statements of ideology. It is also about practices, about how actions and debates are actually carried out. In this respect, we continue to pursue some of our key questions about the *pedagogy* of these sites— the ways in which they address and seek to engage their users, and how users themselves actually participate. Since several of these organizations at least nominally target young people as their constituents, questions of generational power are central to the cases we examine. In what ways do the websites express or conceal their makers' organizational dynamics—that is, whether these dynamics are hierarchical or democratically distributed? Is information allowed to flow in a free and open manner, or is it highly controlled? How are recalcitrant participants dealt with? And how are different types and levels of participation distributed throughout the organization's activities?

These kinds of issues have been addressed in a number of previous studies. Stephen Coleman (2008), for instance, distinguishes between "managed" and "autonomous" youth websites. In managed e-citizenship, youth are invited to participate in safe, contained spaces: they can learn and have their say, but only in ways that are moderated and controlled by responsible adults. By contrast, autonomous e-citizenship makes use of the apparent openness and freedom of online communication. According to Coleman, these positions reflect broader ideological differences: while proponents of managed participation tend to favor the existing status quo of democratic politics, those who adopt the autonomous approach are critical of what they see as "a narrow, quiescent and consumerist model of civic action" and prefer a more anarchic or radical ideology. Farnak Miraftab (2006) makes a similar distinction between "invited" and "invented" spaces of citizenship. While the former tend to be constructed and legitimized by governmental and official bodies, the latter are created through collective actions that directly challenge those in authority; and while the former promote ways of coping with existing structures, the latter promote resistance and change.

We can certainly make distinctions between these top-down and bottom-up or between vertical and horizontal modes of online communication among our case studies here—although, as Coleman suggests, these differences might better be seen as ends of a continuum rather than as a binary opposition. However, in some respects these distinctions do not do justice to the complexity of the issues. In particular, we would warn against the assumption that differences in the mode of communication necessarily map to differences in political ideology, or indeed that a seemingly decentralized, bottom-up mode is always and inevitably preferable.

A key additional factor here, and one that emerged very strongly in the previous two chapters, is the relationship between online and offline communication—although here, too, we would caution against a binary view. In assessing the politics of online interaction, we also need to explore the links between online and offline activities and the different methods utilized by each group or organization for reaching its stated aims and goals. We have therefore selected as case studies organizations that exemplify different approaches: those that operate primarily online (and to a lesser extent offline), those that work primarily offline (and to a lesser extent online), and those that seek to develop a more equal and dialogical relationship between the two domains. As we indicate in the subsequent discussion, the ways in which different organizations prioritize and conceptualize their online and offline activities have considerable implications for the form and content of their actual sites.

Part I: Formal Politics—Case Studies

From the Hitler Youth and the Young Communist League (established in the US in the 1920s) to the youth wings of contemporary mainstream parties, there is a very long history of formal political organizations seeking to proselytize to young people and involve them in their activities—especially in the years immediately before young people reach voting age. But to what extent are young people themselves active participants in these organizations? How far are they able to determine the ways in which they work and the positions they adopt? And what part might the Internet play in these respects? In this section we consider three contrasting examples from different parts of the political spectrum in order to raise broader questions about the characteristics, consequences, and limitations of using the Web to promote formal political engagement among young people.

Juventudes Falangistas de España (Young Falangists of Spain)

URL: http://www.juventudesfalangistas.com. Researcher: Magdalena Albero-Andrés

The Falange is a right-wing, Catholic, Spanish nationalist movement consisting of around eighteen splinter groups, some with electoral ambitions and others without. The party has a history going back several generations to the right-wing nationalist leader Jose Antonio and predates the Franco dictatorship (Büttner 2011, 181–182). In the 1930s, Antonio used populist rhetoric to woo voters away from the communists, and there are still vestiges of anticommunist rhetoric in the party's current arguments, despite the apparently minimal share it has gained in recent elections. The party's quasi-fascist ideology is summed up in its slogan, "Neither capitalism, nor communism, but national syndicalism."

In line with other youth wings of far-right parties and groups (Atton 2006; Whine 1997), the Juventudes Falangistas de España website reflects the wider movement's priorities on issues of religion, immigration, and race. On its home page, the site invokes both this history and a contemporary interest in youth, expressed in the slogan "We are the young people of Spain" (figure 6.1).

In its "About Us" section, the organization describes itself as follows:

We are the youth section, non-university people, of the Falange. We're people under 25 years old. We consider ourselves militants of this political party, and creators of its future, because we're young. We're in charge of fighting today for a future that belongs to us and that has to be better than the present.

Through such rhetoric, the group presents itself in the guise of an alternative to bourgeois or elite youth and in favor of a more egalitarian Spain. The topics that appear on the left-hand menu of the home page might suggest that the organization concerns itself with grassroots issues of concern to young people, such as housing, low salaries, and drugs. However, the extreme right ideology of the Falange's politics focuses mainly on the unity of Spain and opposes the type of semifederal state that was enshrined in the Spanish Constitution of 1978. The youth website reveals its real agenda through slogans such as "Let's fight for Spain" and articles condemning

Figure 6.1
Juventudes Falangistas de España home page, 2008

"separatism," for example in the form of Catalan and Basque nationalism, and what it sees as the national government's complicity with separation movements. The site also displays strong anti-immigrant sentiments, in line with other far-right parties and groups in Europe (Langenbacher and Schellenberg 2011). The Falangists also oppose abortion, which is described on the site as a form of "approved genocide" endorsed by "all the capitalist-liberalist-socialist parties in Spain . . . as a symbol of women's freedom." Resistance to the incumbent government is sustained through symbolic imagery such as the gun sights in the central banner (see figure 6.1), suggesting that violence could be a possible method of achieving the organization's goals.

Other content offered on the site includes a survey of what young people think are the most important problems affecting them (such as drugs, low-paid jobs, housing, education, and immigrants). There is also the option to download sing-along songs dating from the 1930s to the 1980s, and whereas these songs reflect the party's links to fascist politics through the ages, they also target young Spaniards with no regional political affiliations through their attentiveness to national popular culture. While it is emphasized that *young people* have to fight to defend their beliefs, the young people being exhorted of course exclude those from ethnic or religious minorities or of non-Spanish descent.

In 2008, the few images on the site were largely confined to symbols such as the Spanish flag and the party logo. Aside from images of demonstrations, there were no videos or photographs of members, unlike other youth political sites, which tend to celebrate their young members in this way. By contrast, news items were frequently highlighted as a way of giving the content more credibility. In line with Caiani and Wagemann's (2009) findings about the online networks of the Italian and German far right, there were also numerous international links to websites with a similar ideological standpoint. The site offered users the option to create their own blogs and write their opinion on topics such as Catholicism, homosexuality, abortion, and the nation, and these blogs appeared to target young people very specifically, for example through references to football and popular culture. However, this option seemed to be used repeatedly by the same small cohort of bloggers. There were also forums and chat rooms, although participation was limited to party members.

After what appeared to be an incident of hacking in 2011, an updated Falangist youth site launched at a different address, http://www.jfe.es (figure 6.2). This site is brighter and has several more images, particularly of general party leaders or nationalist and fascist figures, as well as of demonstrations. There are also embedded videos of the activities of the young Falangists, such as creating anti-immigrant graffiti, and the option to like or follow the group on Facebook. There are links to videos on

Figure 6.2
Juventudes Falangistas de España home page, 2012

YouTube in which the young Falangists are seen taking part in a variety of pro-fascist, anti-abortion, and anti-immigration rallies, although there is very little evidence of activity on behalf of young people per se. All this implies that the Falangists, like other far-right parties, are learning to harness the Internet for their purposes: while much of the rhetoric remains the same—a potent mix of religious fervor, calls for ethnic purity, and an apparent concern for social justice—the design and technological affordances of the site have become much more contemporary and potentially much more appealing to young people.

AKP Youth, Turkey

URL: http://www.akgenclik.org.tr. Researcher: Asli Telli Aydemir

The AKP (Justice and Development Party) is a Turkish center-right nationalist party that espouses a quasi-religious and broadly conservative form of democracy (Ozbudun 2006). The party has been accused of attempting to bring about Islamic rule and, more recently, of increasing authoritarianism and an autocratic leadership style (Fabbe 2011). Its youth branch website has been established since 2003, although the interface changed twice before reaching its current format. The youth organization boasts around 750,000 members across Turkey, and the website appears to receive around 100,000 unique visitors per year.

First impressions of the site strongly suggest that the main parent party is the umbrella organization and is central to the ideology of the youth wing. As on the Spanish Falangist site, the national flag is placed both in the banner at the top and in the first part of the home page, perhaps to counterbalance critiques from secular Republicans. The banner at the top prominently displays the image of the party leader and prime minister beside the Turkish flag, with the party logo at the far end. Below the text is a second banner condemning terror and once again displaying the Turkish flag. The design is exceptionally formal and makes no concessions to youth culture (figure 6.3). For ambience, the site has background music in the form of a youth march played by Ottoman-origin instruments—a further reflection of the party's conservative ideology. While none of this might in itself prove alienating for young people, it symbolizes the website's commitment to serve the needs of the party rather than the youth cohort it purports to be addressing.

The specific ideology of the youth branch is not as clearly signaled as that of the Young Falangists. In fact, the mission statement of the organization is not provided on the home page or in the main menu. However, there is a link to a declaration by the president of the youth section at the bottom of the home page, although strangely, this document is in English. Even this declaration is somewhat evasive, however: there are many assertions about the party's "different approach to youth" and its "dominant youth perception," but little more specific indication of its political program:

Figure 6.3
AKP Youth website home page, 2008

AK Party believes that youth, being self-confident, democratic and bonded to national and moral values, are the building blocks for the construction of a developed and equitable country. AK Party believes that youth are the guarantee of the future of the country and the nation. For the Party, youth are not only the wealth of the country but also the source of the dynamism. Having a young population is a great advantage for the country.

The repeated word "youth" clearly plays an important rhetorical role here, at least for an assumed audience that reads English, although this emphasis is undermined by the lack of other content or imagery representing youth on the site. Thus, in terms of voices, none can compete with that of the party leader: his rhetoric and ideology are dominant throughout the site. The youth section leader also has public statements, but they go no further than reflecting the party ideology and principles. The party program itself is included, but sections in the program referring to youth are not specifically touched on, again suggesting that the appeal to youth is generic or rhetorical rather than involving a concrete commitment to improving the status or experiences of real young people. Even though the primary target audience is supposedly young Turkish citizens, there is virtually no evidence of this target audience on the website itself.

On the site itself, there are further exclusions. The coordinators of different sections of the youth wing are all male, reflecting the conservative gender values of the party. The content editor of the website told us that their female members generally transfer to the women's branch of the party, creating an odd division between "youth" and "women." The fact that the youth organization is active in "81 cities across Turkey" with members "of varying ethnic origins" is emphasized, although there is little other evidence of ethnic tolerance or multiculturalism. According to the site's editor at the time of our interview, the AKP Youth wing sees Turkey as an emerging power in the Middle East and has started exchange programs with China and other Middle Eastern countries, as well as receiving visits from their youth delegations, although all such contacts are conducted in a highly formal political manner.

In terms of design, the APK Youth website is dominated by written text, mainly speeches. In addition to background music, a web radio channel has recently been added. There are some moving elements (both textual and visual), such as flashing slogans. The site links to a forum apparently moderated by youth section members in Ankara, although in actuality this forum is used mainly by the party's adversaries. A survey on the bottom right of the home page asks questions to determine the user's political views, and there is also a webmail option and a mail window for reaching the editor. While the web team does upload research data and other "materials that might interest the public," new announcements accumulate on top of old ones, making it impossible to find a document if you do not know exactly what you are looking for. As all this implies, interactivity is very limited.

Ultimately, it appears that the website exists because the party had to acknowledge the existence of the youth section rather than because it really wanted to engage its youth members. Top-down relations in the party are explicit. The content editor recounted for us one of their most innovative and "interactive" schemes, which was to go out and interview young people about their views on the party's leader:

We have to keep a certain standard and respect the party etiquette in our website. The youth branch site cannot be too different than the main party site. . . . Instead of including comments of supporters in our website, we . . . asked young people whether they think our party leader is charismatic. We have recorded their responses.

When we enquired what happened to negative or critical comments, we were told that of course these could not be put up on the website. Yet the lack of autonomous youth activity on the site appears to mirror the situation offline, which is overwhelmingly dominated by the central authority of the parent party.

Young Socialists, the Netherlands

URL: http://www.js.nl. Researcher: Fadi Hirzalla

Established in 1977, Jonge Socialisten (henceforward JS, Young Socialists) is the independent, member-based youth wing of the Dutch Labour Party. JS currently has

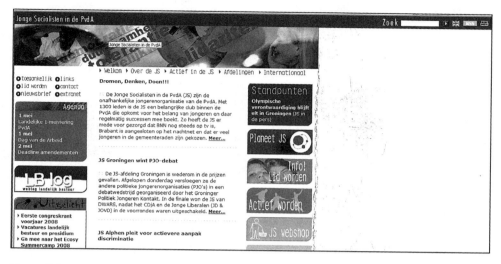

Figure 6.4
JS home page, 2008

twenty-five local departments across the Netherlands, with 1,300 members aged between fourteen and twenty-eight. It is affiliated with two international organizations, the International Union of Socialist Youth (IUSY) and the European Community Organization of Socialist Youth (ECOSY), although most of its activities are oriented toward young people in the Netherlands. In its official mission statement, JS declares that it wants to raise political awareness among young people and to advocate for young people's interests by organizing festivals, debates, workshops, demonstrations, and courses. Most of its activities take place offline.

The JS website, which is accessible, is divided into five main sections. The home page (figure 6.4) introduces JS and highlights news items emphasizing its "successes," as well as linking to other aspects such as a poll, a webshop, and a blog. The "About Us" section provides extensive information about the party's ideals, principles, history, activities, and personnel. An activities section covers a range of offline courses, task forces, and projects, with invitations to participate. Another section lists the party's twenty-five local departments in a menu and a multicolored map of the Netherlands, while an international section lists the international events and organizations that are supported by JS and includes a succinct summary in English.

Emphasizing the general tone of political seriousness, the design of the site is solidly text-based, with barely any images and few contrasting colors. White and dark red, the official colors of the parent party, are the dominant colors on the site, and the only artistic touch appears in the right frame of the site, where thin gray lines provide a loose sketch of an unidentified object. Unlike the formal language used by the AKP site, the language here is informal and clear, with some suggestions of a more youthful style, although it is relatively functional. There is also a little more by way of technological interactivity than the other party sites examined in this section. For example, there are forms for membership applications and those who wish to receive the newsletter, a collection of links, an "intranet" for members, an RSS-feed, contact information, and a weblog written by JS board members. Nevertheless, there are no forums, chat facilities, or opportunities for open responses.

In terms of content, the site refers to a whole range of social and political issues, but a substantial part of its "official" ideology is articulated in the form of abstract societal ideals that are named but not defined or explained. JS's "principles" are, for example, "freedom, equality, solidarity and durability":

These are the most important principles to fulfil our ideal (happy and engaged citizens) . . . . Each person has the right to live in freedom. . . . People are equal. . . . Solidarity results in social cohesion. . . . To ensure a sustainable world for future generations, we must handle the world in durable ways.

Interestingly, and in contrast to some other political party websites, there is little mention of social problems or of issues affecting young people in particular.

At the same time, the site does contain a "Points of View" section that clarifies at least some of the official stances taken up by the Young Socialists, mostly using examples from mainstream news reports of statements or activities by party officials. These address a wide range of issues, suggesting that youth citizenship requires a broad-ranging political engagement and knowledge and an ability to operationalize these in the public sphere. Indeed, the party's organizational goals make it clear that offline activity is critical in enabling young people to "improve their skills" in this respect, for example, in debating. As with AKP Youth and the Young Falangistas, the party's key emphasis is on offline activities aimed at mobilizing political participation. To this end, it organizes debates, courses, congresses, and other offline activities for young people to discuss political and social issues.

However, these skills are not seen to be developed to any significant extent online. While some moderated comments are allowed in the blog section, information far outweighs discussion or interactivity across the site. And herein lies its primary purpose: the site exists to announce and describe the actions and values of the party rather than to provide a significant platform for critical debate and participation among its members, or indeed among young people in general. As in the other two sites we have considered here, this has to be seen as an institutional choice rather than a necessity, or indeed as a failure to "catch up" with the interactive possibilities of the medium.

Each of the three organizations we have introduced in this section decided in advance not only what role their youth wing would play in relation to the parent party but also what role the website of this youth wing could and should play. Of course, the authoritarian or democratic ideology of each of these organizations to some extent determines the scope for party members to critique or stray from the party line: the narrowest spectrum of views and the sharpest homogeneity are apparent on the Falangist youth site, although neither of the others is exactly overflowing with disagreements or lively debate.

The degree to which each of these youth branches feels it has achieved institutional or even governmental legitimacy is also crucial in determining how far the technological interactivity offered by the Internet is excluded or embraced. Blogs run by the party faithful are in some ways the least disruptive means of appearing to move with the times, since they can be little more than disguised polemics, and dissenting comments do not have to be shown. By contrast, forums that take more time (and hence money) to moderate and require a greater degree of engagement with opponents are not much in evidence, and open comment sections are entirely absent.

For at least a decade, there have been recurring discussions about how far the Internet's potential will be used by political parties or movements—whether for promoting democratic debate or simply for more astute political marketing (Römmele 2003; van Selm, Jankowski, and Tsaliki 2002). From the three cases we have outlined here and from our wider research (CivicWeb Deliverable 14, 2009), we conclude that the youth wings of political parties are mostly using the Web for political marketing and the dissemination of information rather than as a democratic forum in its own right. While this might tell us something about the authoritarian nature of such organizations—especially, perhaps, when it comes to their younger members—it also tells us something more straightforward about their priorities. For all three parties, offline debate and action are much more important than anything that might conceivably happen online because it is offline action that will serve their purposes most effectively and make the best use of their resources. For all three, the primary function of their website is simply to present information. In saying this we do not imply criticism; indeed, there is some indication from our interviews with young party members and with web producers that the Internet can be very valuable in this respect, especially when members reside in disparate parts of the country or when the party is out of power and hence less likely to feature in other media (see Norris 2000).

But what of the propositions that young people are at the forefront of the technology revolution and have a natural affinity for online interaction? Evidence from our case studies and from our wider research suggests that the age of the users has little to do with the way in which the sites have been developed or function. Institutional factors seem to dominate, even in relation to design, although the occasional bow to young people in the use of informal language and an openness to debate is more evident on the Dutch Young Socialists site. Nevertheless, an insistence on traditional symbols such as flags points to something much more relevant for a study of young people, politics, and the Internet, namely, young people have historically had as much of an affinity for tradition and rules as they have had for anarchy or cutting-edge technology. Both tradition and rules are high on the agendas of most political parties and movements, not just of authoritarian or conservative ones.

Part II: Activism—Case Studies

As we saw in chapter 1, concerns about young people's lack of engagement with mainstream politics have been counterbalanced by an apparent rise in political activism. Young people may be disaffected with the world of formal politics, it is argued, but their political interests and commitments are merely finding new forms of expression—forms that are at least facilitated, and in some cases actively created, by the Internet (see Bennett 2008). There is an extensive academic literature on these so-called new social movements, and on youth activism in particular (see, e.g., Gordon 2009; Sherrod et al. 2006), although much of it tends to focus exclusively on what can loosely be called left-wing activism. This is the politics of direct action, single-issue campaigns, boycotts and "buycotts," and civil disobedience; and, in the case of young people, it often focuses on issues such as the environment, education, peace, and social justice. These new forms are typically decentralized or "networked" rather than having clear authority structures, and while they frequently operate from the grassroots or within local communities, they increasingly have a global dimension. In the terms outlined at the start of this chapter, they are mostly "invented" rather than "invited" (Miraftab 2006): they are organized and driven by young people themselves, rather than at the behest of adults.

Of course, many of these practices are far from new—we might look back to the Paris Commune of 1871, or indeed the Peasant's Revolt of 1381, not to mention the student movements of the late 1960s—and they are by no means confined to young people. However, they may be taking new forms, not least as a result of the use of new media. In the following discussion we consider four case studies of this kind of political activism. Although the political goals of each group are quite different, and although they use the web in diverse ways, a comparison between them will enable us to identify some broader characteristics of this use of online media.

Asfaltsdjungelns Indianer (Indians of the Concrete Jungle), Sweden

URL: http://asfaltsdjungelnsindianer.wordpress.com. Researchers: Fredrik Miegel and Tobias Olsson

Asfaltsdjungelns Indianer (Indians of the Concrete Jungle) is a Swedish activist group dedicated solely to deflating the tires of large cars meant for off-road driving, such as sport utility vehicles (SUVs), to render them temporarily useless. The stated purpose

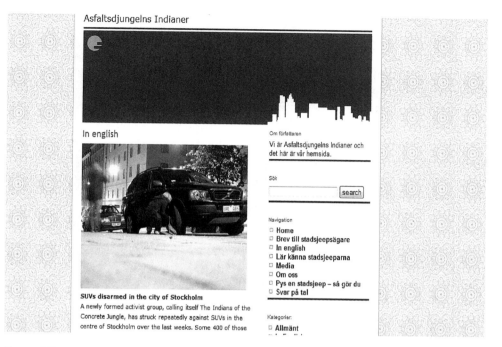

Figure 6.5
Indians of the Concrete Jungle (English), 2012

behind this activity is to protest against the high fuel consumption of and carbon emissions discharged by such vehicles and to encourage "greener" consumer choices. A letter is affixed to the windshield informing the owners why their car has been targeted, and then a photograph of the car with deflated tires is uploaded to the website. The letter suggests that the activists presuppose SUV owners to be wealthy citizens ("As an affluent Swede you will survive longer than most") who can afford to do their civic duty toward the environment by buying "greener" cars with lower carbon emissions.

The group deflates the tires by opening the tire valves and letting the air out rather than by slashing the tires or inflicting other physical damage; the group emphasizes that it supports an antiviolence ideology and is not comprised of vandals who inflict mindless damage on the vehicles. Organizationally, the group is a loosely composed network without any clearly identifiable core. The different subgroups performing the deflations are described as independent "tribes" that can be established by anyone, anywhere. The only requirement for being acknowledged is that deflations are performed in accordance with the group's principles of nonviolence and no vandalism, and that the action is reported to the website so that it can be announced there. For obvious reasons, assignations to meet and deflate tires are apparently made by word of mouth rather than through the website.

The website has a simple blog structure. Besides the logo, the main page contains two columns, of which the left one is dedicated to a continuous reporting of the different tribes' actions. The right-hand column contains links to a number of subpages and to some external websites with similar environmental concerns (figure 6.5). The reports on successful deflations can be commented on by anyone who reads them. No membership or log-in is required. The option to comment is frequently used, mostly by supporters, but also by annoyed SUV owners, who explain their personal reasons for wanting or needing to use SUVs or vent their fury at the group for being "childish," "vandals," and "criminals."

Ease of use and replication of the activist strategy seem to be the two top priorities for the site's makers. One of the subpage links leads to brief information about Asfaltsdjungelns Indianer and what they stand for. Another link takes the reader to the letter the activists put on the windshield after deflating an SUV's tires, and another one to an English version of the same letter. While groups of "deflators" in other countries sometimes invoke issues of class and consumption in their justifications (Signoret 2008), the Swedish group focuses principally on the environmental issues, as this extract from the letter suggests:

Those most vulnerable, and already worst afflicted by the global warming caused by Northern affluence, are the people of poor countries. In the end, however, climate chaos will affect us all, poor people as well as rich. This does not have to happen if we impose a radical cut on carbon emissions. Now. Not tomorrow. That's why we have disarmed your SUV by deflating the tires. Since you live in a city with a functioning and accessible public transportation system you will have no problem going where you want without your SUV. (http://asfaltsdjungelnsindianer .wordpress.com/in-english, 2008).

The site also includes a list with pictures and names of the models counted as SUVs, and instructions on how to deflate the tires and print the letter to be put on the windshield after a successful action. There is also information on how to report the action to Asfaltsdjungelns Indianer, and the group's ethical principles. Further subpages contain media coverage of the group and its actions, and describe how the most common objections from people opposing their methods can be met. An ironic backlash has seen the establishment of a similarly designed website created by a group of SUV-owners calling themselves Asfaltsdjungelns Cowboys (Cowboys of the Concrete Jungle, http://asfaltsdjungelnscowboys.wordpress.com).

The website deliberately does not name or show faces of founders of the site or state exactly when it was established. The first Swedish tire deflations, however, took place in 2007 in Stockholm. There now appear to be numerous "tribes" in several Swedish cities, as well as in other cities across Europe, including Edinburgh, Copenhagen, and Lyon. Some of these predate Asfaltsdjungelns Indianer, and all seem to draw their inspiration from similar eco-environmentalist campaigns across North America in the late 1990s and early 2000s (Pralle 2006; Wagner 2008). This is also evidenced by the fact that external links lead to other Swedish and international websites, including other anti-SUV sites such as the British site Against Urban 4x4s (http://www.stopurban4x4s.org.uk) and the American site Anti-SUV Portal (http://suvsuck.org).

Sarah Pralle's (2006) work on SUV deflators in the US picks up on an unresolved and problematic tension between consumerism and environmentalism in the politics of these groups. Although Sweden does not have quite the same tangling of rhetorics of consumption and citizenship as the US does, Asfaltsdjungelns Indianer is no exception to this complicated dynamic. While the mainstream press and legal authorities have done their best to criminalize the actions of the deflators, sometimes painting them as "eco-terrorists," none of the groups' pronouncements suggest that it wishes to undermine the capitalist system as a whole or even to prevent people from buying cars. What one has, then, is a network of activists, primarily young people, who at some personal risk target a particular group of conspicuous (private) consumer-citizens while ignoring others who might be deemed to fall into the same category (for instance, supermarket chains that import food, or business-class frequent flyers). In this sense, this is a classic single-issue campaign.

Yet perhaps absurdly, given the relatively small number of people inconvenienced by the Asfaltsdjungelns Indianer, such groups have acquired the status of urban legends. This might in part be because of the ways in which they reference historical examples of guerrilla and anarchist tactics or, beyond that, the tactics of Native Americans under siege from the new colonizers. Construed as sabotage or "ecotage" or even "terror," these tactics have been used to contribute to the construction of a "climate of fear" (Wagner 2008) in Western Europe and the United States rather than being discussed as imaginative interventions in a political debate about the environment. This overwhelmingly negative framing might in turn account for the fact that many of the websites of such groups that were operational in 2007 and 2008 have now been taken down or have not been updated.

V De Vivienda (H for Housing), Spain

URL: http://www.Bcn.vdevivienda.net. Researcher: Magdalena Albero-Andrés

V De Vivienda, which was very active at the time of our original research in 2007–2008, was created by a movement of young people who wanted to publicize the difficulties they encountered in finding affordable housing. According to Barba and Blanco (2011), the campaign was originally founded in 2003 in response to rising housing costs: the median home price in Spain increased by 180 percent between

2000 and 2005. However, the group had little impact until it started to make use of the Internet: a chain of emails and SMS messages called for the first sit-in in 2006, and the group expanded from this event to form a broader citizens' network, in the manner of many new social movements. V De Vivienda claimed to represent every person who could not afford a place to live. The tactics and interests of the young activists from this group, including open public meetings, demonstrations, and the occupation of empty flats, subsequently found their way into the current (2011–2012) "indignados" ("outraged") movement in Spain as the campaign for affordable housing became part of a larger movement for economic redistribution and greater democracy.

In line with the theme of social activism for economic redistribution, the first impression of the site is that of collective action. The images on the site show groups of people sitting discussing issues, demonstrating, or carrying banners and posters bearing slogans such as "You won't have your own place to live in your whole fucking life." One of the site's basic aims is to give people information, not only about the activities of the movement but also on topics related to housing: it has sections on tenants' rights and on situations in which property developers are apparently acting illegally. Although the site is not obviously addressed to a specific group, it is clear that the young and potentially homeless are the key target. Readers are addressed directly and communally, as "we" and "us," and using the informal instead of the formal "you." Presaging the clear and democratic communication style of the indignados, texts written and posted by the organization are colloquial and direct, with the exception of press releases, whose tone is more formal.

As with the Asfaltsdjungelns Indianer, the design of the site is bloglike and based on an underlying template (figure 6.6): there is a heading, a section of text that records all the entries with their dates and comments, and a lateral menu to find past posts according to date and theme. There are also links to other thematically related sites and blogs, an active forum, a subscription page, announcements of meetings and actions, and recreational activities such as a themed photography contest. There is little sense of an overall strategy or of a professional ethos in the design and structure of the site. There are pages containing only text, and then pages with only photographs or YouTube videos, randomly added and not searchable. The approach is very much of the do-it-yourself variety, and this casualness is reinforced by the use of a stencil-style font in the headings.

The site appears to have two primary functions. On one level, it appears to be addressed to a wider public audience. It seeks to inform people who might be either ignorant or complacent about the issues and to call for action against those who are seen to be profiting from others' homelessness. In doing so, it invokes broader arguments about social justice and equality, emphasizing the right of every citizen to a

Figure 6.6
V De Vivienda, 2008: "No house, no life, nothing."

place to live. Seeing its cause as one not limited to Spain, it also aims to spread the word internationally, and asks for translations of the texts explaining the housing situation in Spain into other languages.

The second and more important function is as a means of information dissemination and communication among the activists themselves. The site has an open-access forum: registration is required, but acceptance is automatic. This kind of ease of use is crucial for the excluded and homeless youth who are targeted, and the significance of such a low threshold to membership becomes even more evident in the forum itself. The forum contains the minutes of the organization's meetings and information about future meetings, as well as links to media reports of its activities. Crucially, it also acts as a virtual meeting point for the extremely localized associations of different neighborhoods in each city and provides a means for them to share information about their activities.

Here, as with the Asfaltsdjungelns Indianer, the emphasis is very much on offline action. The site encourages people to participate in demonstrations and to attend the information and training sessions that V De Vivienda organizes. Because the activities of the group—particularly in occupying empty properties or in challenging evictions—might be interpreted as illegal or as a threat to the authorities, information about offline activities usually focuses on activities in the past, with little information about future events. Only in the more private areas such as the forums is it possible to find information about meetings that are scheduled to discuss future actions.

To some extent, there might be seen to be a tension here between old and new political aims that is characteristic of other new social movements. The organization wants—and ultimately needs—to influence public opinion, and hence government policy, yet to do so, it feels it has no alternative but to take direct action, of the kind that some will find objectionable. Prefiguring the organization and conceptualization of the indignados, and in stark contrast to the youth wings of the organizations discussed earlier in this chapter, the organization emphasizes its total independence from any political party, state institution, or private organization. Yet even as it disavows traditional political channels it explicitly identifies itself as intervening in the civic and political arena.

This tension between avoiding established civic channels while focused on changing civic policy is to some extent apparent when we examine the forum. Participants in the forum clearly share the same worldview and politics as the organization, and no dissenting voices are heard: there is a sense that forum posters are preaching to the converted. In this respect, it might be suggested that the site fails to achieve a role as a mediator between citizens and public institutions in charge of regulating housing access. However, such an appraisal would be to mistake its purpose and to overstate the importance of the site in relation to the other activities of the organization. While the site is partly directed to those in power, its primary function is one of building solidarity within the movement: influencing public policy is something that is implicitly to be achieved by other means, either in the form of offline actions or through the use of more traditional media.

CiJO (CIDI Youth Organization), the Netherlands

URL: http://www.cijo.nl. Researcher: Fadi Hirzalla

Our next case study poses a marked contrast to V De Vivienda, for it represents a very different form of youth activism and a very different political stance. Whereas V De Vivienda and Asfaltsdjungelns Indianer are primarily virtual meeting places, designed to support offline activism, the CiJO site addresses a wider public. Indeed, it has a clear propagandist purpose in bolstering a particular (state-linked) political cause and ideology. This contrast has implications for both content and structure and makes the website, which is also extremely well funded, appear far less amateur and fungible than the others we have discussed.

CiJO is the youth wing of the main Zionist pro-Israel lobbying organization in the Netherlands, CIDI (Centrum Informatie en Documentatie Israel, or Centre for Information and Documentation on Israel). CIDI was set up in the 1970s, and its mission of promoting Israel has gradually expanded over the years to include work on anti-

Figure 6.7
CiJO home page, 2008

Semitism and racism (van de Beek, van de Mortel, and van Hees 2010, 159). The name CiJO is an abbreviation for CIDI Jongeren Organisatie (CIDI Youth Organization). According to the website (figure 6.7), it was established in 2002 by "students who are devoted to Israel and strive for peace in the Middle East." The "CiJO youth," who are between sixteen and thirty years old, organize events for young people about the ongoing Israeli-Palestinian conflict, Dutch multicultural society, and related issues. In its own words, the organization "conveys a moderate voice and searches for constructive solutions by taking into account the positions and feelings of all parties involved in the [Israeli-Palestinian] conflict." It also "fights racism, anti-Semitism and prejudices by providing education about the Jewish community and organizing events in which different religious-cultural groups participate." In addition to its website, CiJO is very active offline, and it has a clear sense of what it considers virtuous civic activity. It organizes events for young people such as debates, socials, workshops, courses, informal dinners, and journeys to Israel, as well as seminars with other religious groups. It also trains its members to teach other young people in schools about the Jewish community and about Israel.

CiJO's website has five main sections. The home page explains "what CiJO is" and has links to articles, agendas of upcoming events, and short photo reports or descriptions of previous events. It also has a list of hyperlinks to pro-Israeli and Zionist organizations and websites, and instructions about how to become a member of CiJO. The section "About CiJO" describes the organization's vision, activities, and structure (including a short version in English). There are also pages about vacancies, advertisements, and how to contact CiJO. There is an "FAQs and Facts" section, although this was still empty on the date of analysis. The "Library" contains a large selection of articles in English or Dutch, mainly obtained from other sources such as newspapers and magazines. Finally, the "Education" section contains information about courses organized for secondary school classes. Because the website offers a substantial amount of content, its design needs to be functional. In addition to these five main sections, which can be accessed through a horizontal menu bar, there are subsections that appear in drop-down menus. Most of the website can be accessed only through vertical paths initiated by the main menu bar.

The overall sense of seriousness and professionalism that is conveyed here is reinforced by other aspects of the site. Blue, purple, and black, the base colors, are also those of the organization's logo. The language conveys a sense of maturity: there is no youth slang or informal address, and no use of emotional symbols (or emoticons). There are few images. The overwhelming majority of references and items are purely textual, couched in quasi-academic or academic language, and are clearly intended for those with advanced levels of literacy. An impression of official status is also reflected in references to high-profile politicians, such as the former Dutch minister for integration, complimenting the organization on its work.

However, CiJO makes no effort to disguise the fact that it supports official Israeli governmental narratives, the narratives of a nation-state quite separate from the Netherlands, where it is hosted. The site explicitly calls itself political, and embraces a Zionist stance on the development and history of the Israeli-Palestinian conflict. In seeking to justify Israel's policies toward the Palestinians, it emphasizes the "horror" of Palestinian attacks on Israeli targets. Jewishness is consistently identified with Israeliness, and there are no opposing Jewish views identified on the site. Nevertheless, as we have seen, CiJO aims to represent itself as a moderate participant in public debates and claims to take into account "the positions and feelings of all parties involved in the conflict." Indeed, it even presents its beliefs and activities as fundamentally "peaceful."

Young people are referred to as having a particularly important task in understanding and discussing the Israeli-Palestinian conflict. CiJO supports youth civic participation in terms of public discussion, youth leadership, and social interaction:

Young people can make an important contribution to the public debate that has been taken "hostage" by the voices of older people. . . . Especially when it concerns the "multicultural society," CiJO considers it important that young people are not estranged from one another but cooperate with each other.

Despite this claim of cooperation, CiJO clearly aims to inculcate a Zionist stance on the Israeli-Palestinian conflict. Having "knowledge" or valid "opinions" about the conflict and about anti-Semitism is equated with sharing the organization's views. Despite its professional design and functionality, the website has limited participatory elements. There is no forum, and users cannot upload their own content. In presenting itself as an authoritative source of information, especially through its extensive library, it also serves a propagandist function, ensuring that young members feel confident that they have both the facts and the debating skills to take on any critics of Israel's policies, not least by presenting them as anti-Semitic.

On the face of it, this site represents a highly structured approach to political education—and an authoritarian form of pedagogy—that is very different from those considered earlier in this section. Nevertheless, young people are active and central participants in its political project: it is equally a form of *youth activism*, though one sponsored by a nation-state. Perhaps the most striking difference here is the organization's efforts to present itself as moderate and even-handed, and as a neutral provider of information—efforts that appear to have enjoyed some success in terms of official recognition. We return to these issues later in the chapter, but this analysis should remind us that youthful activism is not solely the preserve of the political left, nor does it necessarily take a subversive form.

The Pirate Bay, Sweden

URL: www.piratebay.com. Researchers: Tobias Olsson and Fredrik Miegel

Our final case study in this section is rather different from the others, in three key respects. First, it is an initiative that grew from activities taking place—at least initially—entirely online, with no offline counterpart. Second, its key activities would not necessarily be perceived, even by many who engage in them, as political: rather, they have been *constructed* as political both through the response of the authorities and by the arguments of their proponents. Third, and most surprisingly, they have moved from being a subversive preoccupation of activists—who are technically criminals—to forming the basis for a political party that has since participated (and won parliamentary seats) in formal elections.

The Pirate Bay is a file-sharing site for music, film, computer software, and other digital material. It is a "bittorrent tracker," the world's largest, according to the site's promotional blurb. Bittorrent is a file-sharing protocol that enables the fast and effective transfer of large data files between users of the site. In theory, anyone can use the site, although in practice users are more likely to be those with a fast broadband connection and the requisite lack of anxiety about uploading or downloading such files. The website avoids assumptions about the level of technical skill already possessed by

Figure 6.8
The Pirate Bay home page, 2007

visitors: a link to instructions on how to download and use the torrent files is offered on the home page but can easily be bypassed by those already in the know. To upload files, one must register, which is free of charge.

The structure of the site is in some ways self-explanatory, yet its purposes are complex, and its political dimensions may well be evident only to those who follow it over time. The home page (figure 6.8) contains The Pirate Bay's logo, a pirate ship, and a number of links with options for navigating and searching the site ("search torrent," "browse torrent," "recent torrents," "TV shows," "music" and "top 100"). Under the search field, there are tick boxes with alternatives for the type of torrent files sought (audio, video, applications, games, etc.). Via "Preferences," members can log in and change their settings, while clicking on "Languages" leads to a section where the user can choose from among twenty-seven languages. This number of languages suggests not just user-friendliness but also the ambition of the site's producers, who are confident enough that their site will be sufficiently interesting to an international audience to justify spending time and energy on the different language options.

Although The Pirate Bay does not announce an explicitly political or civic purpose, it has come to occupy, both in Sweden and now internationally, a central position in the escalating public debate over the use of immaterial property and copyrighted material on the Internet (see Lewer, Gerlich, and Turner 2008). This becomes apparent if one follows some of the links on the website's main page. For instance, following the link "About," one can read that The Pirate Bay is the "largest bittorrent tracker in the world" and that on its servers are stored only torrent files with information on files the users may be interested in downloading; the servers store no copyrighted or illegal content. The Pirate Bay takes no legal responsibility for what users of the site do with content spread via the tracker. It further promises that any complaints from copyright or lobbying organizations about copyright violation "will be ridiculed and published on the site."

The Pirate Bay was started by the Swedish anticopyright organization Piratbyrån (the Pirate Bureau) in 2003, but has run independently since October 2004. Piratbyrån is more explicitly political than The Pirate Bay. According to its website, it was established "in order to support everyone who is in opposition to the prevailing opinions regarding copyright-free information and culture" (http://piratbyran.org/?view =articles&cat=8, 2007). While Piratbyrån claims that it does not "organize pirating," the two sites continue to sport mutual hyperlinks, and it might be seen as the "political wing" of The Pirate Bay. The sites adopt a position in the legal and political debate on file sharing and copyright that defines it as a countercultural opposition to the bullying and exclusivity of "big, bad" corporations. This opposition is particularly apparent in a section of the site called "Legal Threats," which posts complaints from individuals and organizations that deem their rights to have been violated by The Pirate Bay's activities; among the complainants are major international players such as Apple, Microsoft, SEGA, Warner Bros., and Sony. The site producers' responses are often highly sarcastic and explicitly anticorporate, and provide an amusing form of political satire. In addition to outright ridicule and impertinence, they often refer to portions of the Swedish copyright laws that (they claim) support their activities. In such exchanges, The Pirate Bay likes to present itself as engaged in a David versus Goliath struggle, bravely defending the civic rights of citizens against the profit margins of corporations.

In addition to these "debates," the site also contains a blog section where file sharing, copyright legislation, and related issues are discussed by key participants behind the website. There are also discussions of police investigations into The Pirate Bay, and suggestions that some major film and music companies have hired professional hackers and saboteurs to try to destroy it.

In recent years, these issues have taken on an increasingly political complexion. Since the advent of The Pirate Bay in 2003, established political parties have had major difficulties handling questions about copyright and file sharing, although attempts have been made to implement new laws. In 2006 the Swedish police undertook a controversial raid of The Pirate Bay's web hosting company, confiscating more than one hundred servers and bringing three people connected to The Pirate Bay in for interrogation. Following this, a new political party was established prior to the Swedish general election of 2006. The main aim of Piratpartiet (the Pirate Party) is the abolition of existing copyright and immaterial rights laws. Within three years it became Sweden's third largest political party by membership, surpassing the Liberals and the Christian Democrats, and in 2010 its youth wing, Young Pirate, became the largest youth political organization in Sweden. In 2009 the party gained more than 7 percent of the vote and two seats in the European parliament. While Piratpartiet has no formal connections to The Pirate Bay and Piratbyrån, it has on several occasions expressed its support for their activities.

It could be argued that The Pirate Bay, together with Piratbyrån and Piratpartiet, have created a strong and influential anticopyright movement in Sweden and to some extent internationally, engaging young people (and others) who consider these issues to be of high democratic and political importance. The fact that the site is seemingly unintimidated by the corporate powers it challenges plays a key symbolic role in asserting the power of citizens in the face of corporations. However, as Andersson (2009) has argued, a closer analysis of the actual uses to which the site is put, and the ways in which users discuss their file sharing, suggests that it functions primarily as an *economic* counterculture, while continuing to support and participate in the circulation and promotion of cultural commodities. He argues there is a symbiotic relationship between piracy and capitalism, undermining claims that The Pirate Bay is playing a politically "resistant" role in relation to the cultural market. Mason (2008, 67) goes further in arguing that pirates, like "punk capitalists," are actually necessary to the capitalist marketplace: they target the inefficiencies that build up in economic systems and, by exerting pressure where the system is least efficient, ultimately result in measures that lead to greater profit. In fact, the movement's invocation of the pirates of old should be a sobering reminder of the interconnectedness of altruistic and selfish motives—and indeed of civic and consumer ideals—in its work.

In this section, we have considered a variety of different types of activism taking place online. In fact, in each case, the online element needs to be seen in the context of the organization's other (offline) activities. The functions and characteristics of the four sites vary partly in line with the balance or relationship between these two elements; and yet these elements ultimately need to be seen, not as separate or even opposed, but as parts of a symbiotic whole. For Asfaltsdjungelns Indianer and V De Vivienda the website is a small but nonetheless extremely useful part of a much broader set of actions that take place offline. It helps participants and sympathizers communicate with each other and coordinate their activities, but online participation is clearly not an end in itself. This is also the case with the very different example of CiJO, although in that instance the website also plays a significant role in defining the public image of the organization and in putting its message across to those who are not already involved. By contrast, the main work of The Pirate Bay occurs online—although it is interesting that in seeking to extend and sustain its work, it has become involved in offline activities of a very traditional political kind.

There are also some significant pedagogical differences here, both in the sense of what the sites are seeking to teach and in how they are attempting to teach it. For example, the CiJO site performs a distinctly different pedagogical function from that of Asfaltsdjungelns Indianer or The Pirate Bay, which "teach" an easily absorbed set of activist DIY skills to be deployed offline against a small and clearly identified set of targets (SUV owners, copyrighted products). Behind the actions of the latter lie a set of broader political arguments, although these are not necessarily always articulated, nor do they need to be completely shared by their adherents. Indeed, as we have suggested, the single issues they address could in some respects be seen as quite politically ambivalent. By contrast, CiJO makes a strong attempt not only to arm its users with specific arguments but also to model ways of presenting them as somehow "moderate" and socially acceptable. While none of these sites offers much in the way of actual debate, especially with their potential adversaries, in the case of CiJO, this possibility is almost entirely absent.

The broader political question here, however, is about what counts as activism—and indeed, about its limits. CiJO, which has far more powerful and extensive support networks (both ideological and financial), seems to be perceived as far less of a threat to mainstream political and economic interests than the other groups. It cultivates a form of civic activism that is designed to be regarded favorably by adults in positions of power—although its consequences in terms of the violence that is inflicted on the Palestinian population are infinitely more severe than the possibility that the tires on an SUV might be deflated. As this implies, exhortations to young people about the value of civic participation, even participation that is normatively defined as "nonviolent," need to take much greater account of the politics and power dynamics of the arena in which this participation is to take place.

Part III: Alternatives

In the final section of this chapter, we present two contrasting case studies that are to some extent less overtly political than the sites we have considered thus far. These two, slightly longer, examples, one an international charity youth site and the other a community-based blog portal, point to some rather different, perhaps more diffuse, forms of "political activism" with which to compare our earlier case studies.

Oxfam Generation Why, UK

URL: http://www.oxfam.org.uk/generationwhy

Our first case study is of a website that no longer exists, Generation Why, Oxfam's UK-based youth organization. Our rationale for including this now defunct site is that it exemplified broader trends, both toward "ethical" consumption and marketing and toward activist rather than humanitarian conceptions of charity. Yet while it was outwardly addressed to youth in general, it appeared to speak implicitly to the concerns and expertise of a quite specific demographic—highly educated, middle-class youth—thus representing a broader problem with some forms of youthful activism.

The Generation Why site existed independently of its Oxfam parent site from 2004 to 2008. Its declared aim was to get young people involved in campaigning on Oxfam projects through the activities they presumably already enjoyed, such as popular music, shopping, sport, cinema, and writing. "Do what you love doing but change the world while you're doing it" was the catchphrase displayed on the site. Despite this emphasis on pleasure and entertainment, the site's dark grays and yellows made quite a severe first impression, and the site did not immediately try to appeal via childlike primary colors or graphics (figure 6.9). Just before its demise, the web team had plans to alter the color scheme, perhaps to emphasize light green and make the connection to the main Oxfam site and organization brand more prominent and obvious. In the event, the content was absorbed and homogenized, and the redesign never took place.

Generation Why (like the current integrated Oxfam site) was partly designed to promote forms of offline action, ranging from fundraising and volunteering to buying Fair Trade produce. The site's conception of civic participation and action included activities such as campaigning around trade laws, lobbying government and international corporations, demonstrating, writing letters, and signing petitions. However, the site also published a range of "sticky" content that, it was hoped, would engage more casual users in its own right. Shopping opportunities featured prominently (see figure 6.9), as they do now on the parent site, especially around the time of Christmas, Easter, or Valentine's Day. Here, young people are encouraged to shop in an "ethical" manner by considering issues such as the impact of cash crop farming in certain regions, paying farmers fairly for their trade, encouraging non-genetically modified crops and organic cotton, and so on. The site also had a detailed ethics policy in relation to its purchasable products, covering issues from workers' rights and labor standards to environmental concerns (see Banaji and Buckingham 2009).

While some of the site's features, such as short online polls, appeared to be designed to entice passing visitors, there were also opportunities to purchase more substantial "Small Guides to Big Issues" that detailed the historical background and explained debates around issues ranging from climate change to women's rights. However, these

Figure 6.9
Generation Why home page, 2007

guides were not available free of charge and online, as one might have expected, but in hard copy only, at a cost of around €12 each. Although the books were written by serious political authors such as Jeremy Seabrook, the presentation on the advertising page and the graphics on the front covers were reminiscent of budget holiday and travel guides such as the *Lonely Planet* or *Rough Guide* series, perhaps reflecting assumptions about their users' cultural predilections as backpacking gap-year students.

Roughly a quarter of the site was devoted to user-generated content, selected and vetted by the Generation Why team. All comments and contributions were premoderated, requiring a substantial budget and the services of both paid web producers and volunteers. Invitations to young people to contribute ideas and articles featured on various pages, covering specific Generation Why/Oxfam projects and reports on topical political and social issues. Suggested examples of topics that young users might cover included the environment, ethical consumerism, music bands and their performances, culture and tradition, and spaces and places, as well as how these might be fitted around political activism. For instance, it was suggested that users could purchase a t-shirt with an anticorporate message or send an email about corporate ethics to a big company.

One such article featured a young woman discussing ways of shopping more ethically for Christmas gifts. A response from another young user suggested that she would use only old newspaper to wrap presents and thus save on the wrapping paper. The juxtaposition of the article and the comment implied that the article had successfully persuaded the reader to adopt a greener and more ethical approach to a commercial festivity. By refusing to buy extra toys, paper, tinsel, and other unnecessary ornaments, one might save a large amount of money, which could then be donated to charity and used for the improvement of people's lives in the developing world; while simultaneously being environmentally responsible by recycling and making better use of existing resources.

As this wrapping paper commentary implies, the site appeared to place major emphasis on developing its users' sense of political efficacy, if in highly individualistic terms. While dealing with a range of serious global problems, its tone was fairly relentlessly upbeat and optimistic. Users were encouraged to think that all their actions were "making a difference," and they were urged to "challenge your mates" and "Do It Now!" There were also a great many questions, both pointed and rhetorical, a pedagogical strategy intended to reduce the distance between writers and readers and lend a personalized, intimate edge. In line with the light-touch pedagogical approach, the kind of jargon that might appear on party political sites was notably absent. While readers were assumed to share a common and altruistic concern with issues of global justice and a desire to have their say about such matters, they were also encouraged to have "a bit of fun" and enjoy their youth. Online polls also tended to focus primarily on the environment and "ethical consumption"—issues that users would be able to address on an individual level in their everyday lives.

The politics of Generation Why could be described as broadly left-leaning or liberal. The site did attempt to direct its users' attention to broader issues of injustice and inequality, though on a global rather than local scale. Rather than suggesting that no one was to blame for global injustices, there was a clear sense that business as usual between governments and corporations was not acceptable. However, as on the current Oxfam website, these messages about environmentalism and social justice carried Christian and charitable overtones that might appeal to more conservative young people as well.

Yet while the site did offer information addressed to more politically committed young people, it was primarily targeted to those who might not otherwise have displayed much interest in civic or political participation. Thus, a key aim was to encourage users to buy from the Oxfam ethical shopping catalog:

Why not buy from a charity-shop website, so that while you're still giving something meaningful to those you love, you're also helping to fight poverty and climate change? The Oxfam Unwrapped programme gives you the chance to buy a goat or a loo in the name of a mate and the chance to raise some smiles, have a laugh and make some conversation whilst giving someone something they really need. (http://www.oxfam.org.uk/generationwhy/yoursay/articles/yoursay263 .htm) 2007.

The embedded and intertwined nature of politics, leisure, and "fun" is especially notable here: the language markets a certain type of politics as entertaining while also being morally accountable and making the doer a caring family member and citizen. "Having a laugh" is not opposed to "fighting poverty and climate change" but is an inextricable part of it.

The senior content editor whom we interviewed confirmed that the aim here was to engage the "wider audience" of young people by dropping the overtly censorious tone associated with traditional charity advertising. Rather than patronizing readers or telling them that what they enjoy is bad, apolitical, or irresponsible, the approach was intended to be inviting:

There'll always be a body of young people who are motivated by social justice and social justice issues in its own right and you won't need to engage them through music as they're passionate about justice anyway. But . . . if you're into music or you're into fashion you can still have a positive impact on the world.

However, our analysis of the site, combined with the responses of our focus groups, suggests that this appeal was principally to middle-class young people (particularly young women), most of whom were in higher education. Particular assumptions were made here about young people and their interests, and those assumptions were apparent both in the style and content of the site and in our interviews with its producers. None of this is surprising, but it does suggest that the desire to aim at a generic "youth" demographic is always implicitly bounded by the producers' own knowledge and assumptions about what young people in general are like.

This address to highly educated, middle-class youth was apparent in the sheer amount of written information on the site, but also in the tone and style of much of the writing, including the content uploaded by young people ostensibly visiting the site as users. One example of a "typical" user was "Jessica Vine, 24," doing an MA in modern history, who had contributed extended pieces on issues with titles like "Japan: A Country of Contrasts" and "Are Marches a Waste of Time?" The style of the written content (as on the current Oxfam site) fitted neatly into a particular class style—Standard English with a deliberate "cool" or slangy twist at times, but highly informed and even erudite at other points. Education and the wish to pursue a career in the charity or NGO sector seemed to be a key motivating feature of the site's appeal. It is hard to imagine young people working in low-paid jobs or on state benefit, or those with little access to parental funds or support, being induced to contribute in this way.

These biases were also apparent in the site's political stance. In line with Oxfam's overall position, it appeared more pronouncedly left wing on issues of international development than, for instance, on local issues having to do with inner-city poverty, which barely featured at all. Its mission in terms of young people's civic participation, according to the content editor, was getting "a broad agreement to work with others to eradicate poverty around the world." Yet this broad agreement could arguably be generated only if young people were not encouraged too overtly to think about inequalities in their own society as something problematic or worthy of campaigning about.

Lehet Más a Világ (Another World Is Possible), Hungary

URL: http://lmv.hu. Researchers: Judit Szakacs and Eva Bognar

We move in this final case study to an organization that exists entirely in cyberspace, with no supporting offline manifestation, and that, unlike The Pirate Bay, has not launched an offline sister organization since its inception. Lehet Más a Világ, or Another World Is Possible (LMV), is a community portal—or, to use the site's own definition, a "community haven." It is a collection of web pages and blogs that can be started by anyone who wishes to do so and has the requisite skills; the only requirement is registration on the site, which is free and unrestricted by any other written conditions. The preparations to put the site together started seven years ago; it has been in existence in its present form for approximately four and a half years. According to "L," its founder, the site has no budget. It was launched with a grant of 3 million HUF (approximately €10,000) from the Hungarian National Civil Fund; the funds have since run out, and there has been no follow-up. Everyone participating in the running of the site is, perforce, an unpaid volunteer; there are no paid employees, and no one gains financially from the site (figure 6.10).

LMV does not confine itself to a focus on youth. Indeed, although he too expressed distrust of established politicians and the mainstream media, and anxiety about the effectiveness of political engagement in Hungary, L (who is in his mid-forties) clearly differentiated himself from young people:

. . . young people today seem to be terrified of commitments. Of getting involved, standing behind something firmly, something that could determine your future, it freaks them out. The other thing is, that they are very afraid of other people. . . . So I concluded that they have very, very bad experiences with the older generation, with civic initiatives; they have no idea what they want, they are very insecure. There are quite a few people with failed initiatives in their past by the time they get to their mid-twenties, so they have deep scars and they don't trust others.

L said he founded the site in an attempt to offer a less threatening, more constructive experience of politics and to counteract what he saw as a widespread feeling of distrust and passivity brought about by economic and political corruption.

In line with its lack of budget and "alternative" political aims, LMV runs on Drupal, an open-source content management platform. The site is text-heavy but well organized, with a series of key posts illustrated with a single video or image. There are no loud colors, eye-catching animations, or background music. It is a busy, collaborative

Figure 6.10
LMV (English), 2012

site for issues of local, national, and international political and civic interest. Indeed, according to the mission statement, the site aims to provide a platform for anyone with a cause of importance to "the community":

Every peace demonstration . . . and bike march . . . every human rights movement, every boycott, open letter, petition, public debate, film screening or festival shares one thing: a dissatisfaction with the present and the hope that it can be different. But it will only be different if we become active. And together, in a community, in a network we can hopefully do more than one by one. Supporting this cooperation, this collective process, is the goal of the site.

LMV is a collective enterprise and so does not speak with a single voice. Multiple authors and editors upload material, and all readers are encouraged to become authors on the site rather than merely respond to posted content. Registered users may upload any written text, image, movie, or sound clip, although unregistered users may also respond. Since users are able to customize their blogs or community response pages, there is also no uniform design theme but a variety of ways of displaying and navigating content, and multiple links and further networks are represented. There is not even a "Terms and Agreements" document to read and accept. Quite deliberately, the site producers stand back: LMV lacks an "About Us" section or any information on who set up and runs the site. The contact information is an email address that does not reveal the name of the recipient. The only section where the producers speak openly is the "LMV?!" page, which contains the mission statement and the manual explaining how to upload material. The site's producers are active participants on the site, but it is not apparent which out of all the registered members they are. In accordance with the democratic principles of the site, there is no moderation. L, who has also worked as a journalist on a mainstream Hungarian daily, was very emphatic that the whole point of using the Internet was to avoid what he saw as the undemocratic pitfalls of mainstream media. By contrast, LMV aims to prove its trustworthiness precisely through the lack of controlling and filtering mechanisms or authorial credentials.

According to the mission statement, LMV aims to make the "inner life" of small civic and political groups easier, as well as enable their members to meet new groups, should they want to do so. At the same time, it explicitly seeks to mobilize visitors, not least by providing examples of local self-organization. Engagement leads to action; as the mission statement claims, the world can be different but "only if we do something about it." In practice, the types of groups drawn to the site are largely antiglobalization or anticorporate, left-leaning grassroots social movements. The site's name, Lehet Más a Világ, is the Hungarian translation of the slogan of the World Social Forum, the annual meeting held by organizations "opposed to neo-liberalism and a world dominated by capital or by any form of imperialism."

As such, some of the groups posting on LMV have a broad national and international appeal, addressing causes relating to environmentalism, poverty, sexism, genetically modified products, fair trade, open-source software, or (anti-) globalization. However, many of them are concerned with local issues, and came together when they faced the loss of public spaces or historical buildings because of allegedly corrupt politicians selling public goods to property investors. Examples of these kinds of groups on the site include Kincsünk a piac (The market is our treasure), a group that has successfully mobilized to protect an old market on Budapest's Hunyadi Square, and Nagymező Street, whose residents protest against the proposed cutting down of a line of sycamore trees to make room for an underground parking garage. The Kárpát Commando also reflects this broader sense of the seemingly weak defying the powerful: a few young women mock the far-right quasi-military group Hungarian Guard, established in 2007, by holding swearing-in ceremonies for "clown guards." In other cases, mobilization is not so much against something as in favor of something. Examples include attempts at establishing "direct trade" links to (usually organic) food producers or setting up a "favor bank." This kind of mobilization is also in line with the "think globally, act locally" approach, showing that ordinary people are capable of achieving change. Formal political actions such as voting do not feature on the site, although users are able to create their own online polls.

The style of particular group pages and blogs varies, yet they generally avoid an authoritative voice. While "traditional" blog dialogues are necessarily weighted toward the blogger (Benkler 2006, 217), the group pages or collaborative blogs, which seem to be collectively edited, offer a more democratic chance for discussion. The tone on most pages is very friendly; the informal "you" form of Hungarian is used, along with lots of slang. When users contribute comments, their picture (if provided) is displayed, emulating both face-to-face conversation and online social networks. There are numerous references to specific offline events, parties and outings in which members have participated, bringing the online and offline worlds together in the manner of other social networks.

Despite its home-made (or DIY) approach, several parts of the site make use of quite advanced technological possibilities. In 2008, LMV started to feature a global project video library, where antiglobalization films are available for download. Other contributors employ multimedia and satellite imaging technologies: for example, a group campaigning against real estate deals in the 6th district of Budapest created a Google map marking all the "hot spots" or problem sites. In terms of navigation, LMV was using devices such as tagging well ahead of commercial Web 2.0 services such as Facebook and Flickr. Unlike most such services, it allows users to customize their pages with unique "skins," and does not collect personal information about them at registration.

Clearly, a level of literacy and technological knowledge is needed to find out about, seek out, and register on the site, and a level of political and civic efficacy is necessary for users to feel inclined to contribute in the first place. However, our research identified few sites anywhere on the political spectrum that took democratic communication and freedom of speech so seriously. Even on other sites that aimed or purported to be bottom-up and democratic, we saw practices of control (organizational, technological, and ideological) and even overt censorship. By contrast, LMV was driven by a sense that negative experiences of participation would undermine people's sense of self-efficacy and trust, and turn them away from politics. However, it should be noted that despite the openness of its structure and invitation, there have been no right-wing, nationalist, racist, or homophobic views represented on the site, and according to L, its openness has yet to be tested in this way.

What is particularly notable here is LMV's considered adherence to a horizontal structure that does not play up the achievements or individual personalities of the site's producers, as well as the fact that there is no capital involved. As we saw in chapter 3, the political economy of online nonprofit organizations is potentially exploitative: some people are paid for their work in creating or managing content in virtual spaces, while others are expected to contribute "free labor" (Terranova 2000, 47–50). In this context, a flourishing online organization that does not solicit from, profit from, or pay its users is extremely rare. Even rarer is an organizational model that ensures that everyone's contribution is equally voluntary and equally valued because content does not have to be created in particular ways or to a particular schedule. While accepting that LMV and sites like it are not able to *initiate* civic or political action, L told us they could help to "make visible" people's resistance to power and their ability to effect change, and thereby inspire others. In our view, the site goes a long way toward achieving these goals.

Conclusion

The sites we have discussed in this chapter vary across a number of related but nevertheless distinct dimensions. We briefly identify these as follows:

1. *Politics*   While some of these sites adopt a very formal conception of politics, others directly reject or resist such conceptions. While some include aspects that are close to the world of everyday life, others are oriented very much toward the public sphere of policy and government.

2. *Online and offline*   While some of these sites are primarily intended to service or facilitate offline activities, others are mainly or even exclusively oriented toward the online world. While some implicitly regard online activity as a means to an end, others are more inclined to see it as an end in itself.

3. *Audience*   Where some sites appear to target those who are assumed to be already highly committed, others are addressed more to those who may need to be persuaded. Although young people are among the primary target audience for most of these sites, very different assumptions are made about their characteristics, interests, and likely levels of participation.

4. *Control*   While some of the sites are very much "managed" or "invited," others are "autonomous" or "invented" (in the terms outlined at the start of this chapter). Some attempt to encourage open participation and interaction, while others seek to exclude or prevent it.

It would be possible to map each of our sites onto these polarities, but we fear this attempt would unduly schematize the heterogeneous nature of the sites. As we have argued, each of the dimensions should be understood as a continuum rather than a straightforward binary opposition: indeed, many of our example websites display tendencies in both directions, in ways that sometimes appear to generate conflict or incoherence. Furthermore, these different dimensions do not necessarily group easily with each other, or neatly line up: politics and pedagogy are often contradictory.

While some of the differences between the sites we have looked at in this chapter can be traced to logistical or economic constraints, or simply accidents of production or history, choices were also made by the producers in conceiving and constructing the sites. The nature of the sites to some extent reflects their producers' overall political aims, as well as the intended functions of the sites themselves. It is not our intention here to imply a singular model of "good practice" or a "one-size-fits-all" approach that will work in every situation. Rather, it seems more important that organizations' uses of the Internet should be fit for purpose—that they should be clear about what their purposes are, and about how the Internet might (or might not) help to fulfill them. The production of a website does not need to obey what some might see as the inexorable logic of technology. A highly interactive site, with large amounts of visual material may be appropriate for some purposes but not for others; equally, a site that simply provides information may be entirely adequate for what it seeks to achieve. A more decentralized, open-access site is not necessarily or inherently better than one that speaks with a single voice.

Furthermore, the outward appearance of a site—including its design and structure—may belie its actual uses. A highly professional site that appears to offer neutral or balanced information may in fact be promoting a particular propagandist position. A site that looks democratic and inviting may in practice be reaching a narrow and exclusive audience. A site that appears amateur and anarchic may in fact facilitate very effective forms of offline organization.

Nevertheless, we can hazard some overall conclusions here. Broadly speaking, established political parties and large charities tend to make "invited" (in the sense proposed at the start of this chapter) interventions in the national and international political arena, if from different ideological and structural positions. Their sites are often well-funded and tightly managed, and tend to be addressed as much (if not more) to a general audience than to their existing adherents. This has distinct implications for the authority with which they and their members speak and the actions that they take or support. At the other end of the spectrum, the grassroots websites of activist or campaigning organizations or networks are often unfunded and rely on volunteers' time and energy. Their "invented" civic responses—targeted vandalism, digital piracy, occupations of public and private space—do not necessarily conform to normative political definitions of citizenship and may make them targets for state action. Their websites are frequently perfunctory and often tend to disappear, leaving a fading trail, while their actions are taken up and reinvented by other groups in other spaces. Rather than seeking to persuade a general audience (to win votes or arguments, to attract donations), these sites are primarily seeking to promote communication and debate among their existing constituency. While their users might have an urgent need to "speak truth to power," the website is generally not their primary vehicle for doing so.

This leads us to reemphasize a final key point that also emerged in a different way from our research with young people. Whether for large national organizations or for local groups of activists, a website is typically only a part—in some instances, a very small part—of a broader strategy. Even in the unusual case of The Pirate Bay, whose origins and operation have to do with the Internet itself, it is striking that the advocates of its cause have now taken to offline political action. To this extent, the analysis of websites in isolation can prove not only partial but also actively misleading. The Web can be a powerful medium for politics, but its power depends very much on how it enables its users to engage the offline world.

7 Making Civic Identities

This chapter considers the use of the Web to develop and promote forms of cultural, ethnic, and religious identity, especially among minority communities. The sites we discuss differ widely in their conception, intentions, and construction, but they are similar in one key respect: their invocation of a preexisting sense of communal identity among their intended users. Not all these invitations to identification are overtly political; indeed, most of the sites explicitly avoid positioning themselves in relation to traditional or even alternative and activist politics. Rather, their aims tend to focus on ideas of community service, moral values, or self-advancement. Nevertheless, all the sites in this chapter do have an implicit form of politics, in two respects. First, the actions they propose or embody inevitably *become* political when they are seen in relation to broader patterns of power and authority. Second, and of equal importance to our broader themes in this book, the kinds of civic and communitarian pedagogies that are developed here also entail particular relations of social power. Both these dimensions are explored in detail through our empirical case studies.

The cases we present span four countries—the Netherlands, the UK, Spain, and Hungary; two major religions—Islam and Catholicism; two conceptions of religion—one as cultural affiliation and the other as dogma; a linguistic and regional claim to statehood—Catalan nationalism; and several different ethnic groupings, including Moroccans and the Roma people. The ideological standpoints and aims of the sites are also diverse and in some cases directly opposed. Roma.Hu was set up and run by Roma individuals in Hungary with the aim of enabling a dialogue between Roma and non-Roma people, as well as discussion among Roma populations across Europe. TANS aims to train and encourage Moroccan immigrants in the Netherlands to better their social and employment status. Opus Dei is the online manifestation of a powerful offline Catholic organization, whose members include the pope. Racó Català draws together primarily young Catalan nationalists. Muslim Youth shares aspects of the aspirations of Roma.hu and aims to be a platform for young Muslims to discuss issues and concerns affecting their lives; uniquely among the sites discussed here, it was set up by a young person under the age of twenty-five and continues to be run by young people, for young people.

Cutting across these specific case studies is a set of broader questions, which we explore more extensively later in the chapter. In particular, our analysis points to a persistent concern about questions of democracy, freedom of speech, and censorship online. Is a site or an organization being undemocratic if it censors posts that are abusive or racist toward members of a minority community? What, indeed, is the point of freedom of speech for some (in the majority community) if it negatively affects the ability of others (in the minority) to communicate in the public sphere? Our case studies implicitly challenge popular claims that the Internet is an inherently bottom-up medium that invites a diversity of viewpoints, in contrast to the apparently "undemocratic" tendencies of older media. Calls for freedom of speech and interactivity, we suggest, may need to be balanced against the real constraints of online communication and of the organizations that seek to promote free speech. In this respect, issues of ethnic and religious identity, both on- and offline, can be seen as a key testing ground for the limits of civic tolerance and democratic practice.

Case Studies

Opus Dei, Spain

URL: http://www.opusdei.es. Researchers: Magdalena Albero Andres and Albert Bastardas

Opus Dei is an organization linked to the more traditionalist elements of the Catholic Church. It was founded by Saint Josemaría Escrivá in 1928 and recognized as a "personal prelature" by Pope John Paul II in 1982. Its mission is "to spread the message that work and the circumstances of everyday life are occasions for growing closer to God, for serving others, and for improving society." While Opus Dei addresses adults of all ages who share its beliefs and values, its use of the Internet suggests that it is also seeking to spread its message to younger people.

The site's overt aim is to represent and link the 87,000 followers of Opus Dei around the world, although there is no indication of how many visitors the site actually receives. Subscription to the site is free, and the constantly updated content is adapted into many languages, ranging from English to Chinese, Czech, Estonian, and Spanish. There is a major emphasis on Catholic countries: for example, every Latin American country has its own customized Opus Dei site. Some of the content is shared across all national versions of the site, although much of it differs. For example, in January 2008 both the Spanish and the British sites had articles in common—"God and Our Children" or "Letter from the Prelate"—but other pages were distinct and covered more local topics: the British site featured the story of someone who had suffered an accident and become totally incapacitated, while on the Spanish version the corresponding story talked about the illness of the son of a well-known bullfighter. Unlike on many smaller religious and political websites, all the material is adaptable for those with sight or hearing impairments.

The site has the expected menu ("About Us," "Contact Us," "Frequently Asked Questions," etc.), as well as extensive illustrations and videos about the organization and its founder and quotations from his writings (figure 7.1). It follows a common website design with a frame on the left listing each section, a menu bar across the top, and a central frame with specific content on each page. The site's muted colors—light orange, pale blue, and black—are often used by political or religious conservative groups, at least in Spain, and might perhaps be seen as a visual cue for social conservatism. Extremely formal, even ceremonial language is used consistently to discourage frivolity and encourage subservience and respect for the religious traditions discussed.

On one level, it might even seem odd—or perhaps deliberately provocative—that we have chosen to include this site in a study of civic websites. However, even a cursory glance reveals that the site gives extensive advice about both religious and mundane beliefs and actions that undoubtedly take place in and affect civil society. Indeed, while there are no overt references to political news, let alone to ongoing conflicts between the Catholic Church and civil society or the state (Paz 2001), the

Figure 7.1
Opus Dei home page, February 2012

sense of being a martyred, moral minority within an oppressively secular society pervades much of the content. There is, therefore, a discourse of "the common good," which some have seen as a key characteristic of civic participation (Montgomery, Gottlieb-Robles, and Larson 2004, 17–18), and a concomitant sense of Opus Dei as a key player in promoting said common good.

The key question, of course, is how—and by whom—the common good is defined. In a manner reminiscent of the young Zionist site examined in chapter 6, Opus Dei's Spanish website provides an entirely positive, top-down flow of information about the organization. All written stories are by important institutional figures in the organization, most notably its founder and the former pope, Benedict XVI; and there are also stories and tracts by well-known figures in business or the arts who claim to live by Opus Dei's principles. All published material on the site passes through the Opus Dei press office, and users are neither invited nor given the opportunity to contribute content apart from an invitation to "write to us." Even then, the press office chooses which of the opinions received can and cannot be published. Information published on the site has thus been preselected to fit the organization's ideology. However, since the organization clearly seeks coverage in the mainstream media, it also has a large selection of press reports, audio fragments, and videos about Opus Dei and its work that the mass media may use if they choose. At a more individual level, through a section titled "Preguntas" (or "Questions") people can email the site producers, and the organization promises to send information through the same system—thus also ensuring that users' email addresses are recorded and available for future marketing and fundraising.

The use of links on the site reinforces this sense of closure, which stands in stark contrast to utopian claims that the networked character of online communication is inherently counterhegemonic and antihierarchical (see chapter 1). Far from contributing to a pluralistic virtual public sphere, all the links here lead to sites of organizations that reinforce the Opus Dei worldview. In common with many political sites—of both party-political and activist varieties—the site is thus entirely devoted to promoting a singular viewpoint. As such, it seems largely confined to preaching to the converted, those who are already convinced of the organization's brand of Catholicism; it is hard to believe that this form of authoritarian, top-down communication would be particularly effective in attracting new followers.

Racó Català (Catalan Corner), Spain

URL: http://www.racocatala.cat. Researcher: Magdalena Albero

The website Racó Català aims to provide access to information and a forum to discuss social issues affecting the Catalan area of Spain (Catalunya, Valencia, and the Balearic Islands). The producers of the site are not attached to any preexisting organization, and the site tries to offer an alternative to mainstream media depictions of the region, as well as encouraging user-generated content. The site was launched in 1999 as a personal opinion site and by 2007 had six administrators and 20,000 registered users, of whom 1,200 were active posters of content. In 2012 more than 350 organizations and individuals created pages. The site itself is not addressed directly to youth, but according to the site producers we interviewed, most members who join up as individuals are fifteen to twenty-five years old. Despite the apparently open invitation to participate, the site is essentially a venue for Catalan nationalist youth to discuss their concerns. Participants appear to share the site's nationalist ideology, and there are no dissenting views.

The main social issue represented at the time of our analysis in 2007–2008 was the political, economic, and cultural situation of the Catalan region, its definition as a "nation" without a state (Conversi 1990), and its options for the future. The Catalan nationalist cause was (and still is) represented by a collection of articles that discuss these issues and by comments on these news items and articles. News affecting other locations that are thought to be in a similar situation to Catalunya are also featured prominently, for example in items about a possible referendum on independence in Scotland and in Flanders. The independence of Catalunya remains a contentious political debate, and it should be pointed out that conservative right-wing parties (such as the Falangists, discussed in chapter 6) are strongly opposed to it. As such, the site could be said to implicitly address a more left-wing Catalan nationalist constituency.

Racó Catalá addresses users in general, although using the informal "tu" instead of the formal "usted" might perhaps be seen as more characteristic of young people. Young people's voices are easily discernible in the forums, the activities advertised, and the answers to the online surveys. Although there are no pictures of youth on the site (except in the advertisements) and none of the language or iconography appears to be specifically geared toward young people, most of the products available for sale—t-shirts, silicon bracelets, mugs with slogans—do seem to be more oriented toward a youth market (figures 7.2 and 7.3). The advertisements on the site are not at first evident, but in small clickable spaces at the top of the main page one can find ads for graphics and web companies, and listings that range from schools to translation services to gay movies available online.

Racó Catalá attempts to establish its credibility, authority, and trustworthiness by using news stories as a starting point for discussion. Educational or pedagogical intentions are ever-present, in the sense that all the information that appears on the site is geared toward maintaining and encouraging a very bounded and specific Catalan identity. The site actively promotes forms of offline civic activism (such as lobbying, protest events, and volunteering) geared to defending Catalan culture, which is seen to be under threat from the homogenizing influences of Spanish nationalism. There

Figure 7.2
Racó Català home page, January 2008

Figure 7.3
Racó Català online store, April 2012

is extensive information about offline activities such as concerts, meetings, and celebrations of nationalist achievements. However, the site also seeks to achieve these aims by using more entertaining and participatory functions such as online shopping and chat, which tap into leisure uses of the Internet.

Although the site is dominated by written text, and there are few visual or interactive features, there are opportunities for participation through forums and message boards, and the option to add pages. Many of these user-generated pages are created by groups of young people from different towns, and there is information about music groups that sing in Catalan, the situation of the Catalan language in Europe, and Catalan software. Although the design of the site could be described as fairly static, the salience of the topics seems to generate lively debate, though in some cases among only a small group of users. While the forums are moderated and checked, we were told they are not often censored. Yet in effect, the expressions of cultural identity on the site become self-sustaining and mutually confirming: discussions of music and sports refer only to Catalan music and sports, for example. Even articles published in the "International" section refer to areas such as the Basque country or smaller European nations or regions where parallel issues of cultural identity are seen to apply. Although there is no censorship as such, it could be argued that there is an element of self-censorship at work, or at least a self-conscious construction of identity that is framed in quite narrow and specifically nationalist terms. The site appears to invoke a notion of informed and active citizenship and to invite debate, but competing and dissenting arguments are almost uncannily absent. In this sense, there appears to be a latent tension between the explicit ideals and the actual practices of Racó Català: while by no means as authoritarian as the Opus Dei site, it appears to achieve a similar effect of ideological closure.

Roma.hu, Hungary

URL: www.roma.hu. Researchers: Judit Szakacs and Eva Bognar

Roma.hu was a site created by and for the Roma people in Hungary. It is a curious and illuminating case, for several reasons. Our analysis here needs to be prefaced by a cautionary explanation. In the months immediately following our research, the site disappeared from cyberspace. In early spring 2008, a message was posted on its home page, a sort of frustrated epigram to the effect that "everybody thinks they know more about the Roma than the Roma themselves." In the summer of that year, the site was replaced with a note informing visitors that the domain name had been put up for sale by the owner, who was trying to appeal to potential buyers by pointing out that "roma.hu" could easily be understood as referring to the Italian capital Rome (Róma in Hungarian) or to the football club AS Roma. All that appears now is an error message, while a Google search leads instead to ASRoma.hu. While our original analysis holds good, the fact that this site is no longer available reflects some of the difficulties faced by web producers, especially those attempting to tackle minority community issues in hostile political environments.

The URL www.roma.hu would be the most obvious guess if one were looking for Roma-related Hungarian sites; but it was therefore surprising to find that it did not belong to a governmental organization or to a big Roma NGO. But whom *did* it belong to? There was no "About Us" section or any site imprint, which is apparently mandatory for any Hungarian publication (according to some unenforced—and unenforceable—Hungarian legislation). There was no offline contact information, and the email address provided was not intended to shed light on the people behind the site, either: it was simply foszerkeszto@roma.hu, which translates as editor in chief@roma.hu. There was no response to our efforts to contact the site editors. For a clue about the creators, one had to dig deeper: among the list of registered members, where one could find an entry for "foszerkeszto" (editor in chief), revealing his real name, Zsolt Balogh, and with a picture uploaded. That this elusiveness might not be accidental was revealed when the editor in chief, discussing a newly launched Roma social networking site on the message board, commented that it would be unwise for a Roma person to post too much personal information about himself or herself on the Web. A sense of unease and defensiveness in a hostile environment was thus immediately evident.

The site contained no mission statement either. However, a press release describing the site's aims was available on the website of *Barátság* (Friendship), a magazine for ethnic minorities in Hungary. This claimed that "our primary goal is to create the kind of independent Roma medium which is close to its visitors' taste yet is sufficiently informative." It also declared that the creators of the site "regard interactivity as of key importance," particularly since "it is relatively rare on Roma-related websites." Additionally, in an article in the media journal *MédiaMix*, Balogh did reveal that the site was "created, owned and edited" by him, with one volunteer co-editor.

Roma.hu relied on a free content management system and utilized a fairly simple frame-set in its design, with content in three columns and the navigation bar on the left-hand side. The muted colors—light gray and light blue, with the most important information in red—and the small, simple font reinforced a low-key look. This was further strengthened by the site's simple but sophisticated banner (figure 7.4). The site's name, which was simply the URL, roma.hu, was present only on the banner, and even there in a nonintrusive way. The first impression was one of modesty: it was a site without a flashy name, without showing off, suggesting a much more understated claim to identity than the websites of Opus Dei or Racó Català.

Roma.hu's description in the Google directory stated that it was a portal site containing "articles, studies, photo reports and audiovisual material related to the Roma/Gypsy, for the Roma and the non-Roma." In contrast to Racó Català, it also emphasized the site's political neutrality and made explicit the fact that it was "edited by

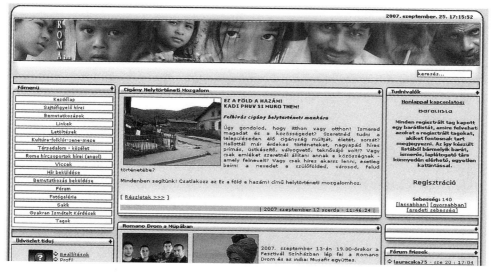

Figure 7.4

Roma.hu home page, September 2007

young Roma and non-Roma volunteers." In practice, however, its definition of "Roma-related" topics appeared to be rather specific. There were few political pieces on the site: for example, none of the widely publicized Roma-related scandals from 2007 made it to the news section of the site (though some appeared in the e-voting archives). The news section contained promotions for concerts, performances, and exhibitions by or about Roma people, as well as calls for applications for scholarships, internships, and conferences on Roma-related issues. There were only two archived news items that did not fall under the category of "culture": one, dating back to December 2005, was a factual account of a news conference held by László Teleki, then secretary of state for Roma issues; the other was an outraged description of an anti-Roma website from January 2006. The former event was preceded by Teleki's visit to an infamous, poor Roma settlement; this visit was captured on video, which was the only video to be found under the heading "Society–Public Affairs" on the site. In contrast, the "Culture-Folklore-Music-Tales" section housed thirteen audio and video files. As this content weighting implies, the official or editor-generated sections of the site conceptualized "the Roma" principally as a cultural and not as a political identity. This strategy was shared until recently by the mainstream Hungarian media, which also tended to show Roma people only in connection with culture, most typically in the form of the age-old figure of the Gypsy musician.

This construction of the Roma was also apparent in the visual dimensions of the site. The images on the banner (see figure 7.4) recalled ethnographic photographs or press images of distant lands; the people pictured embodied the stereotypical Roma man and child. In a similar vein, almost every news item on the site was accompanied by a still image, usually of the performers promoted or the poster for the event advertised. However, the gallery section, much proclaimed in the site's press release, did contain more unusual photographs, videos, and audio files. It included a substantial collection of images of Gypsy musicians belonging to a private collector, some dating back to the 1930s. The multimedia section also contained excerpts by famous classical Gypsy bands and Gypsy folk dances, as well as some poems recited by presumably Roma students. One could also watch excerpts from a mimed performance by a Roma pop star, which seemed to have been captured by a phone or a camera in the audience. While these offerings were all in accordance with the site's cultural perspective, there was also a collection of photographs (apparently taken for the site) of one of the most impoverished, isolated Roma settlements in Hungary, the Hétes encampment in the town of Ózd. This material clearly identified Roma poverty as an issue, although it called for no action in particular.

However, the site also featured a forum and a message board, both providing space for heated discussions on anything Roma-related. In these user-generated sections there were debates about recent scandals, Roma politicians, racism, discrimination, and more. In this way, the site apparently tried to reconcile its official "Roma culture" perspective with a more political debate about issues relating to the Roma minority in Hungary. It is possible that the site's original goal was to focus on culture and that it was appropriated by users in ways that did not match the creators' intentions. However, it is more likely that the creators intended the forums and message boards to address more political issues. This suggestion is confirmed by the fact that some noncultural forum topics, for instance one titled "I have been discriminated against" and another titled "Do we need Roma minority councils?," were started by the site's editor in chief. Thus, while the concept of *political* citizenship was not explicitly discussed, the site worked implicitly to enrich the citizenship of Hungarian Roma and to identify where the institutional will to ensure a firm citizenship was lacking.

The site operated primarily in a "we" mode, with Roma speaking to Roma. This was most obvious from the forums where the editor in chief (or, more precisely, a person with the user-name "editor in chief") described experiences of being discriminated against as a Roma. The site's moderating policies also contained the following call: "Let's show respect to other visitors by translating Roma forum entries into Hungarian." Thus, non-Roma-speaking users were placed in the category of "others," while at the same time being included through a translation policy.

Young people were not addressed directly; although arguably, it is the younger generation of Roma and non-Roma people who would have been computer literate enough to use the site's fairly sophisticated functions. The site also used the colloquial "you" of the Hungarian language on the rare occasions when it addressed the users directly or in an imperative (such as "Choose a game to play!"). Interestingly, the site contained Roma fairy tales recited by children (in audio files) as well as (non-Roma-related) online games and Roma jokes, suggesting that the creators had a young audience in mind, as well as parents looking for resources to support their children's learning of the language and culture. Likewise, the "Our Stars" section provided pictures and links to sites of Roma pop stars (instead of, say, classical musicians or artists), although there was little reference to youth culture across the site as a whole.

Structurally and technologically, Roma.Hu epitomized an open, democratic approach. The site had an open registration policy: all one needed to do to register was submit a valid email address. The profile offered space to enter one's user ID in various instant messaging systems, one's birthday, as well as a personal message or "motto," although, unlike on most other social networking sites, it was the user's decision to provide any further information. Registered members were also able to send private messages to other members, to set up photo albums, and to create a "friends list." Users could also get involved through a message board or chat room, a forum, e-voting, and sending news announcements and links to the editors. The site was also extremely customizable. Every feature was published in a separate content box and could be minimized or removed entirely, and the speed with which scrolling information moved and the way links were displayed on the links page could be set. In all these respects, the site handed a considerable degree of control to its users, and tried to construct a community by facilitating internal connections. As the editor in chief stressed in the press release, this level of openness and interactivity was of key importance for its creators.

However, this open approach also left users vulnerable to constant harassment and racist flaming, which for many mirrored their offline experiences. All the content was created by users, yet this content had to be strictly moderated. Moderating operated both through automated software that automatically deleted obscene words from forum and message board entries (sometimes with uneven results) and through the intervention of the editor. It was "strictly forbidden" to make racist, hateful comments or to use Nazi symbols on the site, and to advertise racist websites; and the guidelines also banned behavior "that is offensive for other users' personal interests" and "any comments that hinder civilized communication."

In stark contrast to the homogenous postings on Racó Català, the Roma.Hu forums did buzz with passionate and sometimes strident discussion of issues such as discrimination and racism. Yet ultimately, the site confronted the fundamental dilemmas that surround the notion of freedom of expression online (see Fabbro 2010). It was bound to restrict some people's free speech in order to guarantee the freedom of others and thereby offer the potential for "civilized communication." In a sense, the "cultural" framing of Roma citizenship in the main areas of the site, which we have described above, might also be seen as a response to this, in that it avoided at least some potential grounds for contention. We can only speculate as to whether the ultimate demise of Roma.Hu reflects the difficulty—and perhaps the impossibility—of resolving these tensions and dilemmas.

Muslim Youth, UK

URL: http://www.muslimyouth.net

There is no dearth of Muslim or Islamic civic and religious material on the Web, and while much of it is in Arabic and has been discussed for its potential contribution to an "Islamic public sphere" online (El-Nawawi and Khamis 2010), a fair proportion is also in English. Some of this content deals with legal and religious matters, some with social and cultural issues arising from life in non-Islamic states, some with feminist issues, and some with Islamophobia. Some of it is highly rhetorical, polemical, and authoritarian, while some is skeptical, reflective, and anti-authoritarian. Several such sites claim to cater to Muslims in the UK and elsewhere, and some provide spaces in which political and religious issues can be debated. However, while some appear to be run by young people, few are deliberately and exclusively designed for this age group.

MuslimYouth.net (henceforth Muslim Youth) was launched in 2002, in the wake of the hysteria about Muslims in the wider British media following the events of September 11, 2001. It grew out of the Muslim Youth Helpline, which had been started in 2001 by a single young person, Mohammad Syed Mamdani, as a direct response to many young British Muslims' experience of being collectively stigmatized for the attacks on the World Trade Center. Muslim Youth is now an independent charity run by trustees, a dedicated youth team, and around seventy young volunteers working between three and eight hours a week. There are some young part-time and full-time paid staff who update content on the site and look after its day-to-day functioning (see chapter 3 for further discussion). The work is funded by grants from local charitable trusts and from local and national government.

The notion of Muslim identity employed by the site is inclusive and is "more cultural than religious," according to the site's producers. The site is staffed by volunteers from different communities of Muslims of Asian, African, American, and European descent, from Sunni, Shia, and Sufi backgrounds, and of different ages and both genders. In addition to the Muslim Youth Helpline, the organization's offline work includes various outreach programs, such as those encouraging voting in UK national and local elections and one aiming to support and educate young Muslim prisoners and their families about the challenges of community reintegration after imprisonment. The site itself includes a large array of relatively busy forums debating topical political, social, and cultural issues, sometimes from inside but more typically away from a religious framework. According to the producers we interviewed in 2008, the site had over 3,000 registered regular users and well over 300,000 unique visitors, a figure that has increased significantly in the intervening years. Children as young as eleven years old read, contribute to, and moderate content on the site.

The central involvement of young people lends the site a degree of authenticity that is rare on youth civic websites. While the organizers do appear to call on adult religious authorities for advice on some of the issues raised (notably on "homosexuality and Islam") and frequently remain ideologically conservative or equivocal on issues to do with sexuality, the site has an open approach to civic participation reminiscent of the LMV site discussed in chapter 6. It focuses on topics that might be perceived as barriers to participation by the users such as racism, ultra-religious dictates, imprisonment, Islamophobia, and homophobia in the Muslim community, and it invites contributions on global and local political issues from young Muslims in the UK, non-British Muslims, and non-Muslim youth, both in articles posted on the site and in forums (figure 7.5). Meanwhile, the Muslim Youth Helpline offers a confidential telephone counseling service for young people, providing advice on frightening, depressing, or difficult situations from trained counselors. The online and offline strategies for engagement are thus very clearly articulated with one another, and both involve discussion, self-exploration, and self-expression. Overall, they appear to militate against conformity to a singular definition of religious or communal identity and to challenge conservative influences within particular diasporic, national, or local Muslim communities.

The tone of the site is serious but conversational, nonpatronizing, and yet respectful of the differences between its users. This seriousness of address, which is maintained

Figure 7.5
MuslimYouth.net home page, April 2012

throughout, does not rule out the expression of strong emotion in the forums. Exemplary the following explanation of the site's swearing policy, as it stood in 2008:

Why are swear words used in some of the articles?
Many young people, including Muslim youth, use swear words to express their feelings and emotions. Whilst we do not tolerate personal insults, abuse or graphic language, we are committed to removing barriers and censorship which restrict young people from expressing themselves and convey distorted, "palatable" images of social problems.

The producers' acknowledgment that certain formalities deter young people from participating even when they want to do so by making them feel frustrated or inferior is characteristic of their thoughtful approach to issues of age and maturity, as well as their slightly iconoclastic approach to the realm of politics and religion. The fact that some swear words are allowed means that the written text becomes more closely aligned with spoken language, and the voice of the writer comes across much more clearly than on sites with a parent organization's identity to protect, such as Oxfam's Generation Why or the Dutch Young Socialists (discussed in chapter 6).

Nevertheless, the site is highly moderated: posts that contain "racist, sexist or offensive, threatening language, personal attacks on the writer or other posters" are banned. The policy is generally to allow one of the more regular young contributors to be a moderator on a particular day. There is little trolling, although open and sometimes aggressive debate does take place. Even in this context, only informed self-censorship is a guarantee of absolute safety—as the site's producers explained when asked about their policy on issues related to discussions of terrorism. As we have noted, authoritative adult voices are also present in some areas, and indeed, the above statement about swearing might also be seen as intended for an audience of adults, even potential funders, rather than only young users.

The forums on Muslim Youth are divided into straightforward categories, including "Advice and Support," "Culture," "Politics," "Introduce Yourself," "Chit Chat," "Writer's Lounge" (for fiction), and "General." Investigating a level further, the "Politics" forums in February 2012 included threads on Syria, Egypt, and Bahrain, alongside those on "Muslim stereotyping by media," "Islamophobia," and others on Prime Minister David Cameron's views on multiculturalism, the "big society," and cuts in public spending. Although Muslim Youth have been approached by politicians interested in the site's potential for counteracting what they see as the "radicalization" of young Muslims in the UK, this is not a top-down or even a consultative exercise in e-democracy. On the contrary, the discussions on the site suggest that it serves as a means for young people to negotiate a range of cultural, religious, and political issues. They debate with both Muslim and non-Muslim peers; with adults in general; with the British media and government, who might want to label them in one way, and with the Islamic religious establishment, who might want to label them in other ways;

with those who espouse political or even extremist forms of Islam; and with those who see all Islam as political and extremist. From discussion to discussion and thread to thread, young people identify themselves in many different ways, which can result in a sense of confusion, inconclusiveness, and circularity.

While the site is not conventionally religious in that it does not confine itself to good works and the interpretation of scripture, religion is definitely an important element for many users. Cultural and political issues are sometimes addressed from a religious perspective, even from the perspective of local mullahs and religious leaders. Some conversations or postings might be inaccessible to non-Muslims or those with no interest in religion because they contain references to religious "rules" or "statements." Nevertheless, the site is by no means a vehicle for the rehearsal of religious or political dogma. Our research found evidence of users changing their ideological positions and altering their presentations of identity in the light of other users' postings. The site is also at pains to establish the diversity of contexts and ideological standpoints from which participants, volunteers, and paid staff speak. The idea that all young people are somehow politically anti-authoritarian or averse to tradition is clearly debunked by the postings on this site: alongside liberal and unorthodox positions, there are also authoritarian, illiberal voices. While such voices might prove overwhelming on other sites, Muslim Youth's pedagogical approach seems to be better at maintaining continued engagement than ones where mature adults from a particular community seek to teach younger members how to behave or think in the public sphere.

If the overall ethos here is one of tolerance, it should be emphasized that there is often a considerable amount of emotion (frustration, anger, humor, pride) in the forum postings and in the main articles on the site. It would be misleading to see the site as merely promoting a dispassionate form of "rational debate." The emotions expressed and explored are often complex, self-centered, and contradictory, but there is no attempt to force users into a particular register that appears to be "neutral," or else "hip," "cool" and overtly "youthful." As Pantti and van Zoonen (2006) argue, emotions cannot and should not be excluded from the public sphere of political debate, although we need to pay closer attention to the types of emotions and the discourses they feed into. However, we also agree with them that in practice, emotions are not necessarily a unifying feature of politics and citizenship, and that in some cases they can work to exclude, demonize, or endanger others. As the experience of Muslim Youth suggests, getting the balance between emotional engagement and reasoned debate just right in order to keep a broad spectrum of young people coming back to the site is a continuing struggle that is not capable of any simple or easy resolution.

Toward a New Start (TANS), the Netherlands

URL: http://www.tans.nl. Researcher: Fadi Hirzalla

Our final case study in this chapter, Toward a New Start (or TANS), was established in 1997 by a group of highly educated Moroccans (first- and second-generation immigrants to the Netherlands) as a "Moroccan networking organization." At present, it is directed by five board members between 20 and 35 years of age (four men and one woman), who meet once a month. TANS loosely defines its target group as "young Moroccans," but this is not specified any further in terms of gender or socioeconomic status, and it might therefore appear that it is aimed at men and women equally, and at people from different socioeconomic classes. Yet considering the kind of activities that are promoted on the website (such as discussion groups, the "TANS master class" for students, the "TANS gala," and other networking activities) and the kind of job applications featured (which are mainly for consultancy work across different commercial sectors), it appears that TANS is aimed particularly at highly educated young men and women of Moroccan descent who aspire to careers in business or commerce. Given its focus on the enhancement of individual career goals rather than any broader conception of the civic sphere, our choice of this site here might seem questionable. Yet just as the stridently nationalist rhetoric of the young Falangists (discussed in chapter 6) proved to be an interesting starting point for exploring political identities and actions online, so too the interaction between the economic and social achievements of individuals and communities can be seen as a fruitful avenue for exploring civic identities.

According to information on the site, TANS works to achieve several interrelated goals: to "promote the talents of young Moroccans," to "contribute to a positive public image of young Moroccans and counterbalance the negative publicity," to "enable talented young people to form a network and develop themselves by meeting each other in an informal way and exchange of knowledge," and to "be an intermediary and professional agency in Dutch society." To achieve these goals, according to its "About Us" page, TANS organizes "at least six debates, gatherings and projects per year," as well as maintaining its website (figure 7.6). There is no information available about the actual users of the site, and TANS is hardly mentioned in the mainstream media, although our focus group research suggests that it is widely known among Moroccan youth, especially those who are highly educated. The organization is regularly mentioned on other online discussion platforms targeting the Moroccan community and on general social networking sites. In these contexts, it is generally depicted as a positive initiative by successful and entrepreneurial youth, although the organization has also developed a reputation for elitism. Related to this, the networking activities of TANS are well known as good opportunities to engage not only in business enterprise but also for romantic exploration and potential partnership.

The TANS site has nine main sections: a home page featuring news items and items on TANS's agenda, alongside job advertisements (for instance, for the police force and commercial consultancy agencies); a news page, which displays activities organized, supported, or promoted by TANS; an agenda page, which announces events organized by TANS or its partners; a vacancies page, with a list of hyperlinks to job and trainee vacancies outside the TANS organization; a TANS board page, featuring the names of the members of the board with hyperlinks to short biographies; an "About Us" page; a policy page; a volunteering page; and a contact page. Emphasizing the site's "professional" approach and design, the content appears in the same central frame on each page, which can be reached through a vertical menu bar in the upper left frame. At the time of our research, there were some inconsistencies and partly completed aspects—suggesting that a beta version had been rather hastily uploaded—although some aspects of the design, such as rotating high-quality images, were quite technically advanced. It is possible to become a member of TANS and to gain access to an intranet, but this is not announced directly on the main pages and becomes apparent only when one attempts to log in.

The site uses quite formal language to state that its existence and activities are motivated by the problems faced by the Moroccan ethnic minority in the Netherlands (Castles 2000; Entzinger 2006). It claims that the talents of young Moroccans remain underexploited, implicitly referring to low levels of education and employment among Moroccan youth, and that the Moroccan community in the Netherlands has a negative reputation among the native Dutch. It refers briefly to negative press coverage and the growing electoral popularity of anti-immigration political leaders. Especially since September 11, 2001, the Dutch media and politicians have paid an unprecedented amount of attention to the "threat of radicalism" and antisocial behavior among (young) Muslims and, particularly, Moroccans—although for the latter, this attention is generally perceived as a manifestation of racism or Islamophobia (Aarts and Hirzalla 2005; Hajer and Uitermark 2008). On its website, TANS mentions these issues only briefly and does not elaborate on them. Instead, it chooses to emphasize the "positive elements" of the Moroccan community and particularly the "young talent" in fields such as education, employment, the arts, and culture: this talent, it argues, "is developing steadily, but could still use some help, particularly when a public platform is required."

In line with its effort to transcend or dispel negative stereotypes about young Dutch Moroccans, the site chooses to use Dutch as its primary language of communication. The images on the website—several of young, corporately dressed women who seem to be employed in offices—also implicitly attempt to counterbalance stereotypes of submissive Moroccan housewives and to dispel ideas about patriarchal gender relations in this community (see figure 7.6).

Figure 7.6
TANS header, April 2008

Although the TANS website does not elaborate on the historical and social context of its ideology of self-improvement and community advancement, this ideology is quite specific. Rather than seeking to promote a particular version of Moroccan culture, of Islam, or indeed of civic participation among (young) Moroccans, its approach seems to be based on what the site proclaims as "a positive belief in your own power to achieve things." Its activities purport to be aimed at the achievement of three interrelated goals: self-empowerment, social community building, and a positive public image of Moroccans. Thus, in addition to its offline networking events and employment fairs, it offers the "TANS Masterclass," which is aimed at boosting Moroccan students' skills through training programs and traineeships, with the aim of achieving a successful professional career. Compared with these offline activities, TANS has a limited focus online. The website has no discussion forum and no other user upload options, although it does have an intranet and invites visitors to join TANS's account on the popular Dutch social network Hyves.

As an entrepreneurial ethnic minority organization, TANS thus provides a very different approach to civic participation—and a very different use of the Web—when compared with that of Roma.Hu or Muslim Youth, for example. Its civic aims are apparent, but they are defined in self-consciously morale-boosting and individualistic terms—in effect, as a matter of "CV building." To this extent, its politics deliberately remain implicit, although with the exception of Muslim Youth, this is a quality it appears to share with the other sites we have discussed here.

The Politics and Pedagogies of Online Identities

Many academic and popular commentators have celebrated the potential of the Internet as a medium for the construction, representation, and expression of identities. While some early work in the field (e.g., Turkle 1995) explored the possibilities of online interaction as a space for play and experimentation with identity, others (e.g., Abdelhady 2006; Bernal 2006) have seen it as a means through which members of marginalized social groups can build connections and thereby develop a powerful sense of collective identification. Our findings here are somewhat less glamorous and more ambivalent. In exploring the potential of the Web as a means of building civic identities, we deliberately set out to compare some quite contrasting groups, several of which might not be seen as correct or progressive in terms of current identity politics. The comparison between our five case studies certainly reveals some of the possibilities of the Internet as a means of developing civic identities, but also some of the limitations and dilemmas that are entailed.

The ways in which the sites in this chapter appear to conceptualize and use the social and technological possibilities of the Internet are very heterogeneous. While some use it to provide opportunities for participation—to enable users to learn, interact, and contribute to debate—others do so simply to promote the activities and the cause of the organization itself. In some instances, however, our analysis revealed contradictions and fault lines between intention and actualization, or between the organization's stated aims and the actual outcomes of the site itself. These contradictions may also relate to wider contradictions between the self-representation of the particular social, ethnic, or religious group and the historical positioning of that group within the wider offline context.

In the case of Roma.Hu, for example, it was the overtly interactive components, such as forums and message boards, that made this site stand out on the Hungarian civic web, alongside another Roma site, Zhoriben (Szakacs and Bognar 2010). These user-generated sections contained heated political debates, especially if we define "political" in its broader sense to mean more than party politics and government. However, with a few exceptions, the producer-generated content conspicuously lacked anything that could have been viewed as other than cultural. This approach is reminiscent of that taken by most programs on Hungarian public television and radio, where "minority" issues tend to mean people singing or dancing in "exotic" clothes—a safe version of multiculturalism where difference is encouraged as long as it means different food or different music, but not when it concerns more substantial issues such as rights and social justice. By contrast, the approach of Muslim Youth, while not partisan or censorious, seems less inclined to fight shy of overtly political issues, even while it remains primarily defined by a cultural-religious frame. However, as we have implied, a cultural framing of difference may serve as a kind of defense, or perhaps even as a cover; and it may be that the risks entailed for the producers of a minority site in being overtly political may currently be greater in Hungary than they are in the UK.

Our analysis suggests that, contrary to technologically determinist views, the apparently open architecture of the Internet does not necessarily or inevitably result in democratic and anti-authoritarian practices. On the contrary, the characteristics of these sites seem to be much more contingent on the politics and pedagogy of the organizations running them and on the inclinations of their users than on the affordances or possibilities of the medium and the available tools. Thus—though for totally different reasons and in response to different historical cues—sites such as Opus Dei and Roma.Hu work to establish the cohesiveness of the particular group they represent (or claim to represent). In some instances, the sense of homogeneity that is necessary for the representation of a highly distinctive group identity is achieved by providing little space for debate outside the parameters defined by the site's producers. Thus, to different degrees and in different ways, all the sites we have examined here practice forms of censorship, although again, the reasons why a site about a persecuted ethnic minority might need to control content that is posted, and why a powerful, global, conservative Catholic organization might do the same thing, are entirely different. In other instances, as with Racó Català and Muslim Youth, it would seem that such censorship or control is less necessary because the community itself becomes self-policing, although this can never be a wholly failsafe possibility.

Nor do the combinations of good intentions, interactive technological tools, and democratic ideals necessarily mean that sites can generate vibrant democratic and civic debate. Racó Català, for instance, calls for informed and active citizens, and points to ways in which users might become so—at least rhetorically. However, arguments that challenge or compete with regional nationalist views are simply not evident in its fairly well-used forums. All the contributors seem to think in the same way or to write as if they do, and dissenters presumably go elsewhere. The producers of the site perceive themselves as a political and social minority within an unsympathetic country, and dream of having their own independent nation state defined more or less by language. This sense of suppression or injustice generates a good deal of online (and offline) activity, but such content is, apparently, unlikely to interest or appeal to people who do not share these views, and so the site remains ideologically homogenous. It is less clear whether all the users are satisfied by this approach or might welcome a more diverse set of views. Of course, it would always be possible to look elsewhere for opposing views, yet from a pedagogical standpoint, having a spectrum of opinions about a specific issue in dialogue on the same site might well prove to be a more effective means of inducting young people into civic and political debate.

In many of these respects, Muslim Youth appears to be the significant exception. Of the sites considered here, it is the only one to positively emphasize divergence and diversity *within* the group, and it is also the only one that is democratically run by young people themselves. Ideologically, its producers are very aware of political Islam, on the one hand, and of the anti-Islamic politics playing out in the wider UK society on the other. It tries to emphasize the range of Muslim positions and identities, and to connect the (relatively) small community of Muslim young people in the UK to the larger, sometimes more confident and ascendant communities of Muslims outside Europe. Yet at the same time, as is the case with TANS and Roma.Hu, it also conveys a strong sense of representing an ethnic and religious minority in a hostile environment, and as such it is bound to have policies that prevent the posting of racist or inflammatory content. Nevertheless, as with Roma.Hu, content monitoring or self-censorship should not necessarily be seen as alienating for users or as threatening to free speech: indeed, in many circumstances, it might prove necessary to ensure "civilized" democratic debate. In our view, this is a different matter from ensuring that only similar opinions are expressed or represented, as is the case with Opus Dei, or of making a particular style of language or literacy a benchmark for access, as is the case with AKP Youth (discussed in chapter 6).

Ultimately, the differences between these sites need to be understood in relation to their broader social, historical, and political context. For example, the strategy of TANS may be understood as a particular response to the history of Moroccan migrant labor in the Netherlands. The site and its parent organization have an aspirational and integrationist mission, with a clearly defined class character—and this also suggests a particular pedagogical relationship to the young Moroccans who might use it, for example through its messages about positive self-empowerment. In a manner that is perhaps intended to appeal to a politically liberal but economically upwardly mobile audience, it places the onus for generating social change on the shoulders of young Moroccans themselves. Likewise, the particular strategy of Opus Dei should be understood in relation to the changing position of the Catholic Church vis-à-vis the state in modern Spain and the increasing religious diversity and secularization of the broader society (Heubel 1977). The content and the links on its site appear to exist only to reinforce the religious and moral authority of Opus Dei and to maintain its current following. To admit the possibility of debate (let alone to invite it) would serve little purpose and would almost certainly prove counterproductive for a group that regards itself, rightly or wrongly, as an embattled minority. In contrast to the rhetoric of democratic interactivity propounded by some Internet enthusiasts, this website, like many of the others we have described, very much retains the gatekeeper role that is characteristic of traditional media.

Despite their widely differing audience demographics, Muslim Youth and Racó Català are probably the most "activist" sites we have considered here, and as such they bear comparison with sites like LMV, discussed in the previous chapter. However, the fact that even at their most open, both sites rely on a preexisting cultural, religious, or linguistic identity as a defining criterion for group membership and identification makes them quite different. Of the two, Muslim Youth seems the most interactive in terms of generating debate among its users, and this is in no small measure a result of the bottom-up pedagogy developed (both online and offline) by the site's producers. By contrast, Racó Català's invitations to discussion are undermined by its singular adherence to a clearly delineated regional identity formed in reaction to Spanish nationalism, rather than in solidarity with the concerns of a wider group of citizens, as in the case of V De Vivienda (discussed in chapter 6), for example. By contrast, Roma.Hu made extensive use of Web 2.0 technology and seemed to reflect a highly optimistic view of the networking possibilities of the Internet, although this optimism would seem at least premature in light of its subsequent demise (and that of another Roma social network, Zhoriben).

The choice of language on these sites might also be seen to reflect their different stances toward the building of civic identities. While many national civic organizations merely fail or forget to have options for minority languages, these kinds of identity-based websites are bound to make deliberate choices regarding the use of minority or majority languages, choices that may reflect either a sense of integration with a national or international community or a desire to emphasize communal belonging. For example, Roma.Hu used Lovari as far as possible (although other languages were allowed once past the initial stages), and Racó Català is only in Catalan; while TANS uses Dutch, signaling its wish to throw off a separatist identity. Meanwhile, Muslim Youth uses English as a lingua franca, although there are sometimes words and phrases from Arabic, Urdu, or other South Asian languages, indicating that some users are bi- or multilingual. As this implies, the choice of language is a clear indication of political and cultural affiliation, as well as a means of defining boundaries and barriers to communication with potential outsiders.

Finally, it should be emphasized that, for all of these organizations, the interconnection between on- and offline activities is critically important. In different ways, the "debates, gatherings and projects" organized by TANS, the telephone advice and support service of Muslim Youth, and the offline religious practices of Opus Dei all exemplify this connection with offline activites. The websites of these organizations do not stand alone. Indeed, any simple distinction between online and offline soon begins to fall apart once we consider the pedagogical and political strategies of these organizations and their relationships with the communities they claim to represent.

Our case studies in this chapter have shown that the Internet does have considerable potential for building civic identities among minority communities, both for combating discrimination and for bolstering positive group identities. However, they have also shown that the Internet is by no means an inherently egalitarian, democratic space, let alone that this networked structure enables it to redress imbalances of power at a national or global level. The technology does not inevitably produce a particular set of pedagogical or political relationships. We can only understand it in relation to the motivations of its users and the broader social, cultural, and historical circumstances that frame and define them.

8 Conclusion

The research we have reported here began from a seemingly straightforward question: how can the Internet be used to promote civic participation among young people? In this concluding chapter we summarize our key findings on this question, looking across the range of data and the different types of investigation we have presented. However, we also seek to challenge the terms in which the question has been posed, and point to the need to move beyond it.

From Alienation to Empowerment?

Our research supports the view that young people are largely alienated from, or at least feel dissatisfied with, traditional institutional forms of politics. This was apparent both from the responses to our survey and from our focus groups. Most respondents across all our national samples said they saw politicians as corrupt, boring, or hard to understand, mainly working for their own interests, and usually far removed from the everyday needs of common citizens. A large proportion of them felt that things needed to change—and in our focus groups they spoke, often at length, about issues such as inequalities, corruption, lack of housing and job opportunities, high prices, religious, ethnic, or regional discrimination, police harassment of civil protest, and government censorship of the media.

In the context of a cross-national study, we inevitably identified issues that were particularly acute, or that took on different forms, at particular historical moments in different countries. For example, as we have suggested, the sphere of politics is seen as especially dirty and corrupt in both Hungary and Slovenia, and therefore civic organizations often strive to appear detached from politics. This means, ironically perhaps, that voting is not overtly encouraged by youth civic sites in these countries and that even party sites attempt to steer clear of connections with politics. The situation is very different in, for example, the Netherlands, where the existence of a multiparty system makes political choice an especially complex process and online voter advice applications are popular. As this implies, the salience of politics or of particular political issues depends very much on the historical trajectories of particular political systems.

Likewise, the notion of European citizenship and belonging (Tuzzi, Padovani, and Nesti 2007) is viewed in hugely different ways by young people in, for instance, Turkey, Slovenia, and the UK; and civic websites addressing "European" youth issues are accordingly more or less appealing. In the UK, our focus groups suggest that European identity is not at all valued or highly developed except among a small minority of politically left-wing or liberal youth, who see it as preferable to conservative notions of "Britishness." By contrast, in Slovenia we found some degree of positive feeling toward the idea of European citizenship among a wider range of youth. Yet with notable exceptions, most of the young people in our research displayed either a lack of knowledge about European politics or a deep distrust of it. This distrust sometimes bordered on xenophobia and was reflected in the anti-European rhetoric on ethnic nationalist websites. While some limited sense of motivation toward and affiliation with traditional politics was apparent at the national level and in relation to international struggles, and was even clearer at a local or regional level, it was barely visible when participants discussed Europe.

Yet while these young people were generally critical of traditional politics, they were by no means apathetic. Our survey found high levels of interest in some political and more broadly civic issues, and a fair amount of active participation. In our focus groups, we encountered many young people who felt that involvement in social movements (both democratic and antidemocratic), civic groups, volunteering, or protests had increased their confidence and belief in social activism. The experience of solidarity with others, regardless of age, had contributed to a belief in their responsibility as citizens and in the need for civic action, regardless of the outcome.

Nevertheless, these young people generally felt that they themselves were unable to change the things about their societies they found most problematic. This perceived lack of efficacy was especially related to their general feelings about the unresponsiveness, untrustworthiness, and distance of politicians. However, it also derived from their actual experiences of having participated (for example, on schools councils, by signing e-petitions, or in demonstrations) and of not having been listened to or not managing to change anything. In some instances, it also related to fears about how active participation or political critique might affect them personally and make them targets of the state, the police, or aggressive citizens with opposing views.

For many of the civic web producers whom we interviewed, this perceived lack of efficacy was the central problem. Web producers frequently employed the rhetoric of "youth empowerment" and "youth voice." Such a discourse typically sees young people as lacking a voice, or at least as lacking the skills to make their voices heard. When they are given a voice online, it is argued, they will be empowered to express their own concerns in a safe environment, and this sense of empowerment can then be transferred offline to provide them with greater control of their own lives. While some website producers saw greater efficacy offline as a more or less spontaneous consequence of gaining access to online technology, many working in more activist organizations felt there should be more opportunities and training for young people to help them develop the skills necessary to make their voices heard in the public sphere.

Ironically, however, many of the civic website producers were aware that their users tended to be mostly youth who were already engaged or skilled in civic participation. The challenge for all concerned was to find ways of reaching hard to reach and disadvantaged young people, those most at risk of exclusion from civil society and politics. The Internet has thus far not been found to be a particularly good means of doing this, and traditional offline approaches such as outreach on the streets or through youth workers and local youth groups are still the main avenues for contacting economically and socially disadvantaged young people.

These perceptions are reinforced by the findings of our research with young people. We found that social factors such as class, gender, ethnicity, age, and religion significantly affected the ways in which young people approached and used the Internet. In our survey, the interest in civic websites was stronger among older respondents (nineteen- to twenty-five-year-olds rather than fifteen- to eighteen-year-olds), those not living with their parents, those who identified as religious, and girls and young women. Interest in traditional political websites appeared to be stronger among older respondents and those from higher socioeconomic groups. This finding contradicts some commonly held perceptions, such as that girls and young women are less motivated to participate in civic and political activity than boys and young men. However, the strongest factor in relation to Internet use and civic participation across all the countries we studied was social class. There was evidence of a digital divide along socioeconomic lines, both in the quality and extent of access to technology and in the types of civic engagement and political participation.

The Internet emerged in our study as an important mobilization tool for young people who are already engaged in civic or political activities offline. Both our focus groups and our analysis of websites themselves suggest that the Internet is often a major hub for young people who are active in global or local political, religious, or identity-based groups. This was evident in the case of groups as diverse as political parties' youth organizations, activist networks, and communities of civic interest. The Internet also forms an important resource for minorities—political, sexual, ethnic, regional, or religious—and, in some notable instances, seems to offer young people from such communities a space to enact diverse identities, to question notions of tradition, to discuss the meaning of culture and citizenship, or to debate methods of participation and protest.

However, it is important not to overstate the case. The respondents to our survey were primarily interested in websites on entertainment and lifestyle issues, and while a significant minority reported having visited civic or political sites on occasion, only a small proportion reported doing so on a regular basis. This does not necessarily mean that more have not participated in civic discussions online; as we have suggested, such discussions (among people of all ages) may also be found in the forums of entertainment and social networking sites of various kinds. Furthermore, not all young people who are civically active offline participate in such discussions online, and the ones who do participate most often may do so sporadically. Yet ultimately, it seems that the Internet in itself is unlikely to play a major role in promoting civic and political participation among young people who are not already so engaged.

Using the Internet

The Internet is regarded by almost all civic and political organizations as an inexpensive and effective method of disseminating information and making contact with young people. However, our research emphasizes that this is by no means always the case. Several of the producers whom we interviewed pointed out that for a site, blog, or network to be known and used, considerable thought had to be given to promotion and publicity. Most civic website producers have neither the time nor the money to publicize their sites adequately, and hence the core of users remains relatively small, even where social media have been enlisted as tools of promotion. The majority of the websites we analyzed functioned with a combination of one or two part-time paid employees and several volunteers, and staff turnover was often high. In many cases, lack of funding also prevented the sites from being regularly updated or maintained. As with "leaderless" Facebook groups and causes, the stagnation or attrition rate of civic sites is also fairly high.

Among the hundreds of sites we surveyed, both in 2007–2008 and again in 2011–2012, interactive possibilities, especially the opportunity for young people to post their own content, were rare. Despite the availability of more or less interactive applications such as blogs, wikis, message boards, forums, video uploading, podcasts, RSS feeds, and links to Facebook pages and Twitter feeds, most civic sites aimed at young people still take the form of static pages dominated by written text and a few visual images. While in some cases we are convinced the static nature of such sites reflects funding constraints, or perhaps a lack of awareness of the technological potential, the underlying rationale is more complex.

While some of the bodies, including local and national governments, that fund civic websites appear to think that elaborate and more expensive sites are always and automatically "better" than their simpler counterparts, our interviews with producers and young people suggested this was not necessarily the case. Offering interactive facilities did not automatically mean that young people participated. We found several instances of websites that had forums, user content upload facilities, and message boards on general themes that were underutilized or simply full of spam. Claims about the Internet being a completely safe and equal space for participation were also challenged repeatedly by both producers and users of civic websites. Several producers were aware that dealing with controversial issues (especially those having to do with discrimination and social justice) could provoke strong negative responses from some members of the public. Some young people in our focus groups described being "attacked" online, a phenomenon that was particularly apparent on sites concerned with sexuality. Where immigrants or ethnic minority groups have established civic organizations online to challenge prejudice, many of them are subjected to racist critique and flaming, often by organized right-wing groups. In this situation, we found that many organizations had deliberately chosen to prevent such attacks and disruptions by having closed membership or by moderating and censoring posts from users.

As these findings imply, forums, networks, user-generated content, and other interactive applications have to be carefully explained, encouraged, motivated, and managed. Young people are sometimes just as intimidated by what they view as a "requirement" to contribute original content as they are disappointed by the lack of possibilities for commenting or interacting online. Specialized jargon should be avoided or explained. The skills for using applications such as RSS feeds, videocasts, or podcasts have to be taught rather than taken for granted. This requires planning, time, and money for personnel that most youth civic organizations surveyed simply do not have. As a result, several of the producers we interviewed felt it was better to provide a clear, helpful, but static site with the possibility for emailing the organization than to offer potentially off-putting, superficial, or even damaging opportunities for "interaction."

While most producers still saw the importance of promoting their organization or activities through traditional media channels (TV, newspapers, radio), a sizable minority viewed the Internet as a challenge to the gatekeeping of older media, and said their users came to their sites for an alternative and more open perspective. However, both our research with young people and our analysis of the sites themselves suggest that many civic websites still maintain a strong gatekeeping function. Although the reasons for this may relate to safeguarding users or to quality control, the site producers may also be motivated by the desire to maintain a consistent ideological position and to avoid the distractions of dealing with dissent or debate.

Our research therefore suggests that considerable thought must go into how the producers or funders of civic websites actually spend their money. Large amounts of funding are sometimes allocated to website design—and especially to flashy interactive features—without a clear conception of their function. Although such features might conceivably make the organization look good or cutting edge, a large and complex site is not necessarily better for users. As some of the young people and some of our web producers suggested, it is important that sites be "fit for purpose." This means looking beyond the latest gimmicks and beyond some politically correct sense that an organization lives or dies by its website or its social media presence.

The advent of commercial Web 2.0 platforms such as YouTube and Facebook does not fundamentally alter this situation: the cost and the institutional politics of running civic or political campaigns online, or encouraging people to engage with causes or parties or particular ideological standpoints, do not disappear. Indeed, the roles of producers may become more complex. Social networking tools like Facebook and Twitter are increasingly utilized by civic and political actors to kick-start, maintain, or broaden their campaigns, but these same strategies are also used by commercial actors to draw users to particular forms of consumption or behavior. These are ultimately commercial platforms, and one of the main ways in which they make money is by gathering and selling data about their users.

Furthermore, even in these situations there is still a requirement for labor: someone has to do the work, even if much of it is invisible. As such, many of the questions about ideology and pedagogy, ethos and access, control, authority, skills, and remuneration that we have raised here are equally applicable to this "new" set of tools. The opportunity, time, skills, and confidence to post civic content, the positioning of ideologues and activists in groups or networks, the communication of group ideals and demands, the connections between online and offline actions, and the need to engage young people from different sections of society all remain just as significant in the age of social media as they were in the age of print.

Motivating Civic and Political Participation

During our research, we did find a few cases in which attractive website design or the latest interactive features seemed to be motivating civic engagement and participation in themselves. However, these cases were the exception rather than the rule. This finding counters a familiar and entrenched view that it is only by amusing and entertaining young people (on the Internet as well as elsewhere) that one can attract their attention and encourage them to become engaged in civic initiatives. On the contrary, our research strongly suggests that the most lasting forms of civic and political engagement focus predominantly on issues of immediate proximity for the participants: individual and group identities, a sense of discrimination or injustice, and people's current life situations are key. Civic and political interests are often related to having family members, relatives, or friends who are interested in the same issues and concerns: there is a strong intergenerational dimension here that is often ignored in grand claims about the "digital generation." In most of our focus groups, when young people were involved in civic activities that were related to their immediate contexts (both on- and offline), they also felt more confident in their capacity to bring about change or to contribute to critical debate.

While many of these issues could be understood as having a bearing on social equality, justice, and democracy, we are wary of construing them all in this normative way. Although many of the changes sought were egalitarian and anti-authoritarian, some were predicated on the creation of a more stratified, even totalitarian form of governance and on the social marginalization of women and sexual and ethnic minorities. Alongside its democratic possibilities, the Internet has proved to be a powerful vehicle for the dissemination of hate speech and just as useful for the extreme right as for those with democratic civic or political aims.

Despite the affordances of the Internet, most of the civic and political participation, especially sustained participation, described in our research began and ended offline, in local communities or communities of interest and identity. Of course, some civic sites and social network groups are set up as a short-term solution to a problem rather than being integrated into other activities, for instance to prevent the demolition of a skate park or to mobilize opposition to funding cuts. Such sites and social network pages may be intensively used for comparatively short periods of time. By contrast, sites formed by specialist groups (based on religious, cultural, or subcultural identity or locality), aimed at a very specific audience among young people and produced by members of that specific group, tend to support a stronger sense of belonging and community and are more likely to be used over the longer term.

A sense of efficacy is also critical in building the audiences and participants of youth civic and political websites and campaigns. In a number of cases, local civic achievements, the experience of being active together and of group solidarity, or the feeling of having organized an event or campaign and of having received some positive feedback from peers or older adults seemed to generate a sense of efficacy that encouraged and motivated further participation, whether online or offline. On the other hand, such experiences of participation could also have negative consequences: several of the young people in our focus groups had experienced governments' failure to respond, for example when they demonstrated in large numbers against university tuition fee hikes or for better housing provision, or against the war in Iraq. Yet while such seemingly unsuccessful protests might sap the motivation to participate, for some the resulting anger and sense of injustice led to further participation—although this frustration could also result in violence and other forms of antisocial or malicious behavior.

The notion that online civic action and offline civic action occur in entirely separate realms and are pursued by separate participants is clearly untenable. A majority of the website producers whom we interviewed did not see the Internet as a replacement for offline civic and political actions but as a complement to them. For many, participation still began and ended offline, with the Internet sustaining and contributing to offline activism. Many of the producers and almost all the young people we interviewed were at pains to connect online and offline politics and civic action explicitly. This might suggest they were never quite certain about the value or effectiveness of actions that took place solely online. However, many also explicitly extolled the usefulness of civic blogging, online mobilization about social issues, e-petitions, and the provision of political information online. Nevertheless, without a live issue or an offline social and political context for young people to engage with, even the best-designed and well-funded online spaces are likely to remain underutilized.

As we have demonstrated, many of the official governmental sites aimed at young people, like those of many NGOs, seem to rest on seriously limited assumptions about what responsible, civically minded young people *should* be doing. There are implicit—and sometimes explicit—rules about good behavior, implicit constructions of identity, and a favoring of certain kinds of "serious" debate that are embedded in the design of sites, in how young people are addressed, in the kinds of (limited) participation that are invited, and in the ways participation is moderated (Banaji 2011; Miegel and Olsson 2010b). Such practices operate to produce young people as "good little citizens" who will not make trouble but will continue to play the game in particular, and sometimes highly paternalistic, adult terms. In the process, certain kinds of activity may fail to be recognized as civic or as in any way valuable, and certain young people's modes of expression may be delegitimized, ignored, or marginalized. In these cases, we suggest, the Internet actually reinforces particular forms of exclusion. It becomes a forum where young people are invited to participate, but only if they follow the rules and behave according to limited norms of respectability and good manners.

From young people's perspectives, civic participation is most successful when it is *both* peer-to-peer *and* enables opportunities for reciprocal engagement with those in power. Most youth civic organizations offer one or the other, and the engagement with politicians is most often not reciprocal. This can be seen as a disincentive for young people to engage with formal politics online. As one young woman in our focus groups put it, "Why should we speak if no one is listening?" Young people are repeatedly encouraged to have their say, but there is not much evidence that anyone is listening to them, or, if they are, that they are actually doing anything in response. Such superficial forms of participation or consultation may quite justifiably result in an increased level of critical disenchantment, although the young people in our focus groups showed less cynicism than might be warranted under the circumstances.

Nevertheless, there clearly are innovative and exciting forms of political and civic participation taking place online. There is evidence that some civic websites and networks for young people are tapping into newer forms of civic and political activity. This is perhaps most apparent in the case of so-called ethical consumption, which plays on the Internet's qualities as a medium of shopping and marketing par excellence. It is also evident in the circulation of Wikileaks clone sites and political messages through social networking sites, and in the quick mobilization of support for time-limited causes through social media. Questions remain, however, about whether and how such activities are linked to traditional institutional or more activist forms of political participation.

Likewise, we found that the Internet—and YouTube in particular—was being used by groups of young people as a crucial supplement to mainstream media and a means of accessing perspectives and information not widely available in the traditional press or broadcasting. Again, there is a question of how easier access to information relates to increased civic participation, although the importance of having a freer flow of information and a less rigid hierarchy in terms of who can express and broadcast political ideas online should not be downplayed. In countries where the authorities have begun to censor and regulate the online sphere, such as Turkey and recently the UK, the loss of this freedom highlights its importance still further.

We also found good evidence that the Internet enables some young people to take on and refine their role as "monitorial citizens," for instance by tracking elections; keeping abreast of privacy issues; discussing, photographing, and publicizing police behavior; uploading videos about controversial events; debating civil liberties; and getting behind the scenes in conflict situations. In special cases such as file sharing and the free downloading of music or the cloning of protest sites targeted by the state, the Internet itself becomes the focus of and reason for civic action, and it is of particular interest that the young people who take part in such civic actions are not always drawn from those already active in civic or political campaigns offline.

Signing online petitions or forwarding letters to big corporations—termed "one-click activism" by one producer and "feel-good activism" by another—are thus by no means the be-all and end-all of the actions young people are motivated to do online. The information gathering necessary to make up one's mind about a particular cause or the meeting up, discussion, and protest offline can be supported and enhanced rather than replaced by the online actions offered through polls or in forums. In this sense, online civic engagement, however outwardly limited, should not be regarded as a substitute for offline engagement but as a potentially useful complement to it.

Deconstructing the Question

We would like to conclude by taking a step back from the findings of our research and asking some more critical and reflective questions about how the research question was crafted in the first place. Our approach adopted a "social constructionist" perspective, which has been widely used in the analysis of social problems (e.g., Best 2008). We wanted to interrogate the ways in which this particular problem of apparently spiraling youth disengagement from civic and political life has been defined, not least because the definition of a problem also tends to determine the kinds of solutions that can be offered. There are several basic questions that might be raised in connection with our topic:

1. Why does this debate seem to focus on young people specifically? As we have noted, there are some reasons for this attention, but an apparent decline in civic participation is also seen among adults. The focus on young people may well rest on implicit assumptions about young people—for instance, about their relationships with technology—that are in need of critical exploration. There may also be a risk of reproducing some of the time-honored ways in which older generations talk about younger ones, such as the tendency to complain or, alternatively, to fantasize about the younger generation, or to encourage young people to do more worthy and constructive things with their time.

2. What is this civic or political sphere in which young people are seen to be failing to participate? Our initial review of the research in this area suggested that these terms are often poorly defined, or used in inconsistent ways. As we have noted, the term "civic" often seems to imply a kind of normativity. In discussions of civic engagement or participation, commentators often have recourse to some notion of the common good (e.g., Montgomery, Gottlieb-Robles, and Larson 2004), but it is far from clear who defines the common good. Right-wing extremists, for example, frequently claim that their arguments are in support of the common good—and even for the good of the immigrants whom they sometimes seek to "repatriate."

3. Why should young people participate, and what counts as participation? It appears to be assumed on all sides of the debate that participation is a good thing, yet this begs the question of whether there might ever be undesirable forms of participation, or whether participation might be merely a superficial substitute for—or indeed a distraction from—other forms of civic or political action. It also ignores that possibility that in some cases, nonparticipation might be entirely logical, and perhaps even the most beneficial response. Again, there is a recurring assumption that participation will somehow necessarily operate in the interests of democracy, although in our view, this assumption is far from warranted.

4. Finally, why are we looking to the Internet for the solution? Again, there is a risk here of making problematic assumptions about technology, and particularly about the relationships between technology and social change—and as we have implied, the specter of technological determinism is never far away. To focus on the Internet might appear to presume that the problem has fundamentally to do with the medium or style of communication: the problem is not the political system but the ways in which politics is communicated. While this tack might be advantageous for scholars of communication, it could be seen to assume that everything is basically fine with democracy and that the problem can be solved through some kind of communication fix.

This stance might in turn distract attention from the ways in which some democratically elected governments in recent years have actively sought to undermine opportunities for civic and political participation, for example through curbing trade unions or restricting citizens' right to protest in public places. Ultimately, it may well be in the interest of governments to have a disengaged, nonparticipating citizenry.

We could pursue this line of questioning further by questioning the kinds of discourse or rhetoric that are in play here. Debates in this field often invoke some rather ill-defined or contested terms. Aside from "participation," "civic," and "political," several terms recur without ever being adequately defined, among them "democracy," "empowerment," "engagement," and "community." Such discourses often entail binaries. For example, recurring distinctions are raised between old and new—old and new media, old and new politics, old and new styles of communication, older and younger generations—that may be less than helpful. Such distinctions are also frequently entailed in historical narratives, stories of change (and most frequently of decline), in which the grounds for comparison between past and present may be quite elusive.

We might ask similarly challenging questions about the ideals or norms that are implicitly being offered in the texts, which use terminology such as "engagement," "democracy," and "voice." For example, what image is being constructed of what young people are now, and should be in the future? What image are we given of democracy, of the political system, or of citizenship, now and in some possible future when everything will (once more) be all right? Several of the key ideas in these debates—for example, notions of social capital or the public sphere—explicitly embody norms or ideals that are seen to have somehow disappeared or been lost, and are now in need of recovery. Indeed, it could be argued that the term "civic" is itself implicitly normative in this way.

We do not suggest that norms or ideals are unnecessary. Rather, we wish to point out the risk of constructing ideals that have never and will never correspond to the realities of most people's lives. "Democracy" is a prime example in this respect: it is often invoked in idealized terms in academic and policy debates rather than in relation to actually existing manifestations. Vague ideals may command assent, but such assent is often merely dutiful and superficial and may be disingenuous. Indeed, the worthy and normative—and ultimately very bland—assumptions about civic virtue that characterize so many attempts to engage young people may also make it easier for far-right and fundamentalist groups to pose as challengers to the status quo, and as exciting political alternatives.

Civic participation comes in many forms and happens in many ways. Some of the forms of participation that young people engage in are simply not recognized by adults, while others are positively denigrated or else seen as threatening. Smashing up police vehicles as a response to being harassed or "kettled" on a demonstration, spray painting government buildings with political graffiti, or hacking into secret service websites and posting incriminating content online are all routinely described by some commentators as merely destructive vandalism, while others would regard them as highly "civic" in intent (Hands 2011). And so our study has cast up another question: can civic participation be "antisocial" in some circumstances, and if so, which? Or must it necessarily respect the rights of law, privacy, and property ownership even when such rights are being ignored by those in power?

Our final deconstructive move here is to contextualize this debate, historically and geographically. Why are we having this debate *now*? It is not too far-fetched to point out that the debate has arisen at a particular point in the political evolution of modern societies where mainstream political parties have to a large extent converged, where many politicians have ceded much of their power to the "invisible hand" of the market, and where the nation-state is subsidiary to the operations of globalized capitalism. Second, why are we having this debate *here*? On the face of it, this would appear to be very much a European or Western debate. In fact, much of the research literature derives from the US, and some of it at least reflects the very particular characteristics of that context, yet even when we look across Europe (let alone beyond it), it is clearly difficult to translate key concepts or questions. The assumed problem of young people's disconnection from the civic sphere, the ways in which it is framed, and the rubrics used to characterize it reflect quite specific historical or cultural circumstances. This social construction of the problem might well serve particular interests and cause potential or actual damage to those who are involved, or who are spoken about.

Reconstructing the Question

Our project was originally based on a notion of the Web as a collection of more or less discrete sites that were put up largely by organizations, often with a considerable amount of money behind them. In most instances, such organizations use their sites as a means of transmitting a body of content and simultaneously promoting or advertising offline activities, largely according to an established mass media model. In 2012, this model is still the dominant mode for producer-led youth civic participation online. Yet as our work proceeded, it became apparent that different types and degrees of civic participation are also occurring on social networking and file-sharing sites, as well as through a range of other kinds of social software and entertainment forums such as online games and sport fandoms. Toward the latter half of our project we ventured into the endlessly proliferating world of new social media mentioned by young participants in our study—YouTube (Banaji 2013) and Facebook groups or memes in particular—only to be confronted by the same set of questions we set out with.

Indeed, attempting to trace civic participation in these new social media poses these questions in an even more acute form. Where and how might we look for civic activity on Facebook or YouTube, for example? How would we recognize it as such? And how might we assess the specific contribution of these media to promoting civic engagement or participation? These questions might seem to point to an ongoing fragmentation or dispersal of the civic sphere, and perhaps especially of the online civic sphere. However, we do not believe that such a conclusion is yet warranted. The large majority of the Web 1.0 sites that we studied in our research either continue to exist or have been replaced by others that are essentially similar. Likewise, many of the forms of participation we considered can be accommodated within relatively conventional notions of civic participation—which, despite their limitations, also continue to be relevant. The differences between Web 1.0 and Web 2.0 have, in our view, been massively overstated in this respect.

Nevertheless, studying these new phenomena has led us to restate our more far-reaching questions about why we seem to want young people to participate in civic life in the first place, and how we want them to do so. Civic participation is not an either/or phenomenon. Rather than youth being inherently civic or uncivic as a cohort, we have suggested that most young people engage intermittently and contextually in acts of citizenship. From this perspective, we were able to challenge the theoretical assumption that civic participation is a largely individual practice that depends on the possession of individual skills and motivations. On the contrary, our research suggests it is principally about collaboration, solidarity, dialogue, and shared endeavor.

In light of this conclusion, the fundamental question that informed our research—and the wider debate in this area—needs to be rethought. It is not a matter of whether the Internet can reengage young people or enable them to participate when they were not participating before. Rather, it is a question of how the Internet might engage with other movements and modes of participation within society, and how those other movements might use technology in their wider efforts to bring about social change. This becomes a question not primarily about technology or even about young people but about much broader social and cultural processes.

References

Aarts, P., and F. Hirzalla. 2005. Lions of Tawhid in the Polder. *Middle East Report* 235:18–23.

Abdelhady, D. 2006. Beyond home/host networks: Forms of solidarity among Lebanese immigrants in a global era. *Identities: Global Studies in Culture and Power* 13 (3): 427–453.

Andersson, J. 2009. For the good of the net: The Pirate Bay as a strategic sovereign. *Culture Machine* 10:64–108.

Andrejevic, M. 2007. Surveillance in the digital enclosure. *Communication Review* 10 (4): 295–317.

Atton, C. 2002. *Alternative Media*. London: Sage.

Atton, C. 2004. *An Alternative Internet: Radical Media, Politics and Creativity*. Edinburgh: Edinburgh University Press.

Atton, C. 2006. Far-right media on the internet: Culture, discourse and power. *New Media & Society* 8 (4): 573–587.

Bachen, C., C. Raphael, K. M. Lynn, K. McKee, and J. Philippi. 2008. Civic engagement, pedagogy, and information technology on web sites for youth. *Political Communication* 25 (3): 290–310.

Banaji, S. 2008. The Trouble with civic: A snapshot of young people's civic and political engagements in twenty-first century democracies. *Journal of Youth Studies* 11 (5): 543–560.

Banaji, S. 2011. Framing young citizens: Explicit invitation and implicit exclusion on youth civic websites. *Journal of Language and Intercultural Communication* 11 (2): 126–141.

Banaji, S. 2013. Everyday racism and my tram experience: Emotion, civic performance and learning on YouTube. In *Comunicar: Scientific Journal of Media Education*.

Banaji, S., and D. Buckingham. 2009. The civic sell: Young people, the internet and ethical consumption. *Information Communication and Society* 12 (6): 1–27.

Barba, C. H., and V. S. Blanco. 2011. The new social movements in Spain: The protests for the right to housing as an immediate predecessor of the 15M Movement. ECPR 6th General

Conference, Reykjavik, August 25–27, 2011. http://www.ecprnet.eu/MyECPR/proposals/reykjavik/uploads/papers/2277.pdf (accessed January 30, 2012).

Bateman, T. 2011. Has pop gone posh? *BBC Today* report. http://news.bbc.co.uk/today/hi/today/newsid_9373000/9373158.stm (accessed January 28, 2012).

Bauerlein, T. 2009. *The Dumbest Generation*. New York: Penguin.

Baumgartner, J. C., and J. S. Morris. 2006. The *Daily Show* effect: Candidate affiliations, efficacy and American youth. *American Politics Research* 34 (3): 341–367.

Baumgartner, J. C., and J. S. Morris. 2008. One "Nation", under Stephen? The effects of *The Colbert Report* on American youth. *Journal of Broadcasting & Electronic Media* 52 (4): 622–643.

Baumgartner, J. C., and J. S. Morris. 2010. MyFaceTubePolitics: Social networking web sites and political engagement of young adults. *Social Science Computer Review* 28 (10): 24–44.

Baym, N. K., and A. N. Markham. 2009. What constitutes quality in qualitative internet research? In *Internet Inquiry: Conversations about Method*, ed. A. Markham and N. Baym, 173–198. Thousand Oaks, CA: Sage.

Beck, U., A. Giddens, and S. Lash. 1994. *Reflexive Modernisation*. Cambridge: Polity.

Beckett, C., with J. Ball. 2012. *Wikileaks: News in the Networked Era*. Cambridge: Polity.

Benkler, Y. 2006. *The Wealth of Networks*. New Haven, CT: Yale University Press.

Bennett, L. W., ed. 2008. *Civic Life Online: Learning How Digital Media Can Engage Youth*. Cambridge, MA: MIT Press.

Bennett, L. W., C. Breunig, and T. Givens. 2008. Communication and political mobilisation: Digital media and the organisation of anti–Iraq War demonstrations in the US. *Political Communication* 25 (3): 269–289.

Bentivegna, S. 2006. Rethinking politics in the world of ICTs. *European Journal of Communication* 21:331–343.

Bernal, V. 2006. Diaspora, cyberspace and political imagination: The Eritrean diaspora online. *Global Networks* 6 (2): 161–179.

Best, J. 2008. *Social Problems*. New York: Norton.

Buckingham, D. 2000. *The Making of Citizens: Young People, News and Politics*. London: UCL Press.

Buckingham, D. 2006. Is there a digital generation? In *Digital Generations: Children, Young People and New Media*, ed. D. Buckingham and R. Willett, 1–13. Mahwah, NJ: Erlbaum.

Buckingham, D. 2008. Children and media: A Cultural Studies approach. In *International Handbook of Children, Media and Culture*, ed. K. Drotner and S. Livingstone, 219–236. London: Sage.

Büttner, F. 2011. Right-wing extremism in Spain: Between parliamentary insignificance, far-right populism and racist violence. In *Is Europe on the "Right" Path? Right-wing Extremism and Right-wing Populism in Europe*, ed. N. Langenbacher and B. Schellenberg, 181–196. Berlin: Friedrich-Ebert-Stiftung Forum.

Bynner, J., and S. Ashford. 1994. Politics and participation: Some antecedents of young people's attitudes to the political system and political activity. *European Journal of Social Psychology* 24 (2): 223–236.

Caiani, M., and C. Wagemann. 2009. Online networks of the Italian and German extreme right. *Information Communication and Society* 12 (1): 66–109.

Calenda, D., and A. Meijer. 2009. Young people, the internet and political participation. *Information Communication and Society* 12 (6): 879–898.

Cammaerts, B. 2009. Radical pluralism and free speech in online public spaces: The case of North Belgian extreme right discourses. *International Journal of Cultural Studies* 12:555–575.

Carr, N. 2010. *The Shallows: How the Internet Is Changing the Way We Think, Read and Remember.* New York: Norton.

Castles, S. 2000. Guestworkers in Europe: A Resurrection? *International Migration Review* 40 (4): 741–766.

CivicWeb Deliverable 6. 2006. Websites and Civic Participation: A European Overview. http://www.civicweb.eu/images/stories/reports/deliverable6.pdf.

CivicWeb Deliverable 8. 2008. Uses of the web for civic participation. http://www.civicweb.eu/content/view/28/7/.

CivicWeb Deliverable 13. 2008. Young people, the Internet and civic participation. http://www.civicweb.eu/content/view/34/7.

CivicWeb Deliverable 14. 2009. Analysing civic participation websites. http://www.civicweb.eu/content/view/44/7/1/1.

CivicWeb Deliverable 16. 2009. A qualitative analysis of European web-based civic participation among young people. http://www.civicweb.eu/content/view/42/7.

Coleman, S. 2003. A tale of two houses: The House of Commons, the *Big Brother* house and the people at home. *Parliamentary Affairs* 56 (4): 733–58.

Coleman, S. 2008. Doing IT for themselves: Management versus autonomy in youth e-citizenship. In *Civic Life Online: Learning How Digital Media Can Engage Youth*, ed. Lance Bennett, 189–206. Cambridge, MA: MIT Press.

Coleman, S., with C. Rowe. 2005. *Remixing Citizenship: Democracy and Young People's Use of the Internet.* London: The Carnegie Trust Young People's Initiative.

Conversi, D. 1990. Language or race? The choice of core values in the development of Catalan and Basque nationalisms. *Journal of Ethnic and Racial Studies* 13 (1): 50–70.

Copsey, N. 2003. Extremism on the net: the extreme right and the value of the internet. In *Political Parties and the Internet: Net Gain?* ed. R. Gibson, P. Nixon, and S. Ward, 218–233. London: Routledge.

Corner, J., and D. Pels, eds. 2003. *Media and the Restyling of Politics*. London: Sage.

Dahlgren, P. 2003. Reconfiguring civic culture in the new media milieu. In *Media and the Restyling of Politics*, ed. J. Corner and D. Pels, 51–170. London: Sage.

Dahlgren, P., ed. 2007. *Young Citizens and New Media: Learning Democratic Participation*. London: Routledge.

Dahlgren, P. 2009. *Media and Political Engagement: Citizens, Communication, and Democracy*. Cambridge, UK: Cambridge University Press.

Dahlgren, P., and T. Olsson. 2007. Young activists, political horizons, and the Internet: adapting the net to one's purposes. In *Young Citizens in the Digital Age: Political Engagement, Young People, and New Media*, ed. B. D. Loader, 68–81. London: Routledge.

Deuze, M. 2010. *Media Work*. Cambridge: Polity.

Dolnicar, V. 2011. Measuring the dynamics of cross-national digital divides. In *The Contemporary Internet*, ed. L. Haddon, 191–206. New York: Peter Lang.

du Gay, P., S. Hall, L. Janes, H. Mackay, and K. Negus, 1997. *Doing Cultural Studies: The Story of the Sony Walkman*. London: Sage.

Earl, J., and A. Schussman. 2008. Contesting cultural control: Youth culture and online petitioning. In *Civic Life Online*, ed. W. L. Bennett, 71–95. Cambridge, MA: MIT Press.

El-Nawawi, M., and S. Khamis. 2010. Collective identity in the virtual Islamic public sphere: Contemporary discourses in two Islamic websites. *International Communication Gazette* 72 (3): 229–250.

Entzinger, H. 2006. Changing the rules while the game is on: From multiculturalism to assimilation in the Netherlands. In *Migration, Citizenship, Ethnos: Incorporation Regimes in Germany, Western Europe and North America*, ed. Y. Michal Bodemann and Gökçe Yurdakul, 121–144. New York: Palgrave Macmillan.

Fabbe, K. 2011. Doing more with less: The Justice and Development Party (AKP), Turkish elections, and the uncertain future of Turkish politics. *Nationalities Papers* 39 (5): 657–666.

Fabbro, F. 2010. Interactivity as ideological dilemma: A socially situated reading of interactivity discourse in three civic sites in the Italian context. *International Journal of Learning and Media* 2 (1): 81–93.

Fisher, W. F. 1997. Doing good? The politics and antipolitics of NGO practices. *Annual Review of Anthropology* 26:439–464.

Fuchs, C. 2010. Labor in informational capitalism and on the internet. *Information Society* 26 (3): 179–196.

Furlong, A., and F. Cartmel. 1997. *Young People and Social Change: Individualization and Risk in Late Modernity*. Buckingham: Open University Press.

Galston, W. A. 2004. Civic education and political participation. *Political Science and Politics*. 37 (2): 263–266.

Geniets, A. 2010. Lost in translation: Why civic online efforts in Britain have failed to engage young women from low socioeconomic backgrounds. *European Journal of Communication* 25 (4): 398–412.

Gerodimos, R. 2009. New media, new citizens: Youth attitudes towards online civic engagement. In *Proceedings of the WebSci'09: Society On-Line*. Athens, Greece.

Gerodimos, R., and J. Ward. 2007. Rethinking online youth civic engagement: Reflections on Web content analysis. In *Young Citizens in the Digital Age: Political Engagement, Young People and New Media*, ed. B. Loader. London: Routledge.

Gerstenfeld, P. B., D. R. Grant, and C.-P. Chiang. 2003. Hate online: A content analysis of extremist internet sites. *Analyses of Social Issues and Social Policy* 3 (1): 29–44.

Gibson, R., P. Nixon, and S. Ward, eds. 2003. *Political Parties and the Internet*. London: Routledge.

Gillan, K. 2009. The UK anti-war movement online. *Information Communication and Society* 12 (1): 25–43.

Gillmor, D. 2006. *We the Media: Grassroots Journalism by the People for the People*. Sebastopol, CA: O'Reilly Media.

Gordon, H. R. 2009. *We Fight to Win: The Politics of Youth Activism*. New Brunswick, NJ: Rutgers University Press.

Greenstein, F. I. 1965. *Children and Politics*. New Haven, CT: Yale University.

Haddon, L., ed. 2011. *The Contemporary Internet*. New York: Peter Lang.

Hajer, M., and J. Uitermark. 2008. Performing authority: Discursive politics after the assassination of Theo Van Gogh. *Public Administration* 86 (1): 5–19.

Hands, J. 2011. *@ Is for Activism*. London: Pluto Press.

Handy, C. 1988. *Understanding Voluntary Organisations*. London: Penguin.

Henn, M., and M. Weinstein. 2006. Young people and political (in)activism: Why don't young people vote? *Policy and Politics* 34 (3): 517–534.

Herring, S. 2008. Questioning the generational divide: Technological exoticism and adult constructions of online youth identity. In *Youth, Identity and Digital Media*, ed. D. Buckingham, 71–92. Cambridge, MA: MIT Press.

Hesmondhalgh, D., and S. Baker. 2011. A very complicated version of freedom": Conditions and experiences of creative labour in three cultural industries. *Poetics* 38 (1): 4–20.

Hetherington, M. 2005. *Why Trust Matters: Declining Political Trust and the Demise of American Liberalism*. Princeton, NJ: Princeton University Press.

Heubel, E. J. 1977. Church and state in Spain: transition toward independence and liberty. *Western Political Quarterly* 30 (1): 125–139.

Hirzalla, F. 2010. The Internet in young people's civic life. PhD thesis, University of Amsterdam.

Hirzalla, F., and S. Banaji. 2012. Young people's online civic participation. *Encyclopedia of Cyber Behavior*, ed. Zheng Yan, 996–100. Hershey, PA: IGI Global.

Hirzalla, F., F. Muller, and L. van Zoonen. 2009. Young people's situated articulations of internal and external efficacy. Manuscript, University of Amsterdam.

Hirzalla, F., and L. van Zoonen. 2011. Beyond the online/offline divide: How youth's online and offline civic activities converge. *Social Science Computer Review* 29 (4): 481–498.

Hoffmann, D., T. Novak, and A. Schlosser. 2001. The evolution of the digital divide: Examining the relationship of race to internet usage over time. In *The Digital Divide: Facing a Crisis or Creating a Myth?*, ed. B. Compaine, 47–97. Cambridge, MA: MIT Press.

Isin, E. F., and G. M. Nielsen, eds. 2008. *Acts of Citizenship*. London: Zed Books.

Ito, M., S. Baumer, M. Bittanti, d. boyd, R. Cody, B. Herr-Stephenson, H. A. Horst, P. G. Lange, D. Mahendran, K. Z. Martínez, C. J. Pascoe, D. Perkel, L. Robinson, C. Sims, and L. Tripp. 2010. *Hanging Out, Messing Around, and Geeking Out: Kids Living and Learning with New Media*. Cambridge, MA: MIT Press.

Jenkins, H. 2006. *Convergence Culture*. New York: New York University Press.

Kahn, R., and D. Kellner. 2004. New media and internet activism: From "the battle of Seattle" to blogging. *New Media & Society* 6 (1): 87–95.

Katz, J. 1997. *Virtuous Reality*. New York: Random House.

Keen, A. 2007. *The Cult of the Amateur*. London: Nicholas Brealey.

Landry, C., D. Morley, and R. Southwood. 1985. *What a Way to Run a Railroad: An Analysis of Radical Failure*. London: Comedia.

Langenbacher, N., and B. Schellenberg, eds. 2011. *Is Europe on the "Right" Path? Right-wing Extremism and Right-wing Populism in Europe*. Berlin: Friedrich-Ebert-Stiftung Forum.

Lee, L. 2008. The impact of young people's internet use on class boundaries and life trajectories. *Sociology* 42 (1): 137–153.

Lewer, J., R. N. Gerlich, and N. Turner. 2008. The ethics and economics of file sharing. *Southwestern Economic Review* 35 (1): 67–78.

Lievrouw, L. A. 2002. Introduction [to Part Two: Technology Design and Development]. In *Handbook of New Media: Social Shaping and Consequences of ICTs*, ed. L. A. Lievrouw and S. Livingstone, 131–135. London: Sage.

Livingstone, S. 2009. *Children and the Internet: Great Expectations and Challenging Realities.* Cambridge: Polity.

Livingstone, S. 2011. Digital learning and participation among youth. *International Journal of Learning and Media* 2 (2–3): 1–13.

Livingstone, S., N. Couldry, and T. Markham. 2007. *Media Consumption and Public Engagement.* Basingstoke: Palgrave Macmillan.

Loader, B., ed. 2007. *Young Citizens in the Digital Age.* London: Routledge.

Longley, P., and A. Singleton. 2009. Linking social deprivation and digital inclusion in England. *Urban Studies (Edinburgh, Scotland)* 46 (7): 1275–1298.

Marvin, C. 1988. *When Old Technologies Were New.* New York: Oxford University Press.

Mason, M. 2008. *The Pirate's Dilemma: How Hackers, Punk Capitalists, Graffiti Millionaires and Other Youth Movements Are Remixing Our Culture and Changing Our World.* London: Penguin.

McCaughey, M., and M. D. Ayers. 2003. *Cyberactivism: Online Activism in Theory and Practice.* Bristol, PA: Taylor and Francis.

McLeod, C., S. O'Donohoe, and B. Townley. 2009. The elephant in the room? Class and creative careers in British advertising agencies. *Human Relations* 62 (7):1011–1039.

Meijas, U. 2010. The Twitter Revolution must die. *International Journal of Learning and Media* 2 (4): 3–5.

Mesch, G., and S. Coleman. 2007. New media and new voters: Young people, the internet and the 2005 UK election campaign. In *Young Citizens in the Digital Age*, ed. B. Loader, 35–47. London: Routledge.

Miegel, F., and T. Olsson. 2010a. Surveillance and file-sharing: Two issues engaging the unengaged. *International Journal of Learning and Media* 2:55–66.

Miegel, F., and T. Olsson. 2010b. Invited but ignored: How www.ungtval.se aimed to foster but failed to promote youth engagement. In *Young Citizens, ICTs, and Democracy*, ed. P. Dahgren and T. Olsson. Gothenburg, Sweden: Nordicom.

Miraftab, F. 2006. Feminist praxis, citizenship and informal politics: Reflections on South Africa's anti-eviction campaign'. *International Feminist Journal of Politics* 8 (2): 194–218.

Montgomery, K., B. Gottlieb-Robles, and G. Larson. 2004. Youth as E-citizens: Engaging the digital generation. Center for Social Media. http://aladinrc.wrlc.org/bitstream/handle/1961/4649/youthreport.pdf?sequence=1 (accessed February 26, 2013).

Niemi, R., and H. Weisberg, eds. 2001. *Controversies in Voting Behavior.* Washington, DC: CQ Press.

Norris, P. 2000. *A Virtuous Circle: Political Communications in Postindustrial Societies.* Cambridge: Cambridge University Press.

Olsson, T. 2006. Active and calculated media use among young citizens: Empirical examples from a Swedish study. In *Digital Generations: Children, Young People and New Media*, ed. D. Buckingham and R. Willett, 115–130. Mahwah, NJ: Erlbaum.

Olsson, T. 2007. An indispensible resource: The internet and young civic engagement. In *Young Citizens and New Media: Learning for Democratic Participation*, ed. P. Dahlgren, 187–204. London: Routledge.

Ozbudun, E. 2006. From political Islam to conservative democracy: The case of the Justice and Development Party in Turkey. *South European Society & Politics* 11 (3–4): 543–557.

Palfrey, J., and U. Gasser. 2008. *Born Digital: Understanding the First Generation of Digital Natives*. New York: Basic Books.

Pantti, M., and L. van Zoonen. 2006. Do crying citizens make good citizens? *Social Semiotics* 16 (2): 205–224.

Paterson, R. 2010. The contingencies of creative work in television. *Open Communication Journal* 4:1–9.

Paz, J. A. S. 2001. Perspectives on religious freedom in Spain. *Brigham Young University Law Review* 2:669–710.

Perlin, R. 2011. *Intern Nation: How to Earn Nothing and Learn Little in the Brave New Economy*. London: Verso.

Pralle, S. 2006. "I'm changing the climate, ask me how!" The politics of the anti-SUV campaign. *Political Science Quarterly* 121 (3): 397–423.

Prensky, M. 2001. Digital natives, digital immigrants. *On the Horizon* 9 (5). http://www.marcprensky.com/writing/prensky%20-%20digital%20natives,%20digital%20immigrants%20-%20part1.pdf (accessed February 26, 2013).

Prensky, M. 2012. *From Digital Natives to Digital Wisdom: Hopeful Essays for 21st Century Learning*. London: Corwin.

Putnam, R. 2000. *Bowling Alone: The Collapse and Revival of American Community*. New York: Simon and Schuster.

Rheingold, H. 2003. *Smart Mobs: The Next Social Revolution*. New York: Perseus.

Rheingold, H. 2008. Using participatory media and public voice to encourage participation. In *Civic Life Online: Learning How Digital Media Can Engage Youth*, ed. L. W. Bennett, 97–118. Cambridge, MA: MIT Press.

Rice, R. E. 2002. Primary issues in internet use: Access, civic and community involvement, and social interaction and expression. In *The Handbook of New Media*, ed. L. Lievrouw and S. Livingstone, 105–129. London: Sage.

Römmele, A. 2003. Political parties, party communication and new information and communication technologies. *Party Politics* 9 (1): 7–20.

Ross, A. 2003. *No-Collar: The Humane Workplace and Its Hidden Costs*. Philadelphia: Temple University Press.

Scheufele, D. and M. Nisbet. 2002. Being a citizen online: New opportunities and dead ends. *Press/Politics* 7 (3): 55–75.

Schudson, M. 1998. *The Good Citizen: A History of American Civic Life*. New York: The Free Press.

Selwyn, N. 2007. Technology, schools and citizenship education: A fix too far? In *Young Citizens in the Digital Age*, ed. B. Loader, 129–142. London: Routledge.

Selwyn, N. 2009. The digital native: Myth and reality. *Aslib Proceedings* 61 (4): 364–379.

Serrano, J., and D. Sampere. 1999. *La participación juvenil en España*. Barcelona: Fundación Ferrer y Guardia.

Sherrod, L., C. Flanagan, R. Kasimir, and A. Bertelsen, eds. 2006. *Youth Activism: An International Encyclopaedia*. Westport, CT: Greenwood Press.

Shirky, C. 2009. *Here Comes Everybody: How Change Happens When People Come Together*. London: Penguin.

Signoret, M. 2008. Trans. John Smith. 4 × 4s: Urban penis substitutes. In *Cafe Babel*: the European Magazine. http://www.cafebabel.co.uk/article/24527/4x4s-urban-penis-substitutes.html (accessed January 20, 2012).

Spannring, R., G. Ogris, and W. Gaiser, eds. 2008. *Youth and Political Participation in Europe: Results of the Comparative Study of EUYOUPART*. Farmington Hills, MI: Barbara Budrich Publishers.

Starr, A., L. A. Fernandez, R. Amster, L. J. Wood, and M. J. Caro. 2008. The impacts of state surveillance on political assembly and association. *Qualitative Sociology* 31:251–270.

Szakacs, J., and E. Bognar. 2010. Making sense of Zhoriben: The story of a Romani social networking site in Hungary. *International Journal of Learning and Media* 2 (1): 67–80.

Talbot, D. 2008. How Obama really did it. *Technology Review* (September/October).

Tapscott, D. 1998. *Growing Up Digital: The Rise of the Net Generation*. New York: McGraw-Hill.

Tapscott, D. 2008. *Grown Up Digital: How the Net Generation Is Changing the World*. New York: McGraw-Hill.

Tatarchevskiy, T. 2011. The "popular" culture of internet activism. *New Media & Society* 3 (2): 297–313.

Terranova, T. 2000. Free labor: Producing culture for the digital economy. *Social Text* 18 (2): 33–58.

Theocharis, Y. 2011. Young people, political participation and online postmaterialism in Greece. *New Media & Society* 13 (2): 203–223.

Tsatsou, P. 2011. Digital divides revisited: What is new about divides and their research? *Media Culture & Society* 33 (2): 317–331.

Turkle, S. 1995. *Life on the Screen*. New York: Simon and Schuster.

Turkle, S. 2011. *Alone Together*. New York: Basic Books.

Tuzzi, A., C. Padovani, and G. Nesti. 2007. Communication and (e)democracy: Assessing European e-democracy discourses. In *Reclaiming the Media: Communication Rights and Democratic Media Roles*, ed. B. Cammaerts and N. Carpentier, 31–65. Bristol: Intellect.

van de Beek, J. H., S. A. van de Mortel, and S. van Hees. 2010. Eurosphere: Diversity and the European public sphere. Towards a citizens' Europe. http://eurospheres.org/files/2010/06/Netherlands.pdf (accessed January 21, 2012).

van der Meer, T. W. G., and E. J. van Ingen. 2009. Schools of democracy? Disentangling the relationship between civic participation and political action in 17 European countries. *European Journal of Political Research* 48:281–308.

van Dijck, J., and D. Nieborg. 2009. Wikinomics and its discontents: A critical analysis of Web 2.0 business manifestos. *New Media & Society* 11 (5): 855–874.

van Laer, J., and P. van Aelst. 2010. Internet and social movement action repertoires: Opportunities and limitations. *Information Communication and Society* 13 (8): 1146–1171.

van Selm, M., N. W. Jankowski, and L. Tsaliki. 2002. Political parties online: Digital democracy as reflected in three Dutch political party web sites. *Communications* 27:189–209.

van Zoonen, L. 2004. *Entertaining the Citizen: When Politics and Popular Culture Converge*. Lanham, MD: Rowman and Littlefield.

Vromen, A. 2007. Australian young people's participatory practices and internet use. In *Young Citizens in the Digital Age*, ed. B. Loader, 97–113. London: Routledge.

Vromen, A. 2008. Building virtual spaces: Young people, participation and the internet. *Australian Journal of Political Science* 43 (1): 79–97.

Wagner, T. 2008. Reframing ecotage as ecoterrorism: News and the Discourse of Fear. *Environmental Communication: A Journal of Nature and Culture* 2 (1): 25–39.

Warren, M. 2007. The digital vicious cycle: Links between social disadvantage and digital exclusion in rural areas. *Telecommunications Policy* 31 (6–7): 374–388.

Warschauer, M. 2004. *Technology and Social Inclusion: Rethinking the Digital Divide*. Cambridge, MA: MIT Press.

Wayne, M., J. Petley, C. Murray, and L. Henderson. 2008. *Television News, Politics and Young People: Generation Disconnected?* Basingstoke: Palgrave Macmillan.

Whine, M. 1997. The far right on the internet. In *The Governance of Cyberspace: Politics, Technology and Global Restructuring*, ed. B. Loader, 209–227. London, New York: Routledge.

Whiteley, P. F. 2009. Is the party over? The decline of party activism and membership across the democratic world. *Party Politics* 17 (1): 21–44.

Willis, I. 2006. Keeping promises to queer children: Making space (for Mary-Sue) at Hogwarts. In *Fan Fiction and Fan Communities in the Age of the Internet: New Essays*, ed. K. Hellekson and K. Busse, 153–171. Jefferson, NC: McFarland.

Winston, B. 1998. *Media, Technology and Society: A History*. London: Routledge.

Women in Journalism. 2009. *Teenage Boys and the Media: Research Report*. London: Women in Journalism.

Wyn, J., and R. White. 2007. *Rethinking Youth*. London: Sage.

Xenos, M., and K. Foot. 2007. Not your father's internet: The generation gap in online politics. In *Civic Life Online: Learning How Digital Media Can Engage Youth*, ed. L. W. Bennett, 51–70. Cambridge, MA: MIT Press.

Zhang, W., T. J. Johnson, T. Seltzer, and S. L. Bichard. 2010. The revolution will be networked: The influence of social networking on political attitudes and behavior. *Social Science Computer Review* 28 (1): 75–92.

Index